About the Author

Frans Merkx was born in 1966 in Bradford, West Yorkshire to a Pakistani Muslim father and Dutch-South American Catholic mother. He was brought up in a very turbulent and rough time in Northern England. From being never accepted by either Asian or White people, Frans struggled and fought his way to the top through life. His struggles have taken him through being the outcast to the pop star and again hitting rock bottom only for him to rise again to the very top. Frans was and has always been one of those guys who out of nothing did everything.

Nikhil Lakhani is a UK-based author of contemporary fiction and non-fiction. He was born and raised in Kenya with Indian roots. He left home at the age of fifteen, first attending boarding school in India and later making the move to Europe, studying in Canterbury, Switzerland and London where he is currently settled. He has been writing since the age of six and his stories are mostly set in parallel worlds, focusing on existential themes of breaking free from the binds of a conventional life and self-discovery. He is also an aspiring screenwriter, blogger and creative entrepreneur.

Dedication

I'd like to dedicate my book to the following people:
My family: Nadia, Carlton-Louis, Ryan-Ramone, Rishi & Jay-Jamal. You give meaning to my life. To my mother: Mum, a lot of water passed under the bridge and many a time we didn't agree and your decisions were never the best, but you are still my mother. To my father: Daddy, you were never there, but that made me stronger. My brothers: Lateef, your bullying never broke me, and Zak, there were times we lost our brotherly love and friendship, but I think we can get it back. To my sisters: Soroya, I always admired and loved how you fought and are still fighting sickle cell and never give up. Yasmeen, you always brought joy and happiness into my life and to many others' lives and I miss you every day. Rest in Peace big sister. To my other Family: Caleb Black, Chloe Black, Bruce Black, Roseanne Black, Mr. Trevor May, Ben, Ashley, Roger Marsh, Sharon Marsh, Frans Merkx Sr., Nettie Merkx, Linda Merkx, Christian Diesveld, Dave Mallet, and the Bradford Massive (Rude Boys). My other Mothers: Roseanne Black, thank you for making my childhood bearable and bringing love into my life and to Mrs. Marion Marsh, thank you for feeding me and supporting me when there was no one else. I love you both. My other Father: Bruce Black, I always looked up to you. My life has been a rollercoaster and, yes, there are some things that I could have done better or not done at all. But you know what, that's life. I did nothing and everything happened. Peace and Love always *FX*

To Pamela, whom I love most in the world. Thank you for keeping me sane, believing in me and for staying sane yourself. *Nikhil*

FX and Nikhil Lakhani

DO NOTHING!
THE MEMOIRS OF FX

AUSTIN MACAULEY
PUBLISHERS LTD.

A CIP catalogue record for this title is available from the British Library.

ISBN 9781786934192 (Paperback)
ISBN 9781786934208 (eBook)

www.austinmacauley.com

First Published (2017)
Austin Macauley Publishers Ltd.
25 Canada Square
Canary Wharf
London
E14 5LQ

Acknowledgments

I'd like to thank Nik; you're a trooper, a rudeboy and also my brother. Nadia and my kids for always giving me strength. *FX*

This work would not have been possible without the cooperation and collaborative effort of FX, whom I must thank first and foremost.

I'd also like to thank my parents, brother, best friends, Sehrish and Tanuj for their continued support and Shankar and Sioni for their encouragement of my writing right from the beginning. *Nikhil*

CHAPTER 1
Strife

Bradford had seen its heyday way back in the Victorian times. The wool industry was at its peak and this, coupled with the industrial revolution, made the city an important hub for business and it boasted a thriving commercial scene, with opportunities around the compass. That was all in the past, however, for the present-day Bradford was a murky grey city, where racism was rife and poverty was the prerogative of all the poor prisoners; Black, White and Asian presiding there.

Trails of smoke from the chimneys of sullen factories filled the dull skies, which hung over a sunken city of despair, with the traditional Victorian architecture of the buildings marred by new uprisings that had crowded the place, below which hawkers haggled to get by, corner-shops were fashionable, particularly among members of the Asian and Black communities and the piercing cold of that winter's day piling onto the misery.

There was no antidote for the repressive nature of the area, where it seemed unlikely for any dream to come true, but somehow my father remained oblivious to all this, and persisted with his passions nonetheless. Aside from grafting, my father had several other passions, some of which he hid from my mother, but it was only a matter of time until something seeped through the cracks, enraging her and probing her into gathering the pantry from the kitchen, stuffing it into a bag, and calling out to us. "Yasmeen, Soroya!" she shouted up the stairs, and at the foot appeared three young girls in descending order of height.

Soroya, my eldest sister one would be the hardest working, but simultaneously the least healthy with the sickle-cell anaemia, which led to her being given until eleven years old, but which she would combat to survival. Then there was Yasmeen, she was my favourite; fairer, which society took as a stark attribute of beauty, and with my mother's delicate features, she'd go on to challenge me for the title of black sheep, although, like with everything, I'd end up winning.

My stillborn brother, Tariq, never got to see the light of day.

"Lateef, Zahid, Zaker!"

"Move!" My elder brother, Lateef, pushed me right onto the wardrobe door, as he strode forward to heed my mother's call. Throughout my life, I would only ever fear two things: my father and Lateef. It would take a while to confront these fears, but at that time, he would bully me to no end, taking any opportunity to shove me, lash out and slap my head, trip me up as I walked past him and take anything that I ever had. It was unfortunate that I had to share a room with him, but on the other hand I had Zaker as a roommate too, and he was a gem in comparison; cute, small and we called him 'the liar on the roof' because he lied all the time.

And there I was: Mohammed Zahid Lateef Hameed Chaudhary. Even I had trouble remembering all my names. Four years old in the year 1970, neither Pakistani nor Dutch, nor English; a mélange, just like my siblings, of different shades of skin colour and facial features. I had the sturdy look of my Pakistani father, but the lower jaw composition of my mother to soften the appearance. This mix would be the centre of confusion for most of my childhood, leading up to the teenage years.

"The taxi is here," said my mother, trooping us all into a black cab.

"Where to love?" asked the driver.

She did not respond straight away, but urged us all to "get in the cab, now!"

"Where we going?" Lateef complained.

"Get in!" my mother screamed, holding the door open and half-tossing him in, which I thought was amusing. "Zahid, you come up front with me."

I did not argue, but got into the front seat with her, which Lateef thought was unfair. "Why's he get to sit in the front? That's not fair!"

"You, shut it, now!"

"Where to?" the driver asked again.

"Glasgow."

The driver raised an eyebrow. "What love, Glasgow?"

"You heard me, let's go!" We were off without another word. I did not want to ask my mother why on Earth we were driving all the way up to Scotland, as strange as it was. That had been my nature from early on to the present; I would never dwell on a thought, or ponder over it, if my mother told me to get in the car, I would get into the car.

We drove on past the dreary brown and red-bricked buildings, past the rail tracks where the barriers were up, across the main square with the clock tower jutting up out of a well-architected building that typified English town halls. We drove along until we left the industrial clouds, on through stretches of green pasture with livestock scattered about, their black and white hides flashing past the speeding vehicle.

We past town after town, all the while my mother muttered to herself, mostly in Dutch, but I caught phrases like "Son of a Bitch" and "Kill" in English. She was furious about something, the rage burning in her eyes, her target set on Glasgow.

"Can you go any faster?" my mother asked of the driver, who obliged, picking up the speed.

The Glasgow surroundings were as bad as Bradford, and 'weren't any further along the line of post-war developments. Dusk had fallen upon us as we were traveling, and so I had not had the opportunity to see it by day, but I could tell that it was every bit as grim as the city where I resided.

"Take this road, and the place should be up on the left," my mother said. I had to admit, it was impressive how she had managed to navigate us to such a precise location without the GPS devices that would be made available to the public sometime in the new millennium. "There, stop." We pulled up outside a huge apartment complex and my mother got out of the car, grabbing up the bag full of pots and pans from beneath the seat. She marched right up to the entrance and out of sight before anybody could protest.

"What's going on?" Lateef asked around.

"I don't know," Soroya said, peering out of the window to have a closer look at where mum had gone to.

"Should we go check?" Lateef asked again. I did not cast my vote, because I knew I did not want to go and check. Always wanting to do something, the rest of my family did.

"I'm going, you all stay here." Soroya got out of the car and crept up cautiously to the entrance.

It was all quiet for a while, and Lateef had his nose pressed against the glass. "It's too dark, I can't see," he said, squinting. I wanted to retort, but that would get me another beating.

Suddenly, there was a crash and a wail that made the hairs on the back of my neck stand up. Something was happening on the first floor, and it did not sound good. It was followed up by the breaking of glass, and a loud thud that sounded like something huge had been kicked in or broken. Was that my mother making that noise?

And then I heard it, the distinctive male voice, rough and throaty and thoroughly characteristic of a Pakistani. "Let me talk! Bloody hell let me…"

"What for! You leave me…and five kids…to come here and do her and have a baby with *her*?" my mother screamed, her voice demonic, echoing through the night like the shriek of a banshee. There was another thud, and the unmistakable scurrying of feet. "Don't you…don't run away, you coward! Answer me!"

"Let me…let me talk, okay?"

"What have you got to say, you bastard!" The sound of two people tussling ensued, and I understood what the pots and pans were for. The bumps and hits ceased, and there was silence once more.

"Wow, what was that?" Lateef asked again. I wanted to tell him it was obvious that it was a fight, but I resisted again as Soroya came running back to the car and got in. "What happened?" Lateef pressed her. Even the taxi driver was looking shocked and wanted to know what was going on.

"Dad was in there, and there was some woman as well. He tried to lock the door, but mum broke the glass and got in."

"Wow," Lateef said again.

Even at four years old, I knew that it was serious. Sure enough, my mother emerged from the entrance again, her hands covered in blood and her mascara smeared all over her face. I knew where I'd drawn my inspiration for fighting and never giving up from, later on in life. She was panting, and wiping the tears away from her face as she got into the car. "Take me back to Bradford," she shot at the driver. "Also, I can't pay you right away, I haven't got any money."

"No problem love, just call the taxi central when you have it." Even he knew not to mess with a woman who had just ravaged her sneaking husband. The only thing that spared my father, was the fact that my mother had shown Catholic mercy like the Pope, and once she saw that there was a little baby in the house, with that other woman, she did not pursue the beating any further.

That was my father; a womanizing, conniving asshole. Probably one of the biggest assholes I would ever come across in my lifetime. He was oxymoronic, because on the one hand he was diligent and wise, and on the other hand he spared no emotion for his kids, or my mother. While he had nothing to spare for us, he was fully devoted and entirely passionate about his political affairs, and other infamous affairs.

He may have been sharp in business, but he had not succeeded in covering his tracks, and that would be the beginning of the end for him, and the start of a new father-less era for my siblings and I.

We did nothing, and out of nothing we were born. We did nothing, and we were cast out into a world to face the opus, but I marched on through the truffles of doubt to seize the days to come...

CHAPTER 2
Early Hustles

My father wasn't good for most things, but the one thing that really stood out about him was that he wanted it all. He wanted the world to bow down before him and kiss his feet. You could see it blazing in his eyes. He never took nonsense from anyone, and everyone knew not to mess with him. I was glad for that, because even though he wasn't there for me, he definitely rubbed onto me, and even as a kid, I wanted more than just sweets and ice-lolly sticks like the others.

I shadowed my father, and one day, when I was a mere toddler, I had my eyes set on a milk cart. I wanted it. At four years old, it would seem like early days for hustling, but not for this sneaky toddler. I still can't get over the feeling of getting behind the wheel of that milk cart and steering it downhill. It was exhilarating, the adrenaline going wild inside of me as I somehow took off the clutch and braced myself for the motion. Being on top of a hill meant that I had to apply the brakes if I wanted to stop, but it was too late and I couldn't reach the brakes and the cart went hurtling down. I could not even see over the steering wheel! The end result was a smashed-up cart at the bottom of the hill, and a bawling kid who wouldn't score anything for that. It was a failed Grand Theft Auto, but good practice for what would come later.

The tension at home had reached its climax. The atmosphere was palpable; a crease had materialized on my old man's forehead. He had returned home after the Glasgow saga, with his tail between his legs. I noticed the packed suitcases waiting by the front door. They were there without explanation and all of a sudden as though somebody had conjured them out of thin air.

The night before, my parents were arguing. I hadn't heard what they were saying, but it sounded worse than their previous quarrels. My mother's voice was shrill and filled the corridors, and was punctuated by my father's deep, throaty voice. It ended with mum slamming the bedroom door shut, and, sobbing hysterically, she went downstairs and slept on the couch. All through the night, I could hear her sniffing as she cried, and I couldn't' sleep.

Every morning my father would sit with all of us at the table, munching his three hard boiled eggs and talking to my mother with his mouth full. But on that occasion he wasn't sat at the table. It was his last morning.

I heard the horn of a car from outside, where a taxi was parked in our driveway. My father stiffened up and looked at us all in a bizarre way. He seemed, and for the first time, nervous, and unable to say anything. We never usually instigated conversation, and that time was no exception, so we watched as he walked towards the door,

The morbid atmosphere at home was as though somebody had passed away; mum shaking as she sobbed, her eyes puffy and red. Dad stopped and took one final look at his reflection in the mirror above the mantelpiece in the hallway. He combed his hair in typical fashion with half a pot of Brylcreem in it, and avoided eye contact with his wife. He carried that comb everywhere he went, and every now and again, he would use a bathroom break and straighten out his hair. Never judge a book by its cover; the man in front of us looked imposing and sharp in that suit, but he was a cunning bastard that couldn't spare a tear as he made to exit the house for the last time. Not even for his own kids!

One thing I would not miss was the way my father would punish Lateef and I without a care in the world. He'd beaten Lateef so many times, he had become as evil and nasty as my old man.

Lateef wasn't always like that. As a toddler he was as sweet as they came, with not a shred of violence in him. As time carried him along, my father delivered the sort of beatings that would usually result in jail time, if anybody out there had seen it. It was like our very own Ultimate Fighting Championship training, and my father was the ringmaster. And if he wanted more violence, but couldn't be bothered dishing it out himself, he would force Lateef to fight me. Of course, I always lost. The demon was roused, that and several million brain cells that had been killed in the process, and the end product was a fearsome menace and a complete and utter pea-brain that was my elder brother who had made me his punching bag.

My father betrayed me right at the moment of his departure that left a gaping hole in my heart. I boiled with rage, and the refuted words my father would always say to me, "You are my favourite because you remind me of Tariq," left with him. What type of a sick lesson was that? Why was I even trying to find a justification for any of it? The guy was sick in the head, that's what it was, a sick demented ghoul that could not show any remorse for leaving his kids behind. Tariq was the brother that had kicked the bucket, the pride in my father's eyes, but I did not want to be his replacement.

I despised my father and I really wanted him to know it right before he left. As he turned the handle to step out the front door, I mentally screamed, "I hate you, you liar!" At that moment I didn't have the guts to say it out loud.

He was the epitome of a walking paradox, my father was. On the one hand, he had delighted himself in falling in love with my mother, had commenced building a life with her. She always loved him dearly, and had stuck with him during the frugalities, and the hardships. They had pooled in to build a life together, they had flown into a whole new country for the start of something new, in a neutral place, but it is said you cannot really take the village out of the man, even though you can take the man out of the village. Even during the seventies, Bradford boasted a large Asian community, and my father could not resist being drawn into the conflict zone by finding himself a different partner, and making it clear he wanted a relationship with that community and with Islam.

I knew that he really did love my mother, because he could not bear to look back as he marched on. My siblings and I stood and watched. I was six, and still able to register that my mother and father were giving silent eulogies to their ten-year-old relationship.

I would never know what it felt like to really be part Pakistani, because according to their customs, we were from the "other side;" my mother being white and Christian in their eyes. We were the half-breeds, or as we were told many times the half-castes, which they used as a way of making us feel disenfranchised and alienated from their affairs. It doesn't make any sense at all, but it does make you get a taste of the discrimination.

And so began my mother's days of intense pain and suffering. Of course, she hid it from us. She wanted to stay strong for the family. She got herself two jobs at the Bingo hall and also cleaning. It broke her back, but she stuck to it.

Mum had it rough all her life, until she met my dad, and then after that again. She was put up for adoption at an early age because of her mixed-race status, so she definitely knew what it was like being different and not knowing on which side of the scales to tilt.

The only good relationship my mother had had was with her father, my grandfather, who was suffering from chronic alcoholism. She took great care of him, and when she brought my father to him, the man thought the world of her new partner. I guess dad always had commanded respect from just about everybody, but it was too bad he had lost mine by walking out.

It was Yasmeen who deputised mum's duties from that moment on. She fed me, dressed me up, all of it. She and I shared a lot in common, and I loved hanging around her more than the others. She was the coolest of my sisters and kept it natural. She wasn't into make-up and fancy dresses and later would be a kind of free hippy, but she still managed to look amazing. She was the bigmouth of the family, her non-stop chatter would drive all the others up the wall, but I loved it and to top it off she wasn't afraid of pea brain Lateef. It all changed when dad walked out the door. I don't think Yasmeen was the same, and I doubted she'd ever get over it.

My mother once decided to take us along to the Bingo hall. I guess she could not find someone to babysit us for the day. It was a shoddy place just down the road from our house; **crusty** and stunk of old people's breath. There was dust all over the premises, and the tablecloth was moth and mite bitten. All the cats had come out for a chance to get lucky and gain some extra quid. They were all your average working class Joes: not younger than forty-five, foreheads creased, their eyes fixed on the digits printed on bits of different coloured paper. I remember seeing one white man peep constantly at his neighbour's sheet shaking his head.

"Hameedah! What did you bring them here for?" the boss was squat and foul, with a screwed-up face sagging like a scrotum. Even though her name was Maria they would use her married name, which I always found strange.

He shook as he bore down on my mother, who stood her ground. "These are my kids, Dough. That's Zahid, Lateef-"

"I don't care about who these fuckin kids are; this is not a place for kids! I don't want to see them in here again, love, ok! Now get back to work, stop standing around doing nothing!" He was brutally unfair, but I could see my mother swallowing the pill for the sake of the financial security at the end of the road.

I didn't pay too much interest in the Bingo. I thought if luck existed, I was the unluckiest sod alive. My father left us with nothing; I sometimes got to bed without a proper dinner, got up the next morning and went to school without my customary toast and tea. What really did catch my eye was a pair of impressive-looking gentlemen seated at the bar. Wow! They look cool, I thought.

As a kid, I thought it was an odd place for these classy gents to be meeting. I was observational, regardless of my age, and I knew these guys were neither Tom, Dick nor Harry. They had their heads together, and were talking in low voices, using a tongue I did not recognize. Moments later, one of them pulled out what looked like a wad of twenty-pound notes, handed it over to his counterpart. They shook hands and the payer left.

My eyes feasted on the pile of money in the guy's hand, as he counted each crisp sheet of legal tender.

"Hameedah, I told you to speak clearer when you are helping the customers!" The manager had dragged my mother to the side and was holding her by the arm as he told her off.

"I'm doing my best!"

"It's not good enough. I specifically hired you because you said you could speak English..."

"I can! I am!"

"That's not the English I'm looking for, it's not good enough and if you don't improve, I'm going to have to let you go."

"Okay."

My mother thought that I was watching a lady at the slot machine trying to hit the jackpot, but in truth my ears were perked up and I was listening to what was going on. She was as elegant as they came in those days, despite being put down by pricks.

Leaving the hall that night, my thoughts returned to the cash exchange between the two men. And then I thought back to the old lady trying to hit the jackpot. She must have pulled on that lever at least a hundred times while we were there, and each time she received two matching images and one faulty. She seemed to have gone past insanity, and was well into the confines of erratic, and I preferred the ease with which the well-dressed gentleman received the cash from his companion.

I played the whole interaction over and over in my head, and that triggered the spark of wanting it too. I liked what money represented in that transaction: respect, power, class…and for me at that particular point, a solution for my mum's struggles. That is an idea that from that day served as the seed for my will of having it all.

My father as a father was a useless man in my life, but he made sure he passed on the right genes for being a go-getter and an entrepreneur.

CHAPTER 3
Uncles

I did get to see some of my father after he left, but those were not memorable times at all. Through the faint glimpses of him in the street, or at his sweetshop. One day he took my younger brother and I to the circus. That was the only time that I felt like I actually had a daddy and not some kind of dictatorial figure that stared daggers at me all day.

It was the three of us, and the spectacle was great. As we watched, my dad started to laugh and it was actually the first time I saw him laughing. I hadn't even noticed he had teeth before! He laughed and laughed, and all the snide business deals, the nonsense with us, everything was put on hold and we just had a great time.

Like I said, that only happened once. Mostly, we'd go over to his sweet shop down by a corner in Little Horton, opposite a beat-down council estate called Canterbury. It was not as shabby as its surroundings, I'll give my father that. The shop sold a variety of sweets, which were visible through the glass counter at the front.

Sure enough, he had a new piece of candy there: his arm candy. She was the same Pakistani woman from Glasgow that screamed as my mother went Mike Tyson on my father's ass. She was as plastic as you could get: she could have never pulled it off with the amount of makeup and jewellery she'd put on. Her eyes were burly and she wrinkled her nose in our direction as she watched us approach the counter. She really reminded me of the witch in the classic Disney cartoon with Snow White and the Seven Dwarfs. My sisters despised her with a vengeance, and they would often avoid coming along with my brothers and I to seek out our father.

In the beginning, she had tried hard to hide her snarl behind a smirk, but no amount of makeup could cover up the ugly hatred she held for us and in the end she accepted that we loathed her and she us. So it all became a ritual: she'd brandish a bag of the choicest sweets there, and we'd just take it and leave, no words exchanged.

The worst part was my father wasn't even there most of the time, which made it crystal clear that he had no interest in us whatsoever, and eventually neither did we, so I guess we just wanted to get our hands on some sweets.

Truth be told, I wanted to tell her that those sweets were no compensation for the horrors we had been through, and that we actually just wanted to see him, but I did not want to give her the satisfaction of seeing I was desperate or something, even though I was not.

In the end, I got my revenge as I screwed my face up in anger and reached behind the counter, stuck my hand into the till and grabbed a handful of notes before walking away with my loot.

I've got to say that I was the sweetest kid around. I would always hide behind my mum's dress, too shy to show myself if I didn't know somebody. My eyes twinkled with a particular innocence and I was often seen simply sitting and smiling, doing nothing, but deep down inside I was angry. I don't think I could ever forgive my father for leaving us without even the bare essentials.

I wanted to go to the shop and take something, or let him see me, let him know that I existed. That was probably my way to stand for it. My anger towards dad was fed by the fact that he gave his new family everything. Maybe that was why I wanted to show him and his friends that we half-breeds were better than any of those self-proclaimed "pure" bloods.

In the end it was all about my little brother and I going to see what sweets we could get and I would go to see how much money I could steal. I thought of it this way: we weren't getting the love we deserved, so I'm going to take what's rightfully ours. Besides we couldn't just live off sweets!

By this time, he was building his career, and his reputation, and we knew he didn't want us in his life. The rejection stung and left deep scars on our hearts, especially on Yasmeen, who brooded more than ever before..

I think dad gave up on us when he lost the custody battle. My dad being a qualified lawyer from Punjab University, emerging with honours and everything, and having a profound understanding of British Law, I guess he did not want custody. With half an ass he lost the contest, which for him was just a performance and thankfully we went to mum. In any case, I don't think his argument that he wanted to take us to Pakistan and teach us the old ways and arrange my sisters' marriages rubbed well with British Law. It served him better, because in the eyes of the community, we were outcasts, low life, half-breeds, "un-Islamic," we were everything his friends and associates hated.

This was made obvious when one day, my brother and I decided to go to his house uninvited. He was there having dinner with his important friends. To say he was shocked and embarrassed was an understatement; he was livid, and we hardly received a welcome.

We noticed that there were several pairs of shoes left outside the door. I hesitated, exchanged a glance with my brother, shrugged and then took my own shoes off. I knocked on the door, and several heartbeats later, his wife answered it.

She froze, staring at us with her nose crinkled up. She made me feel like I stank or something, and I even had a whiff of my armpits to see, and then leaned slightly to sniff my elder brother. Damn it, perhaps Lateef hadn't cleaned up before we left, and it was the lingering smell of sweat after he'd thrown a few good punches prior to our departure. Maybe he didn't bother grooming himself because he knew they would not notice the difference anyway.

"What do you want? What the hell are you doing here?" my father rushed forwards towards us and scolded us.

"We haven't seen you in age's daddy, and we haven't heard from you either, thought we'd come and see you," Lateef said. My sisters and younger brother had stayed at home, Yasmeen saying outright that she wanted nothing to do with him ever. Going to see my father with Lateef was something we shared in common. It was about the only thing we shared, because everything else was about him dominating, while I was left with nothing.

My father looked at the two of us with disdain and then said, "Here, take this money and go. I'm busy." I had never felt so unwanted in my life, but I thought that I should just take the money and go; it was better than nothing. I also realized that was another way I could fill my pockets with dough. I mostly used the money to buy food, to feed myself when there was little at home. Mum usually came home so exhausted that she couldn't be bothered to cook, and so the money was useful to buy myself fish and chips and a bottle of dandelion and burdock.

Suddenly, as I was about to turn away, one of my dad's friends walked in from the other room and said, "Who are these boys?"

My father replied, "These are my other children... the ones I told you about."

His friend looked at us both like we were aliens or something, and answered with a simple "oh." The house stunk of curry and that pungent smell of oils and incense that did not make any sense at all. It was a combination of turmeric and coriander, mingled with a strong lavender scent, which was enough to make anyone crazy. I remember the carpets being all multicoloured, with strange symbols on them that I could not recognize and I thought what was the point in taking our shoes off outside, to step on the dump inside? That was one of the many rules that made me wonder what being Muslim was in the first place.

I had an uneasy feeling about being there, like a weight had been placed on my head and I was made to endure it. Where there was no carpet, the floor space was covered with mustard yellow tiles that in no way matched the baby blue of the ceiling. There were paintings in the hallway showing glittering gold letters in a language I would only guess was Arabic.

Since my father's friend had seen us, my old man had no choice, but to invite us to sit with them. It was something like an Al-Qaeda meeting with the men sat in a circle in traditional Pakistani clothing which looked more like pyjamas; white tunic gowns that covered their entire bodies, including their feet. They all wore white caps, which must have symbolised something and a few had long beards dyed orange, which I was not sure was symbolic or just a fashion trend I would never follow in my wildest dreams. I could smell tobacco all about me, and I was sure nearly all of them were smokers.

We got into the room, my brother and I, and it was creepy. I cringed as I looked around, while they looked at us and said, "Wa Salam

Aleikum." We didn't respond as we didn't even know what that meant. One of them kept snorting as he brought the phlegm up from his throat, and the other three were drumming on their thighs with their fingers and another was fumbling with a set of beads. I finally got to know the source of the smell, but now that was mixed with their body odour and the oil in their hair and combined with the tobacco and something that reminded me of toothpaste.

My father hesitated as he introduced my brothers and I to his friends. "Lateef, Zahid.

"This is your Uncle Hussein, this is your Uncle Bashir, this is your Uncle Bilal and this is your Uncle Saleem." They were all so-called uncles to us, but I was sure none of them shared my father's DNA. The condescension on their faces was so obvious it was almost as though they were verbally expressing their contempt towards us.

"And these are…your kids, ji?" one of the "uncles" asked politely, his voice appearing a little too sweetened for my liking. Then again, my father was feared by everyone, and so-called "Uncle" Hussein looked like he wanted to shit himself as he couldn't help, but ask. Anyone who stepped out of line with my father would disappear and reappear back in Pakistan or the underworld.

I looked at Dad, and even though I knew how embarrassed he was, he feigned a grin and nodded, "Yes." I felt my neck grow hot as my temper rose and met the feeling of sheer rejection.

I hated those "uncles" and everything about the place from the stink to the weird music in the background. I wanted to scream and get out of there, to just run away and go back to my mother. Worst of all that I felt like an outsider with somebody I thought one of my own.

Everything there was so foreign and new to me because Dad never took us to the Mosque with him, never talked to us about Islam or the fundamentals he practiced. I did not know what the main belief was, what the pillars were, who their God was, and I found that the language was far too difficult for me to understand.

I remember seeing a copy of the Quran once, which belonged to my father, but I didn't know what was contained in it, and I didn't bother opening it to read. I didn't realize it then, but looking back it was obvious that my father kept his association with us a secret from the public, and that was why he never took us to any of the gatherings with him, or anything.

We were raised Catholic, because my father never bothered to show us the Islamic way. My mother was a sturdy believer in Jesus Christ, but with religion, I was once again in no-man's land; forced to lean towards Catholicism, or so I thought because I didn't have orange hair like those beards.

Dinner was one of the least pleasant things I had to ever endure. I couldn't eat because the food was overdosed with red Chili powder. The worst part was, my father would grunt his new wife's name, "Meena," and nod in my direction, prompting her to keep piling curry onto my plate from where she sat across me. She used her hands to serve me some Indian flatbread as well. She hardly looked at me, and whenever I said stop, she'd keep going and going, glancing up at Dad, until he grunted.

I felt the anger bubble inside me and when I asked for a spoon to eat with, because there wasn't any cutlery on the table, my father looked at me and said, "You are not white panchote," which was a particularly nasty swear word. And what was that supposed to mean, I'm not white? "Eat with your hands boy and finish everything on your plate."

He scrutinized me like he had never done in our own household. I screwed up my eyes and tried to control my breathing. I was so humiliated; I wanted to throw that plate out of the window. My stomach was on fire, and it grumbled as I struggled to scoop that spicy mess up with my hands and put it into my mouth. "Use your right hand to eat boy," my father said. He didn't care that I was left handed.

Back when he was living with us, Mum prepared Pakistani meals for him to take to work. Somehow, it was better than what the Pakistani women could do, and that probably played a massive role in how her relationship with Dad lasted more than a year.

She wound up making the best curries because she'd make his food separately, and then add ingredients like chips to create a sort of Western fusion for the rest of us.

She must have been one of the first to do it, and boy was it good! Sometimes she failed in her experimentation, but my father didn't complain. He ate in silence, licking his plate clean with a fork or spoon.

Eventually, Mum grew fed up with trying to prepare curries and we would eat more western food, and that's when we'd see even less of him. As it was, his workaholic demeanour meant he was either driving buses, cabs, with his friends, making deals or doing community service like shagging all the Pakistani women in the city.

I watched him as he ate, while his friends kept up the conversation. He nodded and grunted, and slurped as he licked his fingers clean. So different! Maybe it was the company he was surrounded by, or the lack of my mother's elegant presence, but somehow he seemed just like another one of the Pakistani men I'd see on the street and nothing like the classy man I once knew.

I felt sick to the brim with the food, and my head started to hurt. The men talked loudly between them, conversing in Urdu, while the women moved to the next room and sat in silence, probably conversing between one another using telepathic means. They looked vulnerable and stupid.

I tried to catch my brother's eye, but he looked on the verge of tears. I knew that he was thinking the same things that I was: that we didn't want to be at that table, listening to the men ramble on in a language that was as foreign to us as Mandarin. I would have liked to have been close to my brother, so we could support one another during times like those, but it just wasn't the case. I knew if I had tried to talk to him about it, about us being upset or anything, he would deny it and probably lash out at me. He never wanted to be seen as vulnerable, and any mention of something that made him look weak angered him all the time.

When the "Uncles" were finally done eating, their wives came in and cleared all the plates. My father said sternly, "Zahid, go and put your plate..."

I gave him a look of pure disgust. I loathed him telling me what to do, and I wanted to disrespect him in front of the very people whose approval he had been seeking. I could not forgive myself for appearing at his front door, I mean what was I expecting; a warm welcome, some father-son bonding and love? Why did we come there, if he wasn't going to acknowledge us as his kids? If we were such an embarrassment to him and to the community, why did he marry my mother, why did he have not just one kid as a product of that so-called love, but ended up with six? Seven if you count the one that left early. I was only six, but could really reflect on these daunting questions.

It must have been some sort of a political strategy to get in good with the community, to show he was a family man and that he wouldn't hide anything from them. It was a move to show transparency, and while I can admit that he turned out to be a pretty great politician, I am disgusted by being used as a guinea pig to pull of that kind of stunt.

Meena returned to the table with dessert. It didn't look half as bad as the main course, and I looked forward to the taste of what looked like jelly rings. To be honest, it was even worse than the main course; there was this syrup-like disgusting flavour and it was so sweet you'd think my teeth would rot there and then. It was the worst dessert I had ever had in my life. She kept piling that garbage onto my plate, as a result of my dad's piercing look, knowing that I hated every morsel, and I ate fast so that it would be over quickly.

"Eat slowly, Zahid, and chew, wipe your mouth, Lateef." My father kept shooting snide comments at us, and then he would nod at his companions as though to say, "I still wear the pants in the family."

Everything was different in that house, in my dad's attitude, except for the menace he portrayed. He had always let the belt and his fists do the talking, and I was confused as to why he suddenly wanted to verbally punish us, even after he had left us.

The torture didn't end there. After dessert, we went back to the room and the women went to their room. For about three hours, my brother and I sat in the most awkward silence imaginable. The "Uncles" and Dad resumed their conversation in Urdu. I guess my father forgot to tell me to bring my translator.

I was so glad when my father finally clapped his hands together and rubbed them and the others followed suit. He shepherded us to the front door, and pulled out some money from his top pocket. He gave us a "tenner" each, and without so much as a "goodnight" he closed the doors in our faces and left us standing there in the cold.

It was too much to take in, like we were waiters being tipped at a restaurant or beggars in the street, pleading for some loose change. We did not care about the money, or at least I didn't.

As always, I did not stay in the suffering, or the humiliation and rejection. Instead, I took pleasure in the little things. We were kids, and I had some extra money, which I had not anticipated receiving, and so I could treat myself to something fun.

CHAPTER 4
A New Hope

Things at home were reaching boiling point. My mother was struggling with working two jobs, and was on the verge of getting the sack at the Bingo hall. Apparently she had not managed to solve her rifts with her boss, who constantly pressed her for results, even though she worked perfectly well.

She came home every day and broke down, snivelling alone in her bedroom, and whispering, "I can't take it anymore..."

Who could blame her? She had five children that needed feeding, clothing and looking after, and of course, on top of all that, attention.

I did not know what was worse: a father that had somehow been a support system for my mother, or the asshole leaving us, freeing us from the daily confrontation, but taking everything away from us, including my mother's strength and firmness, and perhaps even her happiness.

He was off living his dream; the king had been dethroned and the next in line was my elder brother Lateef, and he sure did a fantastic job simulating Dad's authoritarian ways of punishment and that included major flogging, with his own signature moves.

Ever since we got back from the dinner debacle at my father's new house, he seemed to have added fuel to his temper. It was killing him, but since he was a "tough guy" he kept it all contained, like a bomb always on the verge of exploding, always seeking a release.

I started avoiding him as much as I could, but I wasn't always successful in my attempts. It seemed as though the anger stimulated a few brain cells, and he actually came up with clever ways of catching me.

I discovered new ways of spending my days out on my own, even during the harshest winters. My favourite place was an old abandoned Victorian coal yard. I used to imagine being there in its heyday as a powerful, wealthy man, walking there amidst the boilers and steam engines, and people would come to me to make deals, like those men I'd seen at the Bingo Hall, and I would look sharp, big and strong in a three-piece suit, with polished shoes. Everyone respects me, including my brother.

"Out of my way, you fuckin puff!" Just dreams.

"Leave me alone," I said.

"You what?" Before I could respond, I received one of those fresh jabs he'd probably just acquired at the gym, straight to the face, knocking out one of my milk teeth. I swallowed a shot of blood and slipped away. I ran and ran without stopping until I couldn't breathe.

I blanked out for a second, and I felt the urge to throw up. Nothing came out, except the remaining blood inside my mouth, staining the sheet of white snow. It was just a milk tooth that had fallen out, but I was a kid and the sight of my own blood shocked me into oblivion. I felt vulnerable, more vulnerable than ever, and at that point I really felt the need to do something about it.

I tried to let everything go as I remained still for a few minutes and the activity of the city entertained me. I was captivated mainly by the interaction of people in the street, hanging out in groups. They looked alike and communicated in their own languages, much like my father and the group of "Uncles." I guess I needed to find my own "Uncles," only how was I supposed to know to which group I belonged?

I also noticed that the groups didn't seem to want to interact too much between one another, exchanging foreboding looks. I guess what my father always said about these people, that they always measured themselves against each other all the time, was right after all.

I wiped my nose with the bottom of my duffel coat, which had once belonged to Lateef. I had half the mind to tear it off and toss it into a gutter. I did not want to wear anything that was owned by him, but it was freezing cold. The coat will live to die another day. I felt at that moment as though I could have hated him, but I knew inside of me that at least he was part of the only thing I could feel a sort of belonging to, which still kept me attached to him.

As I walked down the street, something truly magical caught my eye. It was beautiful; the glinting blue paint, the curved handlebars and shining wheel spokes of a brand-new Chopper bicycle. Life would definitely be finer aboard that black leather seat. I wanted to ride that bike away from Bradford, away from home, away from Lateef. I admired it for a while, and then I decided to take it.

"Eh up!" someone shouted. He was blonde and around my age, with narrow eyes.

I froze with one hand on the bars and stroked the frame of the bicycle. "Wow! Nice bike, what's the speed on it?"

The lad scowled, and put one foot on a pedal. "It's got gears, makes it go faster. Got it last week." I found it to be the most magnificent thing I'd seen belonging to a kid my age.

"It's fuckin great!" I said.

"I'm Caleb."

I blinked and then smiled. "Zahid."

"That's a funny name."

"So's Caleb."

"No, actually, Caleb's a Celtic name." I thought what is a normal name anyway and what's Celtic? "D'you wanna have a go?"

"Really?" I asked, surprised.

"Yeah, go on."

"Where can I go up until?"

"I don't live so far away, wanna come to my house and play?"

"Can I?"

"Yeah mate!" It was the best day of my life until then. I was getting a chance to ride my dream bike. I got on and fell off straight away. The thrill of riding that beauty made me forget that I didn't know how.

Caleb asked, "Can ya ride a bike?"

I shook my head. "No, my dad never bought us one."

"It's easy mate, really. You just get on there, and move forwards with your feet and when you've got enough speed, you just start pedalling, and keep it steady. Go on mate try!"

It was a breath of fresh air for me, meeting Caleb. He was the friendliest lad I'd ever met, and it seemed like he trusted me, even without knowing me, at least enough to let me ride his bike. A pang of guilt struck a chord at the thought of me wanting to steal it.

Caleb lived just down the road from the store, but it seemed a million miles from where I resided. It was a splendid house; a massive stand-alone that touched the sky like a gigantic castle. I had never seen a house quite like that, and it left me gawping in wonder. The best part was that his house was right next to a perm-pressed and perfectly pruned park. Talking about having a massive back garden; it was the best.

"Hang on, I'll ask me Mum..." I waited for Caleb, as he rang the doorbell.

I was anxious, of course, because I did not know what his parents would be like. People in Bradford were usually unfriendly and nobody got along with anybody else, especially when it came to racial integration. Everyone had their patch; on one side there were the indigenous whites and on the other side were the Asians and Blacks.

I kept my eyes lowered as Caleb asked his mother permission for me to come inside. I was about to give up the chance of having a new friend, because I did not want to be looked down upon again, and I turned to walk away.

A voice called out to me. "Hello, love, fall off the bike?" she said in an odd, but delightful accent, which I later found out, was Scottish. It was Caleb's mother smiling at me. She was a charming lady and I felt relief spread to all parts of my body.

"Yeah, he didn't know how to ride it at first," Caleb laughed. "This is Za, Zah-"

"Zahid," I said.

"Well Zaheed," she pronounced my name as though it was written with two "e's" but I did not mind it at all. "It's nice to meet you, and you're just in time for tea, come on in and we'll clean you up as well, you poor thing."

The house was full of natural light and everything was in its rightful place. It was glamorous; the floor a chic marble with velvety blue rugs placed here and there like little blue ponds. The walls were solid wood; dark, intact and not peeling even slightly, and it smelt of delicious cooking.

It had been so long since I had had proper homemade food. My sister did her best, but it just wasn't the same as mum's cooking and I crossed my fingers that this would be my day.

I looked down at my muddy shoes, and hastily wiped them on the doormat outside, hoping not to leave a stain in the spotless abode, and I sniffed my armpits. I glimpsed the green mucus on the end of my coat, and I quickly took it off and tucked it away under my arm, smoothening the front of my shirt at the same time.

"Caleb, why don't you and Zaheed wash your hands before eating? Zaheed, come here, love, I'll put some antiseptic on there." I felt the motherly touch, like a blast from the past when my own mum had more time for caring about us.

"Mum, can we watch TV?" Caleb asked.

"Of course, love." They had a coloured television set. I wanted to be on my best behaviour because I didn't want to screw this up. I felt relieved and protected there as I tasted the true delight of mouth-watering melted cheese and ham, and sipped my warm, soothing tea. The homemade shortbread buttery cookies caught my attention, and I made a grab for one and crunched down on it, receiving a sharp pain in my missing tooth. Even though the rich batter mixed with the metallic taste of blood, it was heavenly.

I had to know where this family was from. It was a spontaneous urge to discover to which group they belonged. "Where are you from?"

"We're from Scotland," Caleb said.

I smirked as I remembered the familiar streets of Glasgow, "I've been there." I tried to look knowledgeable to impress him.

"Really? Where did you go?" I told him what I knew about the place, but I made sure to skip the major details of my trip. He explained that his mother and father were from Edinburgh.

After the 'small-talk,' Caleb said, "Let's go to play in my room!" As we went into his bedroom, which was on the same floor, he asked me what I wanted to play and started telling me about his toy collection. I told him about mine, and he stared at me in disbelief. "You don't have any action figures!"

I replied, "My brother took them all," when in fact his only action figure was me.

"You have to check my collection out! Come on, let's play!"

Caleb was playing with me, while I was playing the normal kid. It was refreshing to look outside the window and see a garden, rather than people yelling at each other all the time.

I loved Caleb's room and everything in it. It was personalized with posters on the wall and he had a large depiction of his favourite footy team, Leeds United, stuck behind the headboard of his bed. "Why do you support Leeds, and not Bradford City?" I asked.

"They have a group of Scottish players called the Scottish Mafia and that's why I like them, but I know that other people don't like them. They're like rebels in a way." I did not know anything about football, but I was drawn to this group of rebels. Right there and then Leeds United was my team.

I heard the door opening downstairs, and Caleb said, "Dad's home." I tensed up, and the nerves danced around inside me. I thought about making a break for it; right out the window if I had to. "Come on! Let's go see him!" I hesitated and sweat dripped down my sides, but I followed him back out into the hallway.

What I did not expect was the backbreaking hug, and the pat on Caleb's head, as his father greeted him. My father used to pat me on the head as well, only a little too hard.

And the most surprising part was when he smiled, noticing me, and asked, "New friend?" He came up to me and shook my hand. It was a firm handshake that transmitted assertiveness and respect. As he looked at me, I did not feel as though he was scrutinizing me in any way. "Hello there, nice to meet you."

"Hello, Mr. Black," I said.

"Please call me Bruce," he replied. "What's your name?"

"Zahid," I said.

"Pleasure to meet you, Zaheed, are you alright?"

"Yeah I'm okay." He smiled at me again, and I grinned right back. It was unusual, being treated like I mattered, and I wanted it to last forever.

I wished I did not have to go, but after three helpings of biscuits and two mugs of hot tea, coloured television, action figures and meeting a real father, Caleb's mother, who insisted I call her Roseanne, suddenly made it clear that it was time. "Caleb, it's time to do your homework. Zaheed, love, where do you live? Is your mum home?" My cheeks grew hot. I did not want her contacting my mother and finding out that I lived with a ghost.

"I just live up the road and yes she's at home," I said, thinking fast and hoping she wouldn't insist on calling.

She shot me a suspicious look, but said, "Alright then, you are more than welcome to come over anytime you like to play. Come by tomorrow, actually! It's a Saturday, so we can all have lunch together and you can play in the garden."

At that very moment Caleb's sister came down the stairs and peered at me. "Hi, who're you?"

"Hello, I'm Zahid," I said.

She smiled sweetly and said, "I'm Chloe." It could have been a moment when two kids from different sides of the scales fell for one another and embarked on a twisted journey of forbidden love. In truth, I was still too busy figuring out my place in the world, or at least my world at that time, which was Bradford in the seventies, while coming to terms with my childhood ending, but yes, well, I guess she did kind of like me.

As I stepped outside, I could not help but feel an overwhelming sense of hope that was enough to fill the fallen milk tooth.

CHAPTER 5
Dirty Harry

It was happy days for me. I got to see less and less of Lateef because he was always at boxing or hanging out with his mates and I spent most of my time at Caleb's house. I really enjoyed the perks of being part of the Black family, including being a normal kid without having to hear arguments in the hallways or being afraid to enter a bedroom, in case a menace was waiting on the other side to jump me.

Roseanne Black became a favourite of mine. She prepared the most amazing pizzas imaginable; the delicious blend of cheese, paste, and a variety of toppings. It was as though she could read my mind to know when I was hungry, and I could eat anything that I wanted.

I savoured every sip of soft drink, relishing the cold metal as I brought the can to my lips. We used to have soft drinks at home as well, but my father forbade any of us from having it. That was reserved for him, and he made it clear that he didn't want to share it with anyone else. It was like the cola prohibition!

Caleb's father, Bruce, made me laugh as he wore tartan pants wandering about the house. He worked as an art director at a university, for which he was perfectly suited with the attire and attitude. Sometimes I was amazed at the way Caleb looked up to him, even when he was making fun of himself to amuse us.

Later on, I even invited my little brother to join the fun, because I didn't want him to replace me as Lateef's punching bag. I introduced him to the family, and he was welcomed to their home as well, and then we were three.

Zaker had always been the good-looking boy in the family or at least that was what everyone said, just like Yasmeen was the best looking of the sisters. He was cocky and always knew how to talk to girls, even from when he was very young. He so often sold his charm to my mother in exchange for pleading his innocence, even when caught red-handed during his misdemeanours.

Sure enough he had his eyes set on Chloe, Caleb's sister and she eventually became his first official girlfriend, which gave me some relief because I never saw her as anything more than Caleb's sister, and hence my own.

Rosanne played a Florence Nightingale role, and tried her best to clean up our acts. I arrived one afternoon in a right state and she insisted I take a bath to clean myself up.

It was paradise in that bath, which was huge and there were all kinds of lotions and bath salts, which I never touched, save an ordinary bar of soap. Once finished, I got out and looked back at the water, which had turned a murky black, and my skin had gone a whole shade brighter.

While Roseanne did her best to clean my slate, Lateef worked double to spoil it. Whilst having dinner one evening, he announced to the table; "Mum, there's this really great teacher at school. He says he'd like to meet you." My mother, desperate for some assistance in keeping the household intact, agreed without question.

Harry Beacher was a strict Englishman, average height, but skinny with a goatee beard and shady glasses. Ultra-conservative and with multiple personality disorders; he was a sadistic welch; a total and utter freak with a kinky appetite for corporal punishment.

He would have been the perfect anchor-man for Fox news. He was a walking fright, like Dracula, I could even hear the horror theme music playing back every time I saw him.

We were invited to a meal at his small bungalow, in Low Moor. My mother had done her best to hide her ghostly features beneath layers of make-up and mascara, and even managed to wag a finger at me, saying, "I'm warning you, be on your best behaviour."

Mr. Beacher's home was as bizarre as a home could get without being written off as a moral hazard. In the first room upon entry, three walls were blindingly white, but the fourth one was plastered with a graphic mural of a forest, giving the impression of living in the heart of the Borneo jungle.

He had all sorts of books with different themes in shelves all around the house, most of them about God and history. The living room was L-shaped, large and well-lit going straight to the dining room, which was the worst place to be because the snob tried to school us in his borstal manners.

"Elbows off, no talking, don't eat with your mouth open you look like a washing machine. When you eat make sure you make a small meal on your fork and eat slowly..." He scowled at us, and placed a bowl of salad in the middle. I got on with it; not looking at anybody else as I munched my salad and sucked it up for my mother's sake.

When it was over, I thought Harry Beacher did enough to scare my mother off. Which was why I did not quite understand it when she announced that we would be moving in with the Yorkshire Ripper himself.

It seemed to happen from one day to the next, when my mother and Grahame Harry Beacher pitched in and put down the mortgage for a semi-detached house in an upper-class cul-de-sac, in Ascot Gardens, which was a very appealing area, differing greatly from the low class, shady terraced home off Kingswood Street.

It was 1973 and I was seven years old when my mother and Harry Beacher got married at a local registry. I stood there witnessing the unholiest of unholy unions, donning a snug pair of bellbottoms that did not suit me at all and just about summed up the whole affair.

As we offloaded at our new home in Ascot Gardens a few days later, some of the neighbours stared at us as though we were lab rats. I felt x-rayed, as though there was something fundamentally wrong with me.

Our next-door neighbours were a hellish policeman, his wife and obese son. At least there was no shortage of security, and I considered that an upgrade.

There were four bedrooms in total at our new home; one downstairs, that would be occupied by my mother and her new husband, and three upstairs. Since Soroya was the eldest and insisted that she needed her space to study, she got her own room, which meant I was bunking with Zaker and the monster Lateef again.

Our bedroom had three single beds, all arranged a meter apart. Lateef, as though it made any difference at all, shoved me into the frame of the door and jumped onto the first bed and claimed it as his. He looked like a nutter in a mental asylum. I could not care less which bed I got, I just chose one of the other two, and Zaker was left with the remaining one.

The first thing Zaker did was place a rubber mat in between the sheets and the mattress, because he would often wet himself at night. With all the tension in the house complimented with the feeling of not being wanted by our father, that was probably his way of dealing with it. He used to joke about his pee dreams with me and it used to crack me up and we both just laughed it off.

I went to bed that night thinking one day I'd open my eyes and our condescending neighbours and my tyrant brother would look up to me and treat me with some sort of respect.

The thing about Harry was that he was unsure of himself. He didn't give orders with the kind of stern authority my dad did. He wasn't bold and confident; he hesitated, with his shaky voice, and seemed caught in two minds before he finally quickly barked out the order.

That's not to say he didn't make his best attempts at demonstrating his power. He'd take his belt off and ask us to bend over, and then he'd whip our backsides raw, which I think he rather enjoyed in his own sick way. Thankfully, he wouldn't do that to the girls, but Lateef and I got whipped every subsequent day, sometimes just because we were slouching when we should have been sitting perfectly straight.

Piece by piece, Harry Beacher took my paradise away from me. For one thing, we now lived quite far away from Caleb, and so my visits to the Blacks' were restricted. The visits grew less and less frequent, and eventually, they ceased altogether.

I started to see changes in my own mother. Before my father left, she was the one we looked to for support and love. Whether or not it was in her heart, she cold-shouldered us as she fulfilled her wifely duties to Harry Beacher.

Across the street lived another kid who was Lateef's age. His father, too, was a policeman! His name was Michael and he was as spoilt as they came. The latest toys, the best clothes and he went away on holiday every so often; he had it all. Lateef made friends with him only because he knew he had money and he'd managed in his own way to "convince" Michael to give up his old toys.

There was one time a very popular toy, which had a helicopter attached to a thin cable and would fly round and round, landed magically in our room along with another toy called 'Evel Knievel,' which was a motorbike you'd wind up, let go and it would race right the way down. Michael had the lot, but that meant Lateef would sooner or later get them. I no longer had access to Caleb's toy collection, so seeing the new collections in my bedroom was a sight for sore eyes, even though I never got to actually play with them.

One Sunday afternoon, while we were just loitering around outside, I saw something that would change my perspective on life forever. A group of white kids came up the road, bouncing a football on the tarmac.

They looked at us as though they were about to make a comment, but then they recognized Lateef, and kept their heads bent as they walked past us. My elder brother stared after them until they were out of sight. There was something about the look in his eyes, something that defied his minimal brain-use, and it was in that look that I saw it all.

He evoked fear and commanded respect and nobody messed with him. He hung out with his two Polish best mates, Matti and Lonya, and even though they were white they were East European immigrants so they fitted in well with Lateef. Together they were a trio not to be reckoned with because they were heavy-duty aggressors and ran the streets with a combination of physical assault and steely looks in their eyes and his pockets of course.

I had to admit, it was inspiring the way he scared the living daylights out of everyone. For a second, I saw my father's eyes instead of his, and I knew he would do my old man proud.

I found that his life was so simple, much like his simple mind. He knew how to take care of himself, and defend himself against potential perpetrators, which was an added bonus, because it meant that he had nothing to worry about.

I, on the other hand, had to deal with rubbish at home, at school, and just about everywhere else that I went, and that made my life much more complicated.

I was never a violent kid, and I never was interested in it, in fact I hated it and still do. Sometimes, I was even bullied by my little brother, who took a leaf from Lateef's book. I was never a fighter, but in the end I would have to bring a fighting instinct to my character. It was all about respect and that was what I was looking for.

The question was by doing nothing would I find my way?

CHAPTER 6
When the Going Gets Tough

There's an old Yorkshire saying that goes: "When the going gets tough, the tough get going." And boy were things getting tough at home, if I could call it home in the first place, and Harry Beacher was the toughest nut to crack. Unfortunately for him, he had toed the line with Lateef.

The tension between them started building up from the day Harry initiated his educational rituals with the help of a belt and an overly done speech about good manners and values that not even he could believe.

In his imaginary world he was a demigod, physically strong and powerful, destroying evil through belt whips, which was his secret weapon. Still, he didn't acknowledge the power of the dark lord's son.

What Harry Beacher did not understand was that my brother was a prodigy of terror. Everyone conveniently forgot to tell him that Lateef was the anger and frustration of my father and that he was deadly.

There was the sound of a scuffle in the kitchen, followed by a few thuds and Beacher's yells. Lateef walked outside yelling back at him not to come near him, but as usual that stubborn wart did not heed my brother's warning.

It was the 'Rumble in the Jungle,' a fighter and a mouse measuring one another up, and the ring was our backyard. In the crowd were Mum, Soroya and I, silent and in a sick way eager. We held our breaths because we knew what was going to happen and we knew exactly who we were supporting and more importantly who would win.

Harry moved forward in an attempt to grapple Lateef and show that he was stronger. Next thing we knew, Lateef had delivered an uppercut to his face and what a beautiful blow it was too, I think even the great Muhammad Ali would have been proud. I would know, I'd received plenty of those, only I never thought it would look that gruesome. He then grabbed Beacher by the hair and at the same time with his other hand brought the garage door crashing down straight on top of his head. There was blood everywhere!

Lateef, for good measure, got on top of him as he lay on the floor screaming, and put all his body weight on the man's back and repeatedly punched him in the back of his head and his ribs and finished him off with an almighty head-butt which sounded like his skull had broken in two. I looked at Mum and saw nothing, she didn't seem to have any emotions at all.

We all loved seeing Beacher squealing as blood splashed all about him. He surfaced from the tangle of limbs with a bloodied nose and an expression of pure shock and embarrassment. He screamed that he needed help and at that moment the self-proclaimed man of the house picked up his broken glasses and ran away, ran far off to the hospital.

My mother knew that Harry was a complete failure when it came to being a stepfather that we could look up to, or get inspired by. She also knew at that moment that her marriage with Harry was in jeopardy, and that her master plan of having a stable, secure relationship was about to go down the toilet. I reckon all she could do about it was pray and hope that things would get better.

From that day Lateef was spared any further assaults by Harry. He was definitely on a streak, because my mother did not apprehend him for what he had done and just gave him a free pass to do whatever he liked. I was happy he had given the freak Beacher a beating but he had gotten even worse with me and beat me for no reason.

I don't know if anybody listened to my mother's prayers, but Lateef spared both she and Beacher by eventually leaving the house, which was a relief for me as well, but he did return every now and again, like a monster, to take things from the house, and practice his boxing with his all-time favourite punching bag.

Harry, too, was hell bent on releasing his fury, one way or the other, and now that he had double the tension from not being able to whip my brother, he took it all out on me, but those floggings did not come free. After every beating, I would sneak into his bedroom and in the wardrobe he hung all his expensive suits. That's where he would keep his cash and I would take sometimes a hundred to two hundred pounds depending on how badly he struck me, but I made sure not to take everything.

It seemed as though Lateef needed a new challenge, when he came up to me and said, "You're going to join the boxing club, you've got no choice you puff, it's about time you manned up." I really didn't want to box and hated the thought of getting beaten up by even more people, but deep down I knew he had a point.

I enrolled at the Bradford Police Boys Boxing Club, and if I thought things were going to improve overnight, and that people would come kissing up to me and Harry Beacher would start respecting me, and I would be able to throw a left hook and down Lateef, I was wrong.

The thousand-mile journey had only just begun with that first step, and there was a whole mountain to move pebble by pebble, so even though everyone expected me to be a tough guy, I knew that I wasn't.

The late seventies and eighties were the decades where boxing was at its prime. It was the time when great rivalries blossomed, and the heavyweight division was the ultimate. My favourite was and still is Muhammad Ali. He defined everything that I wanted to be; he was noble and intelligent while at the same time fearless and brave. He made boxing look like an art, but coupled it with logic, each move calculated, each step perfectly measured, and each blow delivered correctly.

My brother Zaker got into boxing as well. Like Lateef, he was a natural and loved looking good. The benefits of training his body definitely encouraged him to make boxing his thing. The only thing that worried him was whether or not he'd still look good after the match. He was fast, flashy, cocky and had nifty footwork, kind of like Sugar Ray Leonard. He was so good that eventually he was voted the number one prospect in Yorkshire for schoolboy boxing.

Lateef, on the other hand, was mean and ruthless in the ring, with that Mike Tyson vibe, as the other boys would say: "Your brother is hard as nails, mate." His challengers were scared even before the sparring began.

I had to step up to the plate. I wasn't the toughest, nor was I the most handsome of the three but what I did have was mental resolve and I was clever. If boxing was rated by how clever a man was then Lateef or Zaker could shine my shoes.

I remember the first day I was going to train. We went straight from school to the boxing club, which was on the other side of Bradford. There

I was with my plastic bag filled with a vest, a pair of shorts and old pumps or what they now call sneakers, which actually had holes in the bottom.

We got there and there was warm up. We did the usual stuff and worked the bags, sit ups, press ups, which seemed to take forever and my arms felt like lead. The blisters on my knuckles burned and after the first session they bled because the skin had rubbed off.

After quite a few visits, the training seemed to get bearable. Even though I got used to the exercises and the warm up, doing it on a constant basis, repetition after repetition, was still a kick in the gut. The first real test for me came when I was told I would be sparring with a fellow boxer called Spencer.

He was a couple of years older than I was; massive frame, face like a bull, his jaw hard and set. Mr. Walsh, our old Irish trainer, signalled the start, and Spencer circled, eyeing me hungrily. I wasn't experienced enough to make the first move and I knew sooner or later, someone would have to thrust.

It is true that practice makes perfect, because not only had Lateef and my father perfected their upper cuts, I had perfected my pain threshold and at that moment, a jab materialized itself, and I felt Spencer's glove connect with my face. I immediately jabbed back, out of impulse, which took him by surprise. He came at me and pinned me into the corner and let loose with what seemed like a million body shots.

I fought back, which only infuriated him, but I stood firm. He was smashing me about, but he wasn't beating me. I didn't feel any pain; maybe his body shots were too fast, or perhaps I was just that immune to it or more likely the adrenaline had kicked in. After some time, Mr. Walsh called "Time" and we went back to our respective corners.

Lateef, who was at my end, looked at me in sheer disbelief. He said, "You okay, Zahid?" Up until then, I would not believe a miracle when I saw it, but to actually hear the pea brain ask if I was doing alright, showed there maybe was hope for him after all. I nodded and walked out for the second round of sparring.

As I approached the middle, I overheard someone say, "Boy, Zahid looks a mess. Spencer is kicking the shit out of him."

Mr. Walsh signalled the restart, and this time I attacked immediately, rushing forwards and throwing a couple of rookie punches. For the first time in my life I hadn't waited for a beating, but I'd dished one out instead. I actually felt nothing in terms of excitement; I was on automatic pilot and did what I thought I needed to do. I could see Spencer was worried that I was not going down. I didn't disappoint, and kept circling him, leaning forwards and using my body weight to try and find the sweet spot.

And then it happened. I hit him so hard he fell over, and everyone watching started to shout. It was as though I had delivered the final blow in a World Boxing Championship match.

Mr. Walsh told the boys in his Irish accent, "Calm down, lads, it's just sparring!" Still, everybody wanted to see me give this Spencer a beating, because I was the underdog with very little prior experience, and my opponent was an arrogant regular.

Spencer was livid. He got back up and decided enough was enough, and he retaliated with a move that was beyond my amateur skills. He dodged my fist, got under me, and threw a clean punch that connected with my chin, but he did not manage to put me down.

Mr. Walsh called for time again, and I walked towards my corner bleeding from my nose and mouth. Spencer walked behind me, laughed and said to Lateef, "Your kid isn't really a chip off the old block, is he mate."

To my surprise Lateef got in the ring as well. "Move out the way, Zahid," he told me. He turned to Spencer and said, "Yeah, that's tough doing that to my little brother. Now let's see if you can do that to me…" His body shook as his rage climaxed, and he threw powerful punch after powerful punch in quick succession. I was awestruck by the way his anger fuelled him into action, and it eventually took three lads to get him off Spencer, who lay out cold, with his nose and two ribs broken.

"Cunt!" Lateef spat, as the three trainers gripped him tight and steered him out of the ring.

Mr. Walsh screamed at Lateef, "Bloody ell, Teefy, Spencer was supposed to be fighting this weekend!" For the first time, he looked the part of an elder brother, coming in to stand up for his kinsman.

Lateef was furious, but I didn't mind because it wasn't directed at me. He kept muttering under his breath, spitting every now and again, and cracking his knuckles. His cold-blooded fists had worked brilliantly, so much so that I was shocked at how coordinated he could be.

I could say that he and my sisters were covering good ground in building up their careers. Soroya for example was the brightest one. She had gone off to university, to pursue a degree in medicine and had a part-time job at the Leeds Royal Infirmary. She'd tell us stories about a creepy celebrity that was admitted there, called Jimmy Saville, who at the time had a show on television called *Jim'll Fix It*. Later on she would prove to be right regarding her observation.

My favourite sister, Yasmeen, the free-spirited rock music lover, was studying to be an orthopaedic specialist. She'd moved out and away from Bradford to study digs in Otley, and was at the time practicing nursing first, before going off to Edinburgh to further her qualifications.

And since I was good for nothing elsewhere, I kept it up at the gym, and I gained confidence as well as new moves. I never took boxing as seriously as Lateef, but did it as it helped me with my anger. I felt fitter and stronger each time I went in there, which really helped me keep my head up, but I knew I was still several push-ups away from being the real deal.

Boxing had become especially trendy because the film 'Rocky' had released and was a huge hit. I loved Sylvester Stallone, with his bad-ass attitude and deep-toned voice. He seemed like the real deal, and the poverty and hard times was something I could definitely relate to.

My brothers and I sneaked in at the Odeon cinema to see it. Boxing really had brought the three of us together. It was a fantastic film. I remember the 'Rocky' music theme, when he prepared to get into the ring; the way it seemed to pump everyone up. We knew it was just a movie, but the fact that everyday people respected anyone who boxed made us all feel good.

Finally, after quite some time of hard training, the biggest day in my sporting life up until then arrived. Zaker, Lateef and I would fight for the Bradford schoolboy championship. This would be the first time ever that three brothers would contest for the esteemed title of Bradford's finest.

Lateef went first, and it didn't last long. The power and precision was awesome and he dealt with his opponent quickly and knocked him out. Zaker was next and he fought a beautiful fight; running rings around his opponent, tiring him out, throwing a jab here, there, and dodging the incoming blows, easily winning on points.

My two brothers had done it, and so it all came down to me. The trainer Mr. Walsh felt that it would be good to have Lateef in my corner for some tips. The only one he had was, "Kick his bleedin' head in!"

I got in the ring and took a good look at my opponent. He was black, bulky, but short, so it would be difficult to put him down. Trust my luck, he was not only the reigning city champion, but also the county champion. He had badges all over his shorts saying that, as though to rub salt in the wounds.

I kept steady, and took my eyes off the badges. I walked to the centre of the ring, we touched gloves and nodded at each other as a sign of respect and went back to our corners. The bell went and I came out to meet my fate. I advanced towards him and just let it all go and didn't wait.

My mind was as clear as an English summer's day and I was ready to dish out some pain. He jabbed and missed, and I felt powerful and fearless and at the same time calm. The bullying was about to pay off and sure enough, I jabbed back, followed by a vicious uppercut and BANG he was down. I'd hit him so hard I felt the power shoot through me into the ground and it felt great!

The referee didn't even bother to count. With that punch he knew he wasn't getting up. He waved the fight off and lifted my arm as a sign of victory. Thirty-three seconds, that's all it took for me to take out one of the hottest prospects around. I was so proud of myself, and even though he was proud as well, Lateef said nothing. Zaker, the little narcissist, was saying, "Oh did you see how I ran rings around that lad, I mean I could have taken him out in one punch as well ..." Well he didn't and I did, and to me that was something.

My self-esteem and self-belief were sky high. It was the start of the process that would score me respect and points. I was ready...with brains and the brawn.

A few days later, I strutted out of the school compound after another uninspiring day, but feeling confident with my fists. I had no idea what was waiting for me at home, until I got there. The rotten Harry Beacher had two other kids with a different partner, a twin boy and girl named Sean and Fiona.

Sean was his father's spawn; a reincarnation of the grand freak himself. He was every bit as condescending as his old man. I wondered if others saw us as Dad in the same way.

Lateef terrified Sean and even though he did not come by so often, he had picked a day when my elder brother was not there.

He was being an utter nuisance and I said to him, "Your dad's a freak and a queer, chip off the old block you are, Sean." I think it may have been my intense hatred of Harry that I could not stand the existence of two of the same kind; the world did not deserve it.

I had him in a headlock and was pounding his face, until good old Harry Beacher came into the picture. As he pulled me off he took a hold of my arms and then in a split-second Sean had punched me full force in my gut.

He had hit me so hard, all the wind was knocked out of me. I couldn't breathe and felt like I was hurtling at light speed towards a bright light. And then, all was calm and there was silence. Suddenly, I felt relaxed. I wasn't afraid. It was the most relaxing and calming experience of my life.

I took a couple of minutes to be there and enjoy it. I asked myself: What now? Nothing!

I could have sworn there was a reverberating voice about me that I could not recognized. It said, "It's not your time yet."

Before I could answer, I woke up back in my body, with my mother bent over me. She was panting with the effort of resuscitating me and unfortunately for the Beacher crew, she'd managed.

She turned to Sean and said, "Get out now."

He said, "It was an accident!"

"I don't care get out," she said again. She knew that once Lateef heard about this Sean would be a dead man walking.

I think that she also realized clearly that Beacher had nothing in his heart for us. He couldn't care less about their relationship and about me.

Still, Sean's dirty punch had turned the epiphany on, and I found myself meeting realisation upon realisation.

That near-death experience would change everything in my outlook from that moment on. I had been resurrected, but still had to figure out what I was sent back to do.

CHAPTER 7
Cut from a Different Cloth

It was the late 1970s, a period in which the extremist group, known as the Irish Republican Army, or the IRA, started making noise about British rule in Northern Ireland, and how they wanted to end it and unite as one country.

At that time, I didn't know too much about the political implications, but people all across Bradford talked about it because of the bombs that kept going off in Northern Ireland and the threats to England.

I never could understand why one group would hate another even though they worshipped the same God. The fact that people lived in fear, birthed my contempt for any kind of terrorism or religious intolerance. I could not take on the leader of the IRA, not then at least, but what I could do was warm up with the toughest kid and the biggest bully at school: Alan Regiska.

I couldn't stand the fact that there was one guy terrorising everyone by taking advantage of other more vulnerable kids. I knew the feeling of being bullied, and since I was still starting out, I felt empowered to make my stand there at school.

It was break time and I was sat on a step, minding my own business, when I saw Alan patrolling with his group of bullies. He passed me by, and said, "Paki, what you looking at?"

I replied, "Fuck off."

"What ya say?"

I stood up and looked him in the eye. I'd plucked up enough courage to say to him, "See you at the gates."

I guess he thought of me as a joke as he replied, "Alright, you Paki, I'm gonna kick the shit out you."

As the bell to signal the end of school sounded, I headed outside. I was a little nervous, and my body fed me with a dose of adrenaline. I had taken out the county champion in the tournament, and that had to count for something, I hoped.

I decided not to wait. I had seen how Alan had fought and knew how dirty he was, but I could play dirty too…

He was laughing and joking with his mates without a care in the world, because in his eyes he had already won. I used my brain and picked up a stone from the ground and charged him. He turned to face me, but before he could do or say anything, I hit him full force with the stone in his face. I not only surprised him, but everyone else there including myself.

The force of the hit dropped him to his knees as he held his face with blood pouring from his nose, cheek and eye. I employed the "be wild" technique to scare the gang off and went crazy on Alan, jumping on him and displaying a variety of combinations of hits I had up my sleeve; my fists destroying him.

He screamed for me to let go and said, "You win, you win, leave me alone!" All of his so-called friends and others who had been victims of his bullying cheered me on. It was like I had just won the war on terror.

Taking down the school bully was something that I was definitely proud of. And I was making great progress in my pursuit of respect, but I did not want to be the new, improved version of Lateef.

If I was not violent, but had beaten up the bully, did that make me my brother's replica? And if I wasn't, what did it mean for me to smash a boy's face in with a rock?

Those were the things I thought about as I sat on the hill overlooking my school, Mandale Middle, slamming off as usual. I was just eleven, but had always been existential, wondering about my path, and how I was going to get on it. What would I look like at twenty-one, how would I be, where would I be, would I be still in this awful and racist city where every creed and colour hated each other, where violence was the norm? I felt "cut from a different cloth."

I wished that I could sit out there on that hill and contemplate forever, but night-time would surely come, and even I was not foolhardy as to stay out there to welcome trouble, at least not all the time. I had to seek shelter, which was casa Beacher.

I thought that money and stability would solve Mum's problems, but I was wrong. She looked more ghostly than ever before, and even worse with the brand new purple dressing gown she had bought as a treat for herself, which clashed horribly with her pale skin. I knew she was still crying herself to sleep every night because her eyes were all puffy and red when I saw her the following morning before she went to work.

As though to add insult to injury, she received a phone call from her family in Holland, with the news that her father had taken ill. I thought she might have looked more stressed to hear it, but to the contrary she sighed with relief, and told Zaker and I to pack our bags. She wanted to take us with her because we were the youngest of the lot, and the others already had something going for them.

I was excited to be going on my first trip. It was an opportunity for me to see the world beyond the Bradford Bubble, and I was thrilled for my first train and ferry rides.

We left early and got on the train to Hull where we would take the ferry to the Hoek of Holland. Mum couldn't afford a cabin on the ferry, so instead we got reclining chairs, which worked fine for us.

After a couple of hours, the jittery joy in my stomach took a turn on me. I got seasick and threw up continuously over the side of the boat, but that didn't stop me from amusing myself. While Mum slept, Zaker and I paid a visit to the small casino on the ship and watched old people gamble their pensions away.

Holland was unbelievable, very different from Bradford for sure, or any other place I had been to before. There were houses with so many small windows and lots of birds flying close by the port. It was summer time, but it still didn't feel so warm. People spoke in a strange language, which Mum understood. It was one of those times I felt proud to be related to her, seeing her babble away in rapid Dutch with the people at bus counters.

We stayed in Eindhoven, with my mother's foster mother. From what I gathered, she was the reason why my mother's turbulent early life was made bearable. She was the sweetest lady I had met, and I thought a union with her would only bring good fortune to my dysfunctional family.

Eindhoven was my first true taste of Europe beyond Britain. The city was like something from the future, with brand new buildings. Everything was so clean, and law-abiding citizens went about their lives without so much as a hiccup. Apparently everything was new because the Germans in the war had blown the old city to smithereens.

From there, my mother planned on visiting her ailing father in Amsterdam, and she arranged for us to go to stay with other members of her family in Rotterdam.

It was there that I met my cousin from the Surinam side. He was laid back and nothing seemed to faze him. He was also mixed-race, but he didn't seem confused about it like I was. I asked him what it was like being a breed in Holland and he just shrugged and explained that it never really crossed his mind. It seemed as though Holland would be a better place for me than Bradford.

He took me everywhere and some things do run in the family, because he even had the same trick of sneaking into the cinema without paying. I even learnt one or two new ones. I remember we went to see a film called 'Saturday Night Fever,' which was fun, but not really my type and nothing compared to 'Rocky,' but spending time with my cousin meant that I enjoyed the flick nonetheless.

Our time in Holland seemed to end as the Saturday Night Fever credits rolled upwards. It had been short, with a bitter-sweet ending. I had a breather leaving Beacher's lair even for a few days, but my mother was faced with futility after her father passed away before she arrived to Amsterdam to see him. She was devastated, and we did not know what to say to her, but we knew it was the final straw for her.

It was not as though Harry Beacher bothered about my mother's demise, not in the least when I saw him dressed up in her underwear, arranging his non-existent breasts. At first I thought I might have been hallucinating, but there in front of me he was stripped to the essentials, and his true colours had been revealed.

He saw me, and that meant I knew his sordid secret. He froze with fear, beads of sweat appearing on his forehead, and his eyes wide with horror. He was petrified that I would tell my mother, even though I would never dream of doing that because I knew it would be more pain for her.

I could have told my mates what I had seen, and they might have enjoyed it. After Caleb and boxing, I had improved my socialisation skills, finding my crew along the way. Closer to where the Blacks lived, the council estate called Canterbury, I had had a few mates, and then just up the road from where I lived was another council estate called Buttershaw.

In Buttershaw, I'd hang out at the local youth club where I met a mix of English and Jamaican lads, who didn't like the boys from Canterbury. It was a small detail I didn't know, a taste of gang rivalry, but I used it to my favour to bridge the two sides.

I adapted well and I practically became Jamaican. I even used their dialect and ate their food. I spoke fluent 'Patois' which was Jamaican English or as it's known by its alias, 'Pigeon English.' Hanging out with the Jamaicans brought me to Lovers Rock, Reggae, Hip Hop, RnB and SKA and it was the latter that touched my soul deeply.

My new mates suited me well. We could all relate to one another, being mixed breeds. They understood what it was like not knowing on which side of the scales to fall, or where we belonged, and that was great because in belonging nowhere, we ended up together.

When I was not hanging out with my posse, I was testing my business acumen, which was beginning to sharpen. The mission: getting merchandise from the centre and setting the sales strategy according to the market niche...done!

I used to walk for an hour to get to Bradford city centre, where I could find a huge selection of items for me to shoplift and steal. The juiciest spot was a toy shop right in the heart of the city. I would always make like I was just checking out the toys, even though I didn't actually care about them. I think I had had enough of the all-action Spiderman with extra abilities when I used to play with Caleb.

I had sticky fingers, and was slick and quick with doing the deed, snatching up the toy and stuffing it into the inside pocket of my duffel coat without the shop owner noticing. At that time, there was no CCTV, which was good for the small thieves, so my job was successful and clean.

When my stock was up, and I had a full supply, I would leave the shop and make for the amusement arcade, where I would loiter around, casually leaning against the machines, and picking the right moment to use a long piece of plastic to click up credits, which meant acquiring credits to make purchases, which I would then sell at half price.

I was like a mobile toy store at school. The kids would get all excited to see me, as I'd sell them what I'd stolen for twice the price. I was securing a two hundred percent profit, which was not bad at all. I recall that in a week I'd have made a solid ten to fifteen quid just off selling toys!

I really did have an eagle eye for making money, and in addition to selling toys and credits, I signed up for school dances and it was not because I was in any way interested in attending them or thinking I was Michael Jackson or John Travolta.

My posse would make like a group of bouncers and charge the rich kids fifty pence entry to their own dance. They would look at us and say, "I thought it was free?" Well, we were duly paid for our ushering services, because we managed to keep out the bullies.

I had to hide my money, carefully, because I knew if Lateef found out, he'd take it all

by force. I hid it underneath the loose floorboard in the attic. I knew nobody ever went there so I was sure it was safe. The tricky part was making sure nobody was around when I went out to hide it.

The thing with seeing less of Caleb and getting a reputation on the streets was that I was bound to meet some interesting people. Zaker and I used to go to the fair in Wibsey whenever it was set up, which was close by the youth club. We ended up meeting a tiny guy, possibly the smallest black guy I'd ever met, called Dave Mallet.

He might have been small, but he was he quick enough to run from any tight spot or tough enough to stand his ground. He was actually from the Canterbury area and his sister knew my sister, but we overcame the Buttershaw-Canterbury rivalry and we all became good friends and I respected him tremendously. There were other characters like Clive Fergusson, Gaffa, Jacko, Simon Hunter and Roger Marsh to name a few.

Around Halloween that year, I devised a plan to dress Mallet up as a zombie by putting make up on him, and carry him as a sort of puppet around the neighbourhood for some trick or treating.

It was brilliant: we went to the rich neighbourhoods, and we'd knock at their doors and initially, with the smaller houses, we'd get some small change. "Let's try some of the bigger houses," I said. We'd collected at least twenty quid up until then, which wasn't bad for kids like us.

Roger, Mallet and I went up to a humungous house and rang the doorbell. An old white fellow answered it, and said, "I say lads, that looks very realistic. Very good!" To our utter disbelief, he pulled out a wad of money from his back pocket.

Mallet saw it, jumped out of our arms, nearly giving the old man a heart attack, grabbed the money screaming, "Thank you!" and ran off into the night. Apparently, he had no idea that Mallet was a real person!

It was a great night. We had loads of money, but we were also in an unwelcoming area, which for us meant trouble. The other gangs were doing their rounds, and it was only a matter of time until we were spotted and ganged up on. We were far fewer than they were, and it didn't make any sense at all getting into a mix up with them, not to mention we also stood out in the white area.

Sure enough, as we walked on Moore Avenue we noticed a group of older white kids on the other side of the street. They spotted us and screamed, "Let's get those niggers!" We ran as fast as we could and got away.

My best friend at this new point in my life was a lad called Roger Marsh, whom I had met via my little brother as they both went to Buttershaw School. Zaker owed me one after I'd introduced him to the Caleb Black's family and his first girlfriend. Roger and I hit it off immediately and became the best of mates. We were inseparable and went everywhere and did everything together. He was like my brother.

He was stocky, and one of those Afro-white mixes. His mother, Marion, was English, and a lovely lady. I never saw her as a competitor to Mrs. Black in any way, and she had a special place in my heart.

His father, Trevor, was Jamaican. He was an ultra-cool, very laidback gentleman and he treated me like I was his own son. Trevor had so many kids that even he had lost count, and I guess he had added me to his collection, but that didn't bother Roger one bit as he got on well with his dad.

Around that time, my own father had gotten elected as a councillor of Bradford City: the first person of Asian and Muslim origin to achieve that post. His transition to power was complete: to top off all the grafting and misdemeanours, he now had the political muscle to follow through and completely take over. He had garnered a lot of respect from different communities, the Tories as well, and all sorts of different Elites included.

He might have won the respect of all those people, but not mine. Being a councillor now meant that we had to get an appointment to go to see him. I guess we needed one even before he got into government, but the difference now was his wife wasn't the secretary.

It was another awful lady, and she refused us to go and see him, even though we told her who we were. She didn't believe us and it wasn't her fault. It was my father denying us again and now, being so important, with more reasons.

As for my adoptive family, Roger wasn't as bright as me in terms of business, but back then, he was loyal. One time in winter I remember going to his house asking him to join me. He was in bed and stirred as I threw one pound notes on the top of his blanket. He got up straight away and said, "Let's go, Zid how come you always have money, where'd ya get it all from?". I was always on the lookout for new opportunities and always happy to share my proceeds with him.

By that time I was known as Zid. My little brother had seen a film called 'Our man Flint' and started calling me 'our man Zid' and it just caught on from there.

Roger and I were like two peas in a pod. When I was not scheming, trying to make money, we'd be laughing at our adventures or just enjoying one another's company, sitting on middens, which were a kind of low Yorkshire brick stonewall, whiling the hours away eating chip butties and mushy peas or hanging out down town in the city centre.

We really were two of a kind and I loved Roger like my own family.

CHAPTER 8
Victorian Warehouse

It was 1979 and Margaret Thatcher was up for election. She was running on a Conservative Party ticket and promptly ousted other people from different ideologies, most of them from the Labour Party, compromised with migrants' rights.

I remember being sat in front of the telly, listening to her and wondering: wow a woman as leader, she might be good, *'Where there is discord, may we bring harmony. Where there is error, may we bring truth. Where there is doubt, may we bring faith. And where there is despair, may we bring hope.'*

She was a strong and imposing lady who promised to get Britain out of the economic crisis. Everyone was complaining about how difficult it was to find a job and the ones with jobs were losing them. Even mum was worried about losing hers.

The funny thing is that everyone had faith in Thatcher, including our people, the breeds, but she would end up going against us and she was the worst leader ever, a fiend of the North of England. This is something I would personally experience: poverty, discrimination and more discrimination.

When it came to us breeds, Asians, blacks and the white Northerners, it was a recipe for disaster. She was right about the minority increasing, and in spite of her efforts to limit the number of immigrants coming into the country, they kept coming in, and this generated more problems between the locals and the outsiders.

There was racial tension everywhere, and I could feel it as strongly as ever. It was not possible for me to hide what I was, and so I learnt from Thatcher's character and didn't allow people looking down on me to affect me.

Harry loved Thatcher. I'm sure they looked so similar when she wore that blue dress. She was like his alter-ego: strict, rigid, ultra-conservative, hated breeds and in that regard, that included my mother.

By that time, she and Harry were just two people sharing the responsibility of the house; purely pragmatic, nothing emotional. He did his best to follow his role model at home, but his intimidation strategy wasn't working anymore.

My mother did have something to finally distract her from her crumbling relationship with Harry. Around that time, there was a popular TV show named 'Dallas' about a Texan oil tycoon, his dirty business, family and love affairs. Mum was hooked. She'd wait for it and when it came on, her eyes would be glued to the television set and maybe she would be transported to that world to be Miss Ellie.

I personally liked a show called, 'Rich man, Poor man' about two brothers; one was rich and one was poor, one was evil and the other was good. And so it was, in our house there was much love and affection exclusively for our priceless parent-friend Mrs. TV.

Lateef had had his round with Harry, and part two was about to happen, only this time with a new stuntman: me. My elder brother and I were in Harry's garage, getting to work on repairing his rusted Robin Reliant. It hadn't seen any action, and was sitting about gathering dust, so he thought about fixing it up and maybe selling it.

By this time Lateef was a Mod and had a beautiful Lambretta scooter chromed, which he had done up all by himself. I admired his handiwork, and the idea of repairing the car got me interested, and I saw it as an opportunity to do something with my brother.

Lateef really was a genius when it came to using his hands. He knew which bolts went where, and how to assemble the different pieces. He even sprayed it blue and when he was done, it gleamed and was ready to be sold. He attempted to get the engine going, but it didn't start.

We started to push the thing down the road and because it was made of fiberglass, it wasn't all that heavy. It finally spluttered into life, with a dubious sound, but it started and Lateef drove off into the horizon.

I laughed at the sight of that ugly Robin Reliant, repaired and looking quite decent. Lateef had no license, but he had the logbook, which meant he could at least sell the thing, which he duly did and actually gave me something. It was not much, but it was at least something, which was better than nothing especially when it was my brother giving me the money.

Harry, of course, wasn't pleased when he found out that his favourite flower pot, which he made at the rat house function, had vanished. Thanks to his outstanding detective skills, he discovered that we had actually fixed that junk and sold it. He wanted his cut, but he didn't have the guts to ask Lateef. So naturally he came to me.

"How much did you get?" he demanded.

I told him to ask Lateef, and that I didn't want to be bothered at the time, but Harry was persistent. He kept pestering me to know how much I had made, until I finally screamed, "Fuck off!" and started walking away.

He walked behind me into the garden and grabbed me from behind, pulling me down. We tussled on the lawn for a while, and I managed to pin him down. I realized even as a thirteen year old, I was much stronger than he was. I pounded him while he screamed like a banshee.

As a boxer, I knew exactly how and where to punch him. My fury was unleashed on him. It was therapeutic, and all the frustration that had built up during my time with him gave way, and I added a few more for my mother.

He tried to cover his face up with his arms, but I followed up with some of my best blows and he had no guard to my punches. I only stopped because I could tell when a man was beat. I wasn't my elder brother: I didn't have the rage, but I knew all about revenge.

From that day on, Harry kept his belt on, and my buttocks were streak-free.

I was getting older and bigger, and so my stomach needed more food, which meant I had to have more money in the pockets. We lived in a better house, but there was never enough food for us. I'd long since moved on from the toyshop, to bigger loot that was worth more. While the kids at school were trading these little football cards for money, I was out there gambling my life to get the real loot.

Getting to know Lateef's best practices, and his car trading, I realized the business was promising. I remembered when I was younger there was one time where I had been in a car with my dad and he had sat me on his lap and I had watched how he drove it. That was all the experience I needed.

I decided to give it a try. It was an RS 2000 Escort, white and fast. It was quite a beauty.

I used a screwdriver to open the car door by breaking the lock. I dismantled the ignition and as they'd say "Bob's your uncle." I had done well to find such a car, and I was driving for the first time in my life.

I watched around me as I accelerated. I must have driven in first gear for a mile before it started to smell like burnt rubber and I felt the machine was struggling to go any faster. I thought that it might be a good idea to change gears. I approached the traffic lights and the damn thing turned off.

Low and behold, my good luck just couldn't fail me and on the opposite side of the road was a cop car. They looked at me and not even my tactics of looking tough and older were effective because they knew a baby-faced driver like me shouldn't be driving a car, let alone a car like that.

The car was off, but my survival instincts were on, and I put a series of moves down on the ignition system and fiddled with the pedals and after the car stuttered for a couple of minutes, I could finally turn the engine on again and escape.

They gave chase and the heat was up. I found myself sliding into the different gears, working out the pedals and the steering wheel. I drove all over the place and thanks to a combination of nerves of steel, adventure spirit, ignorance and sheer dumb luck, the police couldn't get me. Or maybe it was the traffic.

It was too close a call. I dumped the car in Bingley, just outside of Bradford and started working on my street intelligence service to get an old motorbike. There she was standing beautifully outside of a house in a neighbourhood a few streets away. I waited outside in a hidden spot until it was night-time and even though I knew there were people inside, I broke into the garage and found a set of keys and a helmet.

I had a feeling that one of the keys would be for the bike, so I tried them all one by one and unbelievably one of the keys fitted the ignition. I walked with the bike for about half a mile and then started it. I didn't know how to ride it, and it was definitely a lot more complicated than Caleb's bicycle, but I had managed to lose the heat in an RS 2000, so how difficult could a bike be?

I fell a couple of times because I'd let the clutch out too fast. It was difficult to get the stability right at the beginning. I slowly got used to the acceleration, and tried the gears out randomly. I found the smooth one and was cruising down the road.

I rode all the way home. I must have looked awfully silly in that black helmet but it sure was exciting. I wanted to keep riding, but the night was ending so I had to park it a few streets short; leaving it in a secret hideaway I was sure only I knew about.

I went into Lateef's box where he kept all kinds of stuff and I remembered he had blue paint left over from when he did the Robin Reliant up. I took it and in a field nearby, re-sprayed the bike from red to blue. I knew that wasn't going to be enough, so I figured out how to make the bike look even more different by adding some stolen plates from the junkyard and my bike was good to go.

I made most of my hits on that bike, going under the cover of darkness and visiting different warehouses. I would break into them and take whatever I could before riding off again. The following day, I took what I had stolen and sold it to make myself a small fortune.

Sometimes I'd go alone, but for the more complicated hits I had to count on my partner in crime: a crazy Jamaican lad called Floyd Lawes. I don't think warehouse hits were really Roger's thing, so Floyd it was. His mum ran a West Indian food shop at John Street market and I had met him through other friends that called themselves "Rude Boys," which was a term given to boys who were into Ska music, were rebels and broke the rules to get by.

Floyd was an adrenaline junkie, like me, and he just loved doing anything thrilling. Sometimes I was scared that he enjoyed the narrow escape so much, that one day he'd get us caught.

We never planned any of our hits, and just drove about on the bike until we came across something. One large Victorian warehouse, bang in the centre of Bradford and opposite the university seemed to be the perfect spot. It was noisy there with student parties happening all around, and junkies minding their own business, and so we could go about stealing without too much of a problem.

We bust into the warehouse, which we saw stored textiles; we figured there must be something of value in there.

Everything was working out smoothly. There were no disturbances as we got into the space and took what we could carry off. We were about to get away, when sirens wailed and a voice shouted out to us, "Don't move!"

Floyd and I exchanged quick glances, and didn't think twice before making a run for it. The police were not quick enough as they moved snail-like, shouting behind us. I heard barking, and ran faster because I knew that *they* would definitely be able to catch us.

We sprinted to what seemed like a low wall that we thought we could leap. The only trouble was that it turned out to be terribly high and we crashed at the bottom. Floyd screamed as he held onto a broken leg. I could see his bone sticking out with blood everywhere. I wasn't in pain per se, but I was shocked seeing Floyd's leg all messed up and, before I knew it, the dogs were at my face and barking at Floyd. We had no choice but to sit there like two dummies.

The police officers strolled up to us, barring their teeth like the dogs. They had us. One of them said, "You fuckin black cunts, you're in big trouble now."

Another nodded his head saying, "You're under arrest you wog and what about you nigger, hurt ya leg have ya lad?" They laughed at us.

"You have the right to remain, oh what do these black cunts know, throw the wog in the van, the other one looks a mess, radio for an ambulance. That's what you get when you try and steal." I was cuffed and thrown into the back of the van or as we called it a 'Black Marriah'. Floyd was taken to hospital as he couldn't even walk.

One copper sat in the front turned round and looked through the cage bars and just stared at me. I stared back, fearless, because I had been hardened by my sessions with all the different antagonists in my life, and so a little more could not be any worse.

"So, you think you can get away with this, do you?" I didn't answer. "I said, do ya lad?" Again, I remained silent. It reminded me of when

Lateef would interrogate me, and during those times I learned to keep my mouth shut, and not say a word, otherwise he'd keep going. Maybe he ought to think about working on the right side of the law, he'd definitely make a good officer.

As we entered the police area I got out of the van. The cop walked over and slapped me, and then deciding it was not enough, he punched me full on, then laughed and said, "Seems like you hurt yourself with that fall eh." Considering this was a full-grown police officer, the punch didn't hurt so bad. Either that, or the fall had messed my nerve endings up.

As I stood there being booked in, it did not feel all that real until I was taken to the cells. I was left with the fat copper that had been shouting at me all the way there. He kept laughing at me and saying that I was going to be in there for a long time.

As he was closing the door I mumbled, "Pig," which was a big mistake.

He turned around and said to his colleague, "Hey, this Paki thinks he's tough?" They immediately jumped on me. They had bulging bellies and they had been toughened up by Thatcher's cleaning program. I, on the other hand, was seasoned by Lateef's training program, but of course I didn't have the educational council of the United Kingdom's accreditation so it was not good enough as I was kicked and beaten to a pulp.

They hit me so hard that I nearly lost my eye. I was left in the cell and while I was crying from being beaten up, a lot of those tears were from the anger that had enveloped me.

I paced that cell all night in pain. I didn't sleep, I couldn't, the place stunk terribly and the pain in my eye didn't help.

The next morning a woman came to my cell with a different police officer. She turned out to be a probation officer. She asked me, "What happened to your eye son?"

I blurted out, "Those lot kicked the shit out of me, the bastards!" The officer warned me about my language. Again I shouted out, "Fuck off, you fuckin pig, think you are hard beating me!"

She turned to the officer and said, sternly, "I'd like to have a word with you outside." Before I knew it I was being told that due to lack of evidence, there would be no charges, and that I was free to go. I don't

65

know about lack of evidence, I had been caught red handed. I knew it had nothing to do with the stolen goods, but everything to do with the fact that they'd beaten me up, which wasn't acceptable.

As I was leaving, one of the officers whispered, "Watch your back, wog." My head around my eye especially was so swollen, it looked as though I had cracked my cranium.

I managed to pull myself together and went to a "Greasy café" for a cup of tea and chip butty then walked home like a drunk. I wanted to avoid Mum seeing me in that state, but she happened to be outside in the garden hanging up the washing. "What happened to your face?"

"Nothing, Mum," I said automatically.

Mum took my face in her hands and examined it carefully. "You will be fine, go clean yourself up." I was not really expecting any kind of mollycoddling, but I thought she would freak out after seeing my eye in that state. I went to the bathroom and let the cold water soothe the throb.

I was exhausted, and my feet hurt from pacing that damn cell, and so I decided to curl up in bed for a couple of hours, and just rest for the day.

The Victorian warehouse had been one wild escapade, but it was just a small appetizer of what would be the survival mode.

CHAPTER 9
Headmaster's Punishment

After getting into serious trouble with the police, I knew that I had to take a break from the whole warehousing gig, so as not to rouse suspicion, but my grumbling stomach meant I could not stop finding ways to satisfy it.

After seeing Floyd's messed up leg, and nearly losing my eye to the police, I decided to try out the straight path. I hadn't tried it before and not because I didn't want to, it was because I didn't get the chance.

I wondered how long it would last until I was lured back to the dark side, but I had to at least make an attempt to go clean. The opportunity arose at the right time. I was getting back home from hanging out with Wendall, Jacko and Gaffa, my Rudeboy mates. I knew one of the white kids on our street, Julian. He was one of the few that I got along with, besides Caleb.

There was something he and I had in common, and that was we always somehow had money on us. I just had to know what schemes he used to get his pockets full. I asked him, "Julian, how come you've always got money on ya?"

He said, "Well, I've got this job as a helper to the milkman."

"The milkman?"

"Yeah, but it's a tough job, mate. I get up at four in the morning, but it pays ten quid a week."

"That's alright that."

"Yeah, it's well worth it, mate. Anyway, I've got to go, speak soon."

I thought I could do with that money, and I'm sure my belly agreed. A couple of weeks later, Julian came up to me and said, "Listen, Zahid, I'm going away on holiday with me mam and dad, but the milkman needs somebody for three weeks while I'm away. You interested?"

I jumped at the chance. "Yeah."

"Alright, I'll let him know, mate, but meet me in the morning and I will introduce you to him."

I had no problem waking up early, because I was used to it from boxing and so the following morning I was up before the crack of dawn and I met up with Julian for a briefing with the milkman. "This is John. John, Zahid."

"Hello."

"How's thee doing, Zahid," the milkman said.

"Well, he'd like to deputise for me for the next three weeks, if that's okay with you, John. He's a good lad and me neighbour."

"Okay, son, sounds good to me," John said. We set off right away, and drove all over the place delivering milk, while at the same time taking money out of empty bottles. Those wealthy middle class people would leave the money in the bottle and I had to collect it and give it to the milkman, but what if a bottle just happened to *not* have money in it?

The following Monday I got up at three in the morning, an hour earlier. Lateef had long since moved out of the house, permanently, and that meant I didn't get smacked on my head for waking him up to head out so early. Zaker was a heavy sleeper, and he turned to the other side and kept snoring, or pissing, away.

I guess it didn't last too long, and the opportunity was just too good to be true, and so it was I returned to the dark side. I would say instead that my business instinct was uncontrollable and got sharper and sharper every time.

They say that the early bird catches the worm. Damn right it does. And you know what, I thought to myself, I'm not hurting anyone, those rich people can afford it and it's just for three weeks. I had a good conscience! On top of that, I knew that I could do worse.

Take my elder brother for example. He had gotten himself a tiny apartment in the centre of Bradford. He was still running with his Polish crew, but their misdealing had gotten worse. They were into leading: stripping the old Victorian mills and churches of the lead and selling it on. It was dangerous work, but my brother had balls of steel and a brain the size of a pea, so no sweat there. All I was doing was following the milkman around!

I did the rounds on my own or as much as I knew and took the money from the empty bottles. Then after an hour, at four, I was ready for John the milkman. After delivering the milk, I said, "There wasn't any money in some of them," and because I did not steal from all the houses, he never suspected a thing.

He'd say to me, "You know, lad, I think some cunt is nicking my money." And it was even more hilarious when he said, "These kids round here have got wealthy parents and still they steal from their own parents." I was thrilled, not only because he had not caught onto me, but also because he blamed the rich kids, who I felt deserved it after all those times they gave me funny looks.

After finishing my rounds with the milkman I'd go over to Roger's house and get him to slam school. It would always be a task trying to convince him, but as soon as he saw the loot he'd be up and out of bed. We would head down town to the city centre and hang out at a café called Olympus Café. There we'd just wind down the time by drinking cola, eating chip butties and playing on the video machine called 'Defender.'

I had by then perfected fishing the fruit machines for credits, using my trusted long piece of thin plastic, and still managing to sell them off at half price or play the damn thing myself even though I wasn't a gambler.

The pockets were filling up again, and I was really on a roll. I couldn't resist looking for more, just to make sure I was never short on cash. I got used to having money and enjoyed spending it, especially on others like my mates and giving my little brother some too.

One time, while coming back from the milk rounds I noticed a taxi parked in our street. There were quite a few parked there, actually. I remembered from the times I'd been in a taxi that the drivers kept their loose change under the seat. I thought to myself, I can kill two birds with one stone. I would do the milk rounds and when I'd finished that I'd check those taxis out.

With doing nothing comes great responsibility in making the most of it when something comes out of nothing. I had to be like a ninja again; quiet, quick and precise and mind my surroundings.

The following morning, I bade goodbye to John the milkman and crept up to the first taxi parked outside. I took a screwdriver out, one that I had stolen from Harry's tool box, he'd never know because he never used it. I improvised and rammed it in the door lock. With a series of random movements, I broke the lock and could open the door.

It was no easy job, though. On some of the taxi's it worked and some it didn't, but the ones where it worked outdid the ones where it didn't, and so the benefits definitely outweighed the costs, and I saw a surplus there. School was useful after all.

Looking at my finances, I decided to expand my enterprise, and I went after normal cars as well. I targeted the ones parked outside my area, since I would look suspicious in my own neighbourhood. I took everything that I could get my hands on whether it was worth money or not. If I could carry it then I was taking it.

Business was going great, and as always whenever I did things by myself things were successful.

I tried my best to not let my office hours coincide with school, to not be suspicious walking around during class time. I, however, had no interest in school whatsoever because school had no interest in me. I wanted to learn, but was lost inside that place.

The teachers always overlooked me when they talked about "good" students, even though I was sure I could outdo any of them. The rest of the class thought I was some kind of a psycho like my pea brain brother, and I hated that because it just wasn't true, but there was nothing I could do about it.

There was a girl in my class who I got on really well with. It was strange because I never really thought I'd be attracted to a white girl. I always fancied the mixed-race ones, but she was special. I don't know if it was because of my out of proportions reputation of being the tough guy and a gangster, or that I just lacked the courage, but I didn't ask her out, and it was something I regretted, because I really liked her, but since it never happened, I followed my wisdom and didn't really dwell on it.

I was known for being able to take care of myself, and that anybody messing with me would get it good, but nobody took the time to see me for what I really was: a genuinely lost soul, a boy who hated everything about violence, but that had to use it for every kind of self-protection.

I used to crave direction and guidance, so since I didn't receive it from the ones I expected, I got it from anywhere around me, and I survived just fine. I wasn't the top of my class, but I was the brightest finding new business opportunities, making deals and devising plans against time to not get bust up by cops.

The neglect, the racism, the poverty, the hatred and the waste; that was my schooling background. It was not because I deliberately hated it. In fact, I felt drawn to some of the classes related to politics and business, but even the teachers made it difficult for my interest to linger.

As I was good at boxing, you would think I'd at least excel in physical education, but to me even that was a joke and the PE teacher was a bigger joke. They once put me on the football team and I was quite good playing in defence, but the thought of me depending on ten other fools didn't appeal to me one bit.

One time while playing a match one of my so-called teammates was barking orders at me, "Oi, Zahid, get him!" I didn't react quickly enough and his reply was, "What's wrong with you, Paki, this is not cricket!" I turned around, head-butted him and kicked the living daylights out of him. I wouldn't stand for anybody calling me a "Paki" and "wog" and "chocolate log," and since it was clear the teacher was a closet racist because he heard everything and didn't reprimand him, I decided to reprimand him myself.

The most fun thing that I did do at school was eat magic mushrooms. I found that they were a great way to make the days go by faster. Others would sniff glue, but that didn't appeal to me because the lads who did it looked like zombies. Eating mushrooms was fun, mostly because I did not want to linger in a place I called a "Waste." I had better things to do out on the street and so it was either slamming or magic mushrooms for me.

The headmaster was called Mr. Thompson and his deputy was also called Mr. Thompson and both of those clowns were a complete waste of space. The headmaster Thompson knew what I was going through, but he never offered help or understanding of any kind. He was made out to be a saint in the press because he had adopted some black kid and a handicapped kid, but as far as what I could see he didn't care one bit about his pupils.

Once, things got out of hand when a teacher went to Deputy Thompson, saying I'd just been involved in a fight at the school gates. I didn't start it and was protecting myself, but as usual no-one believed me. It was funny, when it wasn't my fault, I got into trouble, but when it was my fault, I got away.

Deputy Thompson approached me in the corridor as I was about to head home. He said, "In my office, now!" I didn't stand around and made a break for the door, I ran through the door, but at the same time swung the door back at him, which hit him full on. It was quite a mess, and to make matters worse, I was caught by another teacher.

"Get inside!" Deputy Thompson, now sporting a bloody nose, screamed.

"Shit…" I followed him into his office.

He asked me to stand with my hand held out. "Don't think I don't know what you and your friends are up to, Beacher." I hated him calling me Beacher.

"My name is Hameed sir, not Beacher, do I look white to you?"

He got even angrier. "Shut it boy, you are in enough trouble because when it comes to fighting on the school premises that's when you step over the line. You will respect the school while you are here, but what you do outside doesn't concern me."

I laughed at him.

"Excuse me?" he said.

I replied, "I said, I don't give a fuck about your school"

"Put your bloody hand out!" I'd never heard a teacher swear like that. Deputy Thompson reached under his desk and resurfaced with a cane. "I said put your hand out, now boy!" He climbed onto his desk as though prepared to dive into a swimming pool. "Zahid, put your hand out, now!"

He was fuming, grinding his teeth, his sleeves rolled up. I had no idea what he wanted to do, and why he was standing on the top of his desk.

I realized what was coming at the last moment, and I put my hand out. Deputy Thompson didn't disappoint. He jumped up, and brought the cane down, but I moved my hand just in time and he missed, stumbled and went crashing into a desk. "Zahid!" he turned back around and climbed back onto his desk. "If you don't keep your hand still, you will have detention for the whole week!" I couldn't afford to have detention; time after school was money.

I put my hand out again and this time he stood in front of me not chancing another miss. I took the hit. The pain was bad, but I'd had worse. "Get out!" I must have pushed him to the limit; he looked nervous and dishevelled.

I heeded his instruction, and left without another word.

CHAPTER 10
Back to Holland

I was unlucky to be at a school where there was no school uniform, because that was the place it all really showed. The kids there would dress in the best clothes, while I would be wearing two to three year old hand-me-downs because mum forgot to buy me a new set a long time ago.

I measured myself with the rest of the class, and except for my crappy outfit, I was doing better than all of them. They complained about getting one pound less for pocket money that week, because they had had gotten themselves detention for not doing homework. I made my own pocket money and in a way that made me feel accomplished.

I hated the second-hand clothes I received from Lateef, because they were either holed or stinky, or in the special cases, both. He hid his animals and God knows what else in those pockets. I was introduced to personal finances, in my "life school" programme. I rationed it just right and managed to start buying my own clothes, item by item.

I bought a shirt one week, and then a pair of pants to match two weeks later. I frequented a shop in the centre called 'In-step.' They sold shoes for the humble price of a single pound! They'd last no longer than a week before the soles broke and had holes in them, but it was worth it. And when I had no money to buy my weekly shoes, I'd be walking around in the previous weeks' ones with holes in the soles. I put cardboard inside, to avoid the holes and plastic 'Morrison's' supermarket bags over my socks; at least that way they'd stay dry. When things got really bad, and the cardboard wore itself out, the hard, cold tarmac sent chills up my feet.

Like those holes in my shoes, my life was empty. My father was sat behind his desk in his office, being tended to by assistants sucking up to him every other minute, while my mother and Harry really only cared about themselves, independently. Yasmeen was off studying hard, while Lateef was already living with his girlfriend in some torn down place, which just about complimented his style. Zak was young and focusing on the girls, and they in turn focused on him, and I hardly talked to Soroya.

I could not count on anybody to be there for me, not Roger, my best mate, or the Black family, or any family. I had but one option to fill the void, and that was by playing the crook, the tough guy and the anti-social kid, with the rest of the Rudeboys.

It was an easy role for me to play, as I had the look, and the family as a backdrop to sell it. It was all a game to me anyway, and I felt like a vigilante, putting on a different mask every night before heading out to accomplish great misdemeanours. At the end of that road, it was all about survival, which was my only option.

As kids in Bradford, there wasn't much to do anyway. I have no idea where the rest of my classmates spent their pocket money, but I had gotten tired of the arcade, and I never paid to go watch movies anyway.

The movie theatre, Odeon, which we called 'the pictures' was a good place to hang out. I remember that I used to get inspired by some of the movies they played back there. There was Beat Street, which was made in New York, about two crews battling it out to be the best dance group in town. I could definitely relate, because we Rudeboys did the same; we'd head out to different cities and challenge other crews to dance offs.

With the Rudeboys and my busy work schedule, I had gotten myself into a routine that allowed me to put three large-enough meals on my plate and dressed me up with a new style.

Meanwhile, at home, my mother was fed up with Harry Beacher. Their relationship had finally fallen apart. I came home one day to find her packing her bags. "I can't do this anymore, I just can't..." she muttered.

I sat down on the stairs and asked, "What's up, Mum?"

"It's Harry, it's all of this...I can't take it anymore, it's too...too much..."

"What happened?"

"Leave it, Zahid, you are too young to understand." I did understand, the image of the narcissist checking himself out in the mirror, looking gorgeous in Mum's dress gave me a good idea of what was happening. "We're moving to Holland. All of us."

"I don't want to go there; I don't even speak their language," I protested.

There really was no use arguing. At least that way I was assured a roof over my head, otherwise I'd have to worry about finding and maintaining a place to stay. I found Lateef packing some stuff up into a suitcase. Mum had asked him to come with us and he gladly accepted as things were heating up for him in Bradford with his girlfriend.

Mum had already packed my stuff, and had announced that we would be leaving over the weekend. That meant I would be leaving school, which was strange because I'd gotten so used to Mr. Thompson's leering looks in the corridors, and I had just schemed stealing these new collectible footy cards that the kids were crazy about, which would have meant good money.

I didn't even get to say bye to my mates, not that there were all that many at school, but I would somewhat miss the Rudeboys. I guess they'd honour me in some way when they didn't find me in the streets the following weeks.

There we were again, on that stupid ferry. I fell sick again, throwing up all over the place and shivering because of the nausea. We arrived at Europort and then took the train to Amsterdam, which was a peculiar old city in comparison to any I'd previously visited; Eindhoven and Rotterdam included. It was busy with bicycles everywhere, people and places exponentially amplified at least one hundred-fold. My mother led us to a tiny apartment in the south of the city called De Pijp. There were five of us including mum, my two brothers, two sisters and I.

My mother had asked my eldest sister to come along so that she could get a part time job and help her out and also because she didn't want her to be in England alone just in case she got sick with her sickle cell, which meant my favourite sister Yasmeen stayed back to finish her studies.

I would have thought with Amsterdam being a capital city, it would be alright, but reality hit me hard and it wasn't so. It was the trashiest apartment I'd ever stepped foot in; small and cramped, smelling of sewage. Lateef, Zak and I crashed in the attic, which definitely wasn't fun for me at all. We could hardly fit in there, and I thought that it was back to the old days as I bunked with my bully of a brother.

The size of our apartment was not the worst part. There was no shower and no bathroom. Just one toilet for all of us and an additional sink. It was dark and depressing. It was humiliating taking a sponge bath in the sink, and then standing there in the cold while I tried to dry off and pull on some clothes.

I had stayed in cells overnight, sometimes for a couple of nights, and those were like five star hotels compared to this dump. It was different from our stay in Eindhoven, where we'd at least had a better place and family to take care of us. Here, Mum had to make ends meet and that meant what was coming was going to be worse than Beacher's house.

Lateef was surprisingly different in Amsterdam. He was always the tough guy back home, but because we didn't know anyone, my little brother and I were his only company. Sometimes even the hardest ass knows that no man is an island, and that companionship is everything.

We would go out to the canals and spend the day fishing together. It was amusing catching fish, bringing it home, cooking it and, eating it. It was disgusting, since it might have been a mutant or radioactive fish because of the pollution.

During another one of our escapades, we found a sports bag full of multi-coloured money. Lateef said, "It's monopoly money, throw it back in." I took a few notes out and brought them home. I suspected that since they were brown in colour, they might not belong to a board game, and I had to show Mum.

She freaked out and said, "This is five hundred guilders, where did you get this from!" That was a lot of money and I knew we should not have taken the word of two-cell Lateef. We took one look at each other and ran back to the spot, but the bag had gone. We were pissed off; that was some good money, and the Universe had practically gift-wrapped it for us. If only I'd grabbed a few more notes!

We didn't waste time loitering about, feeling hard done. We figured that there must be more out there, so Lateef, with a few points and grunts, somehow arranged a dingy and we put it in the water and like in the TV series 'Hawaii Five O' we went around hoping to find some other secret treasure on the banks somewhere. We didn't end up getting anything else, but we amused ourselves with the attempts and had a good time rowing about the place.

My mother had already gotten in touch with a school before we had arrived. It was forty-five minutes away by tram and was diverse, with lots of different nationalities represented. The funny part was nobody understood each other so making friends was hard. At least there were so many groups, I had a wider selection to choose from than just Blacks, Whites or Asians. Eventually, I settled for the Turkish kids, whom I found to be interesting and I even learnt quite a lot of their language.

After school, my brothers and I would sometimes take a stroll around, but every street looked the same and I thought with the amount of dog faeces and trash all over the place, Bradford looked like the cleanest place on the planet.

Zak and I used to laugh to ourselves about it all. We'd pretend we could speak Dutch as I gibbered away and then said, "Ja," and he replied "Nee." It was hilarious because that's all we'd say and people looked at us as though we were fluent Dutch speakers!

Whether it was Thatcher's Britain, or the so-called Cosmopolitan Amsterdam, a racist was a racist. On the tram to school, I would hear people muttering things like "Kut Allochtonen." Apparently that referred to a person who wasn't born in their country, and that was probably the nicest thing they spat at us.

My mother knew that none of us were enjoying it there, so she contacted the local boxing club, which was called the Albert Cuijp Boxing Club. It was ironic because she wasn't a fan of the noble art, but knew she had to do something to keep us from causing trouble or getting frustrated at home and destroying one another.

A man called Ruud van der Linden ran the club, and he was eager for us to join because boxing in Holland was nowhere near as good as in England. He was great and seemed genuinely interested in us.

Getting back into the sport and joining the club was the best decision we'd made. It not only kept us busy, but due to the premise that we were members of the boxing club, we were allowed to use the 'Bath House.' This was a place where the homeless or poor could shower and get cleaned up and it was next door to the gym. It beat the sink at home, with a sponge that was starting to gather too many of Lateef's pubic hairs.

Times were hard and we could see that by the food we were eating. Even though there was a market five minutes from our apartment, Mum

78

couldn't afford much from there, and so we were restricted to the absolute bare necessities, sometimes a little too bare for my hungry belly.

Out of sheer desperation, Lateef had gotten himself a job as a helper to a mechanic in a bid to mitigate his own financial crisis. I should have told him earlier that he was meant to fix cars, not the mechanic's face, but after a spanner or two to his boss's head, he was fired. I kind of felt sorry for him, because the language barrier, the people and the food wound him up.

Through all the tough times, and the boredom, the boxing club was our true oasis. We made friends and life seemed a bit easier. The black kids were our brothers in arms and like in England that's whom I would always hang out with.

A few of the boxers were brilliant and could have boxed in England. Mohammed Said, Romeo Kensmil, Ramon and a few others really had talent, but the rest were rubbish.

There was one boxer called Pedro van Ramsdonk who was the pretty boy. He was the blond-haired blue-eyed hope of the Arian nation and so-called star at the club. My brother loathed him, which was great because it would be fuel for the fire.

Mr. Van der Linden asked Lateef to spar with the star. As he got in the ring, Van Ramsdonk laughed and said in his broken English, "Eh boy I'm gonna teach you a few tricks." That was it: Lateef exploded and this was no sparring match. He pulled off a series of combinations, in full on berserker mode and in the end they had to drag him off the poor fallen star. I guess the beauty could not beat the beast.

Friday was the best day of the week. We'd go to the disco, which was held at the club to raise money for themselves. All the local slappers, or girls, would be there and we'd just hang around, observing. I laughed with Zak, as I watched him eyeball the dancing girls. Somehow, he always knew what to say even when those slappers didn't understand him.

The Friday disco night was held twice a month, so when that wasn't on, I'd sneak out of the apartment and onto the streets. A few times, I ended up at a club not far from where we lived. They'd let me in and I'd just sit there all night observing the crazy people who'd come in and go out.

It was interesting seeing how they dressed, watching the expressions on their faces as they talked, trying to make out the stories they were telling. I saw them ordering different kinds of drinks at the bar counter, which I couldn't afford so I'd stand around with a free club soda in my hand, and sip it slowly while I watched the scene. When I got back home, Zaker asked me where I had been and my only answer was, "Out and about"

It was confusing times living in Amsterdam. I did not feel welcome there at all. I did my best to get into the thick of things, and just let time pass me by, and sure enough I started to settle down again.

"We're going back home, to Bradford," Mum said. Beacher had lost his job and had moved out and refused to pay the mortgage. "I put so much into that house. I can't just let it go. I'll work as many jobs as possible to save the place." Since she was heading for a divorce, she had to mobilize and marshal an onslaught.

She told Ruud van der Linden of her plans and that we would be leaving the boxing club. Mr. van der Linden was terribly disappointed because he enjoyed having good boxers like us around the gym. He suggested that since it was the school holidays that we should stay on. "Lateef, Zak and Zahid can stay at my house in the Bijlmer," he said. That was in the South-East of Amsterdam, and my mother agreed as it would give her space to sort out the troubles that awaited her in Bradford.

"I'm not staying here, no way," Lateef refused.

"Well you come back with us," my mother said. I guess she thought he would not be a burden as he'd stay out on the streets mostly.

And then there were two; it was Zaker and I and Mr. van der Linden's apartment was phat. The area was great; a succulent residential space, not as heavily populated as the South, and with people from different backgrounds, which meant less insults. I could breathe again, and you wouldn't imagine the relief as I sat on a proper couch for the first time in ages.

That summer we went to the local festival called Kwakoo, which was held in the area. It was a Caribbean, South American bonanza and it was an extravaganza. The music carried us on during the day, the food they had there was delicious and the people were warm. Zaker and I would brag to them that we too had a Surinam connection through our grandfather and that seemed to gain us even more acceptance.

Our time in Amsterdam finally came to an end and it was time to go back. What had that all been? A hiatus from the craziness, or part of the craziness itself? Whatever it was, it pushed all of us to our limits, strengthened some brotherly bonds, raised up self-esteem with the boxing, or it was just like a holiday abroad, but because we couldn't afford a glamorous one, we got one based on our budget and luck!

Back to Bradford we went, but with a little more perspective and a few choice Dutch words.

CHAPTER 11
Lost Love

It was 1981 and if things were bad before, they had gotten worse. My mother was back to busting her back working multiple jobs again to pay off the mortgage and all the other expenses, taking abuse as usual and getting the regular beatings from her mental patients as she returned to the hospital.

We were eating scraps off the plate because Beacher had left us with nothing. Apparently he had assaulted a pupil and was given the sack at work. He had moved out and taken another small apartment on the other side of town, leaving all the debts to my mother. The silver lining was that he was out of our lives.

During this time, I got closer to Roger and spent a lot of time at his place. His mother, Marion, was adorable with me, always concerned about whether I ate that day or not. She wasn't wealthy when it came to net worth, but if a person's wealth was a measure of how generous and caring they were, she'd be the wealthiest person alive. She had three kids to look after on her own, but she always had a place at her table for me, something I'd always be grateful for.

I hated being at home, with Mum gradually losing her mind and acting as though I didn't exist, doing a sort of 'Dad' on me. I couldn't blame her: she was under constant stress and pressure, and I mostly kept out of her way, but it didn't do either Zaker, Soroya or myself any good to sit in the dining room, and look upon empty plates.

There definitely wasn't anything there to eat, unless Mum was hallucinating that she fed us. I needed to find a job as soon as possible, either legally or illegally, but considering my origins and more importantly my age, there was only one result.

It was inevitable to compare my mother with Marion: the fact that she had problems of her own, but showed no less love to any of the members of her complete family. This idea was in my head and feeding a new-found feeling of reproach. I even preferred being out in the streets than at home, and when I wasn't at Roger's place, I was sleeping out in the cold, and it was back to the coal yards, freezing my ass off.

I didn't complain about a thing, or go up to Mum and beg her to love me, but I would have liked to have a Marion at home. Maybe it was the teenage years kicking in, and everything started to look so difficult for me to fit in, even at home, where I didn't have a dad or a Harry to blame.

I was back in with the Rudeboys and Ska was the in thing at this point. It was massive, probably at its peak with the Specials, Selector, Bad Manners and The Beat to name but a few.

Getting into music was easy, and more importantly free. I realized that music made me feel alive and happy. If it weren't for these guys I'd probably have followed my mother down the looney trail a long time ago, but they kept my life together, through the toughest times and I would look forward to going out with my mates and enjoying the music.

We kept it up as a gang with the dance offs in different cities, and of course got into fights: all a part of being a Bradford Rudeboy. I didn't mind it because outside of that, I was or had nothing, and it was a way to get the respect of people.

There was one time we were in the club and as I was entering one of the bouncers tried stopping me. I got into a heated argument and either I was fearless or stupid, because looking back that was one giant bouncer.

Things got out of hand and before I knew it a massive fight broke out. The bouncer threw an almighty punch, which hit my jaw full on. I fell back against the wall, but I wasn't knocked out. As I was trying to position myself to put up a fight I saw the bouncer coming in again to finish me off. It was like slow motion as I realized the next punch would surely drop me or even knock me out.

Then out of nothing I saw and heard a familiar voice to my left, "Zid?" I noticed a black kid with the biggest afro fly into the bouncer with what can only be described as a flying 'Head-butt'. The bouncer was laid out cold and to my surprise it was Dave Mallet who had saved me. He grabbed me and said, "You alright, star?'

I nodded and said, "Mallet, you saved me, I owe you."

He just laughed and said, "We brothers, no problem now let's get the fuck out of here."

The business of being Rudeboys was fun, but risky, so to mitigate the risk, you got your brothers to count on, but when they didn't come in handy, I could count on great friends like Mallet that just happened to appear there and then.

One thing about Mallet was he was quick, brave and clever. He was a 'happy go lucky' guy always making jokes, except when it came to kicking some asses or devising spontaneous strategies to get some money from random situations.

The fights we got into were fairly violent. Mostly, it would be against the 'National Front,' a racist organization, always lurking somewhere. Sometimes we'd win the battles and sometimes we'd lose.

Once, while sat in the bus on the top deck at the back we encountered them. We were eight and they were three, so they were outnumbered, which didn't bother us because they would always attack us when they outnumbered us.

This time we had one of the few white guys who would hang with us and his name was Sykesy. This Rudeboy was as fierce as they came. We surrounded those racists, and I could see they were terrified.

As I walked back to the back of the bus laughing at how pathetic they were, Sykesy just lost it and started screaming at them that they were the scum of the earth.

They made one big mistake and one of them screamed back, "What are you doing with those wogs and niggers, you should be with us!" That was all Sykesy needed to hear. He pulled out a huge screwdriver and stabbed it straight into the neck of the lad, who screamed, blood splashing about all over the place.

That was our queue to leave the bus. I shouted at Syksey to hurry up, but he wasn't having any of it. He said, "Not until I get my screwdriver back, it's me dad's!" and he yanked the thing out the lad's neck. It was gruesome but he did get it back.

Outside of the fights, I thought it would be appropriate to learn to play an instrument. It occurred to me when a trumpet crossed my path coincidentally, during one of our earlier escapades.

One of my best mates, Wendall Jefferson, played rhythm guitar and I'd hang with him listening to records and trying to play along. We'd sit there together the whole time eating broken biscuits, which he bought cheaply because they were rejects.

My favourite artist was Dick Cuthel who played trumpet for various Ska bands, and who inspired me to give it a go in the first place. Wendall was another superb friend, and an amazing person. He had the fastest Ska shuffle you could ever see and just like Mallet he always had a smile on his face.

Stealing started to exhaust me and I decided to go clean and do some honest work for a change. Summer arrived, and that for me was a time to do something to help myself, which in turn would help Mum out as she wouldn't have to worry whether I was eating or not. Not that she worried, but it's what I told myself to make me sleep better at night.

I'd noticed at the top of the hill they were building a new house. I walked up to it and enquired whether they would need labourers. The manager on site said he could use an extra set of arms, and I told him I'd get him two sets.

Roger and I were hired to help build a house near Buttershaw council estate. We would spend the entire day there, working our asses off, putting in maximum effort in the blazing summer heat.

It was basic construction work and it was fairly straightforward, really. I'd go there, the boss would give me some instructions to follow, and I'd do exactly as he'd ask and get paid for it at the end of the week.

We'd shovel concrete straight into the foundation, which was heavy work, but the motivation, besides the money, was that the job was like something of a workout. We'd crash at Roger's mum's house after work, which was something to look forward to for a wind down. It was difficult, but I needed the money and I wanted to try out the straight path.

That was five quid a week, which wasn't nearly enough to buy Roger, our mates and me fish and chips. I wanted to have enough to get three meals a day, including drinks and something for my mates. I looked at it this way: Robin Hood did it and it was fine. That was it, it was time for me to put the mask back on and edge over.

"I've not been paid by your foreman, nor has Roger, and on top of that I hurt myself shovelling concrete for the foundations, look at the blisters on my ankle, I don't have the boots to do that work boss," I said.

"I didn't know, I'll have to check with the foreman on this, as for you getting hurt, well I'm sure there's something I can do about it." I guess he didn't want to get in the bad books with the health and safety authority, and fill out all the paperwork, and so he agreed to pay me double to keep me happy.

It worked out great; I'd gotten it up to ten quid a week. Even though I wasn't rich it was double than what we were supposed to get. I really had meant to walk the clean path, but desperate times really call for desperate measures, and there was nothing for it. Those masks would have to do because I just could not run away from what I needed to be to survive.

I felt better knowing that other kids did it purely to amuse themselves, and to show that they were gutsy enough to steal, and shoplift right under the owners' noses, whereas I had no other choice. It was either that, or starve, and I was not going to choose the latter.

I may not have had much choice out on the streets, but I still had a choice at school. I was readmitted after mum begged and begged Mr. Thompson, who reluctantly agreed, saying that I needed to pull my socks up and behave.

All the preconceptions about me being a lost cause, et cetera, et cetera, triggered something in my ego for the first time. How hard could it be to do well at school? If I gave it a try, like the way I was giving most things a try at that point, I was sure I could pull through.

I saw the perfect opportunity. Exam time was upon us, and for the majority of the class that meant endless studying. I wished I had that much time to study, but unfortunately I had to feed myself, and I couldn't read my biology notes while working the forklift.

The exams began. Everybody around me was nervous, but I wasn't. I had nothing to lose; the whole school had already failed me, even before I officially came back. I took a look through the paper, and I thought, "This is easy, I can answer at least a third of it correctly, two thirds maybe, and the last third I didn't need to give a damn about because I'd have aced it by then."

A couple of weeks later the results came out, and I did ace it. I performed brilliantly, and ended up scoring in the top percentile, which drew suspicions all around me. The teachers and other pupils scratched their heads and tried to figure out how this boxing brother of Lateef the psycho had gone on to do so well when he's hardly ever at school!

The results gave me some kind of hope. I had a flicker of a thought about pursuing it all the way, and maybe go to University and get qualified. I had to admit, it felt great being one of the top students, showing everybody up, and letting them know that I was intelligent.

Headmaster Thompson, staring down his nose at scurrying students, found me in the corridor the day after results came out, and said to me, "A word, please." I pushed my chest out and followed him through, happy to take the praise after I proved him wrong. "Zahid, your attendance is not only abysmal, but disruptive?"

I nearly laughed again, like I did on my previous visit there, because I was so puzzled about the question. "I don't understand."

"Your term record shows you have attended less than half of your classes, have submitted probably a tenth of your assignments, you didn't turn up for your mock examinations and you still managed to score highly."

"I'm not sure what you're-"

"I suspect you cheated, but I cannot prove it, but what I can prove is your continuous truancy and disruptive behaviour here at Grange Upper School and after repeated warnings I and the school board are unanimous in our decision to expel you for truancy."

"You are required to immediately vacate the school's premises, we have already informed your mother to let her know that you are no longer permitted to enter the school, and that you will not be attending this school any longer."

I was furious, and my voice shook as I yelled, "You bastards, you never gave me a chance!"

My foolish thoughts of being a good student vanished in a flash. I guess when you are something people don't expect you to be, even if it is conventionally good, they put you back in your place since otherwise, you challenge the system and so they gamble on it and destroy you. That was a free lesson of perspective, courtesy of Mr. Thompson.

As I took the walk of shame all the way home, I came to the bitter realization that rejection was stamped on my forehead. I was rejected at home, rejected at school, rejected everywhere. Even Amsterdam, which I had thought would be better, ended up being more racist, much more confusing, and even more messed up than Bradford.

I sat on the grass. My mind was blank, but in my heart I was angrier than I had been in a long time. There was nothing I could do. Absolutely nothing resonated with me, nobody wanted to give me a shot, and they all just turned their backs on me. I did not want to go home to see that Mum couldn't care less that I'd been expelled.

I'd rather she yelled at me, reprimanded me, demanded I go back to Headmaster Thompson and beg him to take me back, but Mum was officially a part of the ghost mothers again, and that meant she had no idea what was going on outside her little cocoon of survival.

What about Dad? Maybe he'd give me a beating or two for old times' sake, and tell me how disappointed he was that I'd been kicked out of school, when he had so many expectations on me, but the thought of going back to the curry stink more than put me off that option.

At least I had my Rudeboys and Ska. Still, none of them would understand. Nobody spoke about family life or their feelings, it just didn't happen and I wasn't one to tell people. I also did not want them to think I was soft. It was bye-bye school and I now had plenty of time to find more hustles to survive with no distractions.

One night, I was walking in a snicket, which is a pathway between houses, while garden hopping. I was alone, because everyone else had gone home, or had other things to do.

All of a sudden, there was a commotion, and the familiar silhouette of a big-bellied copper blocked my path ahead. "You're under arrest for attempted burglary." He cuffed me and held me by the neck. "Attempted burglary, you're in big trouble now you wog..."

"What you talking about?" I asked.

"See that house there? We've had reports coming in that you've been jumping the fence. Breaking and entering as well, then?"

I looked up to see the house the cop was pointing towards, and I nearly laughed out loud as I recognised it as my own house. "That's my house."

"That's not your house, dirty little wog like you doesn't live there."

"I swear it, that's my house. My mum's in there, ask her yourself!"

By then some of the neighbours had woken up because of the commotion and had come outside in their slippers and gowns. I felt like I was on national television; it was so embarrassing.

I breathed a sigh of relief as I saw my mother appear in our driveway. She stared at me as though she had never seen me before, and I told the cop, "That's my mum, ask her yourself."

The cop turned to mum. "Is this your son?"

For a split second, I thought she was going to deny it, but then she hesitated, nodded and said, "Yes that's my boy."

The cop cleared his throat. "Oh we actually arrested him as we heard reports of a burglary. So he lives here?"

Mum, looking tired, said, "Yes." I looked to the cop to get those cuffs off me. "But I can't control him...can you take him away, please..."

I froze in shock, and felt bubbling acid rise up my sternum. I found myself wishing that my own mother had not just said that. The very same mother I had done my best to put up with, and tried to love, for whom I had gone through so much trouble so she wouldn't have my blood on her hands, had uttered the tongue of the hellish beast.

If there was ever a moment I thought I would break down and cry because of something said to me, it was then. The anguish I felt sapped all the love I could possibly have for Mum, and I was left empty; emptier than ever before. I knew it was irrevocable, that she meant it, and in front of all those snobby neighbours standing outside.

"I'm sorry love, you said he lives here, so we've got to let him go I'm afraid," the copper said. He turned to me and said, "Okay, I'm taking the cuffs off, try to take it easy." It was evident that even he felt sorry for me, but not as sorry as I felt for myself.

I was always kept alive and running with the consoling thought of things someday getting better, and that my mother would be able to rest and come out of her madness to be an actual mum. In the empty holes that had sprouted all over the place that was the tiny spotlight that had been anything for me to keep striving towards.

I felt betrayed, as though she had taken the clothes right off my back, and left me standing naked in the streets for everyone to see. I could almost hear the neighbours muttering amongst themselves about how awful it was that a mother would leave her boy out in the cold, would ask the police to take him away, all that without once feeling bad about it, or attempting to shake it off and pass it off as a misdirected comment.

It was just Mum and I standing there. She was not able to look at me, and I was left with a huge hole in my heart that would never again be filled.

I had no love in my life anymore, or maybe I never had it to begin with.

For my mother and I, it was well and truly over.

CHAPTER 12
Abducted from the Cocoon

The good news was that the police did not take me away, that I was still at the house the following morning, and was hoping to pass my ghost mother by unnoticed, but she was as sneaky and as clever as the SAS or Navy Seals.

I was about to creep to the front door and escape the lair, when I was spotted. Mum approached me and said, "I want you home this evening because there is somebody coming to see you." I did not reply and left the house.

It was only out of curiosity that I returned home in the evening and waited for this person who wanted to see me.

Around half past seven, a man named John arrived and Mum received him with interest. I watched them in wonder, but then it occurred to me that this must be the social service.

John shook my hand and said, "Please sit down, lad." I did and he sat opposite me. "Now, you are Zahid?" he asked. I didn't answer.

"I want him out of the house, I don't want him here," said Mum. Under normal circumstances I guess any kid would be upset, but I despised her. I had become so immune to emotional pain that I was ready for whatever the world or my mother was about to do to me.

John said, "Zahid, we have a lovely couple who are prepared to take care of you." I did not respond in any way, because it was not as though I had a choice. My fate was already sealed.

At the last moment, I thought to give it one last shot, to try to appeal to Mum's heart in one way or another, that she would be moved if I sucked up my pride and confronted her. I hadn't spoken to her since the previous night, but the words came tumbling out of my mouth before I could stop myself. "Mum…why are you doing this?" I asked, but she refused. She couldn't even look me in the face.

"Zahid, don't you worry…"

I turned to him and asked, "Who the fuck are you? You don't know me! You don't know shit about me. When I'm sixteen you won't be able to do this, fuck off, all of you!"

He was perplexed and my mother screamed, "You see! This is what I mean! I can't deal with him, take him away!"

It wasn't fair, and she didn't even want to look me in the eyes. I could not see a reason why she was insistent upon kicking me out the house. It didn't make sense to me, because I wasn't even a burden to her. I fed myself, clothed myself, entertained myself, and that meant she didn't have to do anything, or even try. I even improved at school.

There was no use fighting, and as I walked outside, I was powerless to stop this from happening. Mum didn't even bother to say goodbye.

Social Service didn't care about me at all. John was just like one of those people smugglers that took a troubled kid and kept him stored in a warehouse, and then struck a deal with some family, delivering the kid to the house in working condition, or in my case used condition after being played by Mum.

He tried speaking to me in his car as we drove to a place called Haworth, telling me that for now this was the best option and once I was sixteen I could go my own way. Until then, Haworth would be my new so-called home. This was a place that was world famous because the Bronte sisters came from there and wrote 'Wuthering Heights' and 'Jane Eyre.'

The whole idea of foster care was nonsense to me. It didn't make sense at all that a family would take in a street urchin and raise him like their own, especially somebody with my track record. I couldn't see any other family being like Caleb's, the only ones that accommodated me unconditionally and took care of me as one of their own.

I could have escaped, but then I'd need to find some place to stay because winter was arriving and the cold would eventually get me out in the street. I had my first epiphany: life really was a box of bullets, and at this point I had no idea who or what was going to get me first.

We arrived in Haworth, in the famous Bronte sisters' village. This was in the Bradford Area, but in the middle of nowhere, a place as unfamiliar to me as Amsterdam when I first got there. Everything in that damn village was older and greyer than my previous surroundings.

I was introduced to my foster parents, Brenda and Hughie, who were an English couple with three other kids; two girls and a boy all younger than me. I stood out like a dark spot right in the middle of five twinkling fairy lights of perfection. I thought about how fun it would be when we were introduced to guests or friends. They would have to look some way up the family tree to find somebody whom I'd inherited my darker hair and darker eyes from.

"Zahid, this is your room. you'll be sharing with Matt," Brenda said, leading me to the place I'd be crashing.

It was more appealing than my previous home, however I felt like a total stranger living under somebody else's roof. At least it was better than being a stranger in your own home, I thought.

Hughie turned out to be terrific; good natured and with a sense of humour. He was from Newcastle and spoke in that odd Geordie accent from that area, which was like its own language.

I wish I came with an instruction manual: unpacking your brand-new breed, with chapters like caring for your breed, how to troubleshoot your breed and what to feed your breed. They must have lost that manual in the packaging, and poor Hughie and Brenda had to figure it out all on their own. "What would you like to eat?" they'd ask, and I would shrug, prompting them to exchange glances.

I felt like I was living on Coronation Street, like that television series about working class people going about with their mundane lives. Adapting to my new surroundings was going to take a while, because I was the only breed within a ten-mile radius. At least the neighbours had gotten used to my siblings and me when we stayed at Harry's, because they stopped their gruesome staring, but now it was happening all over again.

Hughie would work all week and then sit in the pub all weekend downing Tetley beer and he'd always want to show me off to his mates. I appreciated how he was proud of looking after a breed, and probably wanted to start a trend, but I don't think it went down too well with his mates, who looked at me like I was a walking, talking pile of trash.

For the first couple of weeks I'd join Hughie at the pub on Maine Street, but after a few visits, sitting with white people who smelled of beer and cigarettes didn't really appeal to me and I had to break it to him that I didn't want in.

Out on the street, abuse was rife, and I was a fat, juicy target for the lot of them. It was diminishing having white kids come up to me saying, "Go back to where you came from, Paki!" I put my foot down and used my fists to respond. I was outnumbered, but I didn't care.

I had nothing to lose, and so I fought and fought and took them all on, and even though I got kicked about and smashed against walls, I did not stop. Pain and pleasure were more or less the same thing for me, sometimes I would not even be able to tell the difference, and at least I took a few of them down before being left a bloodied mess, but unbeaten, to go home and clean up.

Whenever I'd arrive back at Minnie Street with cuts and bruises, swollen eyes, Brenda and Hughie wouldn't know what to do or say. Matt had never received so much as a fleabite on his arm, so I guess they didn't even stock antiseptic cream in the house in anticipation of a gory, bloody mess that stumbled through the doorway.

They looked at me and scratched their heads, and even though I thought they were lovely people, I couldn't help but get frustrated at the fact that they could not respond. I was a nobody fighting for survival. After sometime, I thought taking on whole gangs at once was a bad idea, and so I picked them off one by one, and it took a while, but they eventually laid off me.

Sharing a room with Matt was bizarre, but we got on alright. He thought the world of me, and would often say, "You're the coolest guy ever, Zahid. So glad we are brothers." Even at that early age you begin to realize that racism comes in all sizes and colours, but Matt, who was a typical white kid, saw me as his big brother and not some half-breed Paki.

I got myself a part time job, working in a scrap yard to add a bit of money to my pocket. They paid me ten quid a week, which would have been fine under normal circumstances, but not for all the insults I took.

Passers-by would see me there and whisper to one another, sniggering in my direction, sneering at me and belittling me.

Most of the time I'd be covered in black grease, which attracted jokes like moths to a lamp. "Eh blacky doesn't bother you being covered in dirt because you came in looking dirty, anyway." The trailing laughter would ring in my ears for most of the day and the night.

No amount of abuse could ever make you feel like you are ready to ignore it. Still, I couldn't go around bashing everyone up, but what I could do was enact silent revenge. I used my head, and my talents, and starting stealing from the company's small safe, and in the end it was almost like a swear jar for a foul-mouthed kid.

I used part of my wages to go back to Bradford as much as I could. I had to take a bus through Keighley to get there, but it was worth it. I met up with Roger and my other mates, and we'd hang all day until I had to get back.

I was glad that Hughie didn't have a problem with it, because it meant less work for me not having to sneak out and back in. All he'd say was, "Look, lad, if you can just keep your nose clean, son, then I'm okay with you going out."

Fortunately for him I was about to hit sixteen, and then I'd finally be able to shake Social Services off and find my own path.

I couldn't think of a place I could go to afterwards, but I fell asleep every night, hoping that I'd find something, somewhere along the line.

CHAPTER 13
Paris

There wasn't really much of a ceremony as I turned sixteen and prepared to leave Brenda and Hughie's home and it meant that I could finally shake Social Services off, whom I hadn't heard from since I arrived to Haworth.

I had enough saved up from my job, including the "bonus" pay, and so money wasn't an issue for me. I just had to figure out where to go. I didn't have too many options; back to my mum's was out of the question, Lateef would sooner let in a stray homeless man than welcome me to his new home.

I didn't want to be Roger or Caleb's charity, I don't think I could ever get used to the curry-stink but then again dad wasn't even an option and I hadn't had much contact with my favourite sister, who was living far away on her own.

Every hole has its treasure, and while Haworth didn't do anything for me, I didn't want the life that most working class families had accepted. I saw it with Hughie and just about every other person that lived there. They'd work hard all week in an office cubicle or at some factory or driving a lorry and then sit at the pub to intoxicate themselves and have those momentous displays of courage, where they'd say they were not going to stand for minimum wage, and they were going to break free and follow their dreams, only to find themselves back at the job; rinse and repeat.

I did not want that for me, and while it was going to be a challenge finding an alternative, I didn't have a choice because I wasn't in school anymore either, so it was no use going down the path more taken.

I found a bench in the park, and ate my crisps and drank my Lilt, which was my food for the day, and I pondered. For some reason, a television series I loved came to mind. It was called Abbot and Costello, and it always gave me a good laugh. The series also featured the Foreign Legion: an army of lost souls.

A light switch flicked on, and I decided on the spot to join the Foreign Legion. Why not? I was a fighter, so being a soldier was not so different. I had no family, so that could be my new family and people really respected those soldiers.

I never agreed with wars, but respected the courage the soldiers had by joining and fighting. At that age, from what I knew, here were lads who fought and died for their country without fear. Most people would be afraid to join the army. They would be afraid to die, but not me.

The few times that I actually went to school, I had read books about the Foreign Legion. I knew that their headquarters was somewhere in Paris. Harwich was where I could take a ferry from, and I'd have to make it to France, from where I could take a train or bus to Paris.

I was still a little short on money, and so I did a few hustles to make enough for the journey. I had to first get my passport, for which I'd had saved enough up. It was quite quick getting one of those, but the ten year ones took forever, and I didn't have that sort of time.

I got prepared with my rucksack and I made my own favourite peanut butter and jam sandwiches. I had the Foreign Legion on my mind, and I was excited about going on my own trip, doing it all on my own.

That Sunday morning, I walked all the way to the Bradford Interchange Station to save me money. I jumped on the train to London, from where I'd get to Harwich. Sitting on that train I'd see all kinds of people, most looking stressed and unhappy, but I was motivated, energized and determined to achieve my goal.

After travelling for what seemed like forever on the train and then getting back on another ferry and throwing up as usual, I found myself in the port city of Calais. I had bought myself a cheap book with phrases in French, and I used it to approach passers-by and ask them where I could take the train to Paris.

It worked out well, though, because people appreciated my efforts and I could see that. They responded kindly in English, saying, "You take the city express, goes straight to Paris. You can buy a ticket there at the office."

I exchanged my pounds to French Francs, which was a lot more colourful than English money, and bought the correct ticket with the help of the assistant behind the counter.

I finally managed to get to Paris, and my eyes widened in disbelief. The city was impressive; the buildings stood out with their historical remnants, the river flowing under several bridges. There were fountains and statues everywhere, and archways that gave me a royal welcome. It was just like in the movies, with the teasing smell of fresh bread all over the place, mingled with the subtle hint of tobacco.

The women were drop-dead gorgeous, and that snobbish air about them gave them extra sex appeal. There seemed to be people from all walks of life. I loved the language, the way it was articulated, the way in which the women pushed their lips out to pronounce certain words.

I found a small café, and I got myself a *croissant,* which was a kind of bread, with coffee and it tasted divine. It was fun watching people chatting there, while others sat alone, reading, all minding their own business. I felt my energy change as I was surrounded by a completely different and more electrifying ambiance, and I walked around for some time.

Sometimes I felt that I had passed by the same place more than once. I was getting exhausted when I saw the police and decided to ask for help. I finally got to the Foreign Legion's office and I couldn't believe that I actually made it there, but I had to wait two hours before they called me in.

I saw people in uniform looking imposing. It was a full-on mix; there were white guys, black guys, guys who looked like me and guys who didn't and I thought, this is the place for me.

I was called into a room and sat in front of me was a man who seemed rather important. He looked like the meanest man imaginable; his face scarred and his eyebrows furrowed, not to mention his uber-large build, but when he spoke, and in excellent English, he asked, "Why are you here, my friend?" His tone was receptive and not bullish as I'd have thought it would be.

I was rather taken aback by his kind tone and I explained, "I've come from England, sir, got nothing there, sir, no family and no future there, that's why I decided that I want to establish myself as a member of the Legion and make something of myself."

He raised an eyebrow, smiled and said, "My friend. It takes guts to do what you have done. It is not common for somebody as young as you to come in here like that." His words raised my spirits. He was right, it did take guts to do what I did. I didn't need to be a thief or hide under a mask, I could be just like the guy in front of me.

He stood up, smiled and said, "We have men here like you, and what we can offer is honour and a sense of family."

I sat there ready to be enlisted and I said to him, "Sir, where do I sign?"

Again he smiled and asked, "What documentation do you have with you?"

"I've got…this, it's just temporary, I couldn't afford the permanent one," I said and gave him my temporary one-year passport.

He looked at my photo and then up at me. He said, "Firstly my friend, you are too young, you need to be at least seventeen and a half. Secondly, we would need to see a full passport and your actual birth certificate." He wasn't stern, but firm, and I knew that there was no use arguing. "Come back again when you have everything and when you are a little older, and we will be more than ready to put you through."

I sat outside the office, trying to take it all in. I had been thwarted, yet again, just when I thought I was there, at the peak of my powers and getting my shit together. I groaned as I realized it would be difficult getting back to Bradford with my limited funds, but I knew I had no choice, because there was nothing in Paris for me anymore.

I had come there on a one-way ticket, thinking that was it and I wouldn't need to return thereafter, which was stupid because now I was stranded. I had enough money to get the ferry back, but after that I had no idea how I was going to get to Bradford.

I had to act fast, and the wallowing in self-pity would have to wait as I moved and I was just not in the mood anymore. I got up and went all the way back to Calais, and hopped onto the ferry back to Harwich.

That was the point I'd completely run out of money. I remember watching it several times on television; somebody would be walking down a road, sticking his thumb out until a car or lorry stopped for him and gave him a lift to wherever he needed to go.

I thought I'd try it out. Two cars in twenty stopped, and a couple of lorries as well, but when I said I needed to get to Bradford, they all apologized and sped off away. I didn't stop; I kept going until finally a driver asked, "Where you headed to?"

"Bradford."

"I can take you up to Leeds, that alright?" he said. That was good enough, I thought, and I took the ride.

It wasn't all that bad, actually. In fact, it had been great. I hung out in a small café, drank in the beautiful Parisian flair. I mumbled a few words in a new language, found the Foreign Legion office and introduced myself, and they even liked me.

Even though it had come to nothing in the end, I was proud of myself for making it to Paris and then managing to hitch a ride all the way from Harwich to Leeds.

The way things worked out took me by surprise. In Bradford, I was old enough to be out on the streets and even got lost trying to find a way, but in Paris I was too young to have the chance to be taken off the streets.

CHAPTER 14
Playing with Fire

The Paris escapade left me broke. I still needed to eat, and so I dropped by Roger's place every now and again. His mum welcomed me with open arms, and I was allowed to crash there.

I knew my limits, and didn't want to overstay, and so the following day I trekked all over Bradford, thinking about how I was going to find a place of my own, and once found, how I was going to pay for it.

As I walked past a Pakistani restaurant called, "International," I remembered that I'd seen my dad there many times. He was like an old-school Mafia boss; the way he sat there with a suit and the grim look.

Boss or not, he was a miser. He'd have a whole pack of gold Benson and Hedges cigarettes in his suit top pocket, and he'd still have the audacity to ask people for a smoke. I needed to learn how he still managed to have their respect, even when he did things like that, because I still found them kissing up to him.

I had to find a way out, any way out, and as I glanced up to the heavens for some sort of inspiration, I spotted an announcement in the window above the restaurant for a bedsit that was available. That was my opportunity.

I asked the people who worked at the restaurant about who owned that bedsit, and to my surprise, it was owned by the same man who managed the restaurant. He knew my dad well.

"Yes?" he asked.

"Just wondering, that place upstairs available?" I said.

"Yes. It is thirty pounds per month."

"Good. I'll take it," I said.

"OK, you pay deposit, which is rent for one week, and then on the first of every month."

"Yeah. Right. You know who I am? I'm Councillor Hameed's son." I knew that slimy sleaze ball knew it, but he was trying to play it stupid with me and I was not about to be played by him.

"Of course, of course brother, you are..."

"Zahid. So anyway, I'll take that room then." The deal was sealed, and I had my own place without paying a deposit or the first week's' rent, although I would have to pay the subsequent weeks'.

It was on Pemberton Drive, opposite the Bradford University, which meant it was a student-infested place. I was younger than most of them, but looking at their faces as they walked to the University, or heading off to a pub for drinks, I found that they were not nearly half as intelligent as I was.

None of those students were remotely interesting to me, and I'd only speak to them if I needed tea or sugar. While walking back to my bedsit one day, I bumped into a lad I knew from going out in the city. His name was Javaid, and I got on alright with him.

We'd hang out from time to time, especially at the Olympus Cafe, where we'd just lounge about, eat chip butties and gibber for hours on end just like I had done with Roger. Jav and I were geniuses at putting credits on a game called 'Defender' and we'd play on that for prolonged periods of time.

In some ways he was similar to me; his dad was Pakistani and his mum English. Big difference was that he spoke the language and knew the Pakistani customs, but that did not make him pure in the community's eyes, and I understood what that was like.

There was still the looming figure of thirty pounds a month as I needed to pay rent. Down the road from my bedsit was a corner shop run by an old man. I'd go in there with my Rudeboy Crombie on. A Crombie was a long, black overcoat. A real Crombie overcoat was too expensive, and so I settled for the cheap version. At least it kept me warm and had a number of useful additional functions as well.

One such function was that it was so big that I was able to steal food from the corner shop and put it in the lining, which meant I would at least have something to eat. Roger would still bring me the odd baked beans and rice pudding, which he stole from his mum's pantry, but the dark side called out to me, stronger than ever before.

Crisps from the shop and rice pudding were not going to pay my rent and so my real reintroduction to the criminal ways was a sweet gig involving Commodore Sixty-Four computers. That night, I got together with the usual suspect. That's right: it was good old Floyd and I.

We went across to the other side of the city and broke into a school. We ransacked the computer laboratory. I heard the familiar bark of dogs, and knew it was only a matter of minutes before the police got in and busted us. Floyd took a whole computer screen and I took the rest of the pc and hid it in the lining of my Crombie.

As we headed out over the playing fields of the school, I noticed I was alone. I looked back and noticed Floyd had fallen again and was being held by the police. Damn that clumsy git, I didn't wait and just kept on running.

There was no chase and I guess they were satisfied that they had caught one of us. Later on I'd learn that Floyd never grassed on me and proved he was a real trooper. I kept on running until I reached the centre of Bradford with a stack of the PCs hidden underneath my coat and then walked calmly to my bedsit to hide the goods.

It was worth it, because just one of those babies would get me enough money to get by for weeks to come and I had a few of those.

Lateef had eyes on every corner of every street, and sure enough he paid me an unexpected visit to my bedsit. He knew, in spite of his brainlessness, that by hook or crook I was always making money. He barged in, went through my things and found the computer parts hidden at the back of my cupboard and took the lot. To pile on the misery, he took my stolen VCRs as well. I tried to take them back from him, but just like when he got something from Dad that I had wanted all those years ago, he shot me a warning look that said, "'Don't try or you die."

It was infuriating; he sold the lot and I knew from friends that he got over three hundred and fifty pounds for the computers and gave me just fifty quid. I really needed that money and unlike Mr. Pea Brain, I had backups.

Every Sunday around five in the morning, I would sneak into the restaurant using a spare key. I had discretely made a copy of it so no one knew anything. I would go in there and empty the fruit machines and take the illegal booze, which went to waste in the restaurant because from what I knew about Muslims, they did not drink. I wouldn't take everything and leave just enough to confuse them, like I'd done to Harry Beacher.

I was covered, but I just had to make sure that Lateef didn't follow me and intercept me again.

The situation was critical for me, so I had to figure out how to compensate my losses. One day I was hanging with Jav again, when a group of Pakistani lads walked in and came over to where we sat. "You brothers want to make some serious money?" one of them asked.

I said, "Doing what?"

"There's this small job, nothing difficult for brothers like you, and you get two thousand quid for making the hit."

"What's that?"

"We need you to get down to our warehouse and burn it down."

I thought, if it is so easy, why don't you do it yourself? I laughed and shook my head.

"No thanks, I don't want in." I looked at Jav. He seemed to be hesitating as though he was actually considering it, but he looked at me, smiled at the Paki and said he wasn't interested either. What made me suspicious is that he said something in Urdu to them, as they made to exit and they nodded and left.

They walked away without another word, and I turned to Jav and said, "You'd have to be really stupid to do that, isn't worth a penny."

That night, at around two in the morning, somebody came bursting into my room, panting.

My survival instinct came through and I reacted, grabbing the lamp next to my bed ready to defend myself because I thought I was being robbed. I caught a strong whiff of something that smelled of petrol and smoke. I heard Jav's voice speak, "It's me, shit can I stay here tonight..."

I had no idea what was going on partly because I was only half awake, but the smell of petrol was beginning to get to me. "Nah bruv, best you leave, I'm sorry."

"Shit, I need somewhere to stay!"

"Not here mate." He seemed on the verge of insisting, but probably decided against it after realizing I was being serious. He got up and left without another word and no explanation of why he needed to stay at my place.

The relief was momentary. A couple of hours later, somebody else burst into my room, nearly breaking the door down in the process.

Before I knew it I was pinned down on the bed. I felt the full weight of someone leaning on top of me, and the familiar chink of handcuffs and sneering tone made me realize what was going on. "You Paki, I know it was you. You're under arrest for attempted murder and arson." I was dragged out of my room, out of the bedsit and taken to the police station with just my shorts on.

They made me wait in a cell for hours, before I was called into the interrogation room for questioning.

"Look, we know you didn't do it, but I'm sure you know who did." They waited for my answer, but I wasn't a grass. I was from the streets and that's a big no-no. That, and I didn't actually know for sure who'd done what or what had happened.

"I don't know what you're talking about," I said.

"People have been badly hurt in the fire. I suggest you tell me what you know. Somebody burnt down a warehouse, and we think you know about it. Tell us, who was it, what do you know?" he insisted, his eyes bearing into mine.

I shrugged saying, "I seriously don't know."

The detective looked at me, but I kept my face straight and looked him right in the eyes without blinking. He nodded and said, "I know you are bullshitting me, you'd better watch out from now on, wog."

They released me, but the cop remained true to his word. At that time my younger brother Zaker also started to hang out in the city. The problem for him was that he wasn't the greatest hustler.

A few days after the police interrogation, I was walking back to my bedsit when a police car pulled up beside me and out stepped the same copper who had asked me about Jav. He said, "Alright, Zahid, we'd like a quick word with you at the station."

I asked, "Why what's up? I haven't done anything, am I under arrest or something?"

He said, "No," but shot me a twisted smile. "Your brother Zaker is at the station and is under arrest, best you come down and have a chat with us." I agreed to go there, and we walked down the street together, arriving at the station.

I got into the interrogation room and the cop said, "You know, Zahid, we have some unfinished business with you. Now here's the deal, if you admit to these offenses, we will TIC the rest," which meant 'take into consideration' the rest of the charges. "We will let your brother go and not charge him with theft and burglary, so what's it going to be Zahid?" That dumb little brother of mine had broken into a house and stolen a rather expensive camera. Witnesses had identified him and he was in big trouble unless I took the fall for him.

"Can I see him?" I asked and they agreed. When I saw him I noticed dried up tears and fear in his eyes. I didn't want him to live my desolate life. After all, I was his big brother and I loved him and unlike Lateef I had to be there for him. I asked him, "You alright, Zaker?"

He wiped his face and said, trying to act tough, "Yeah no problem."

I returned to the interview room and said, "Okay, where do I sign?"

"There's a good lad, thank you for your cooperation. Now, you are officially charged with these crimes, you stupid wog."

A few months later I was summoned to the Magistrates, where I was fined and warned, but my little brother was safe and off the hook. The police were happy because they had found the one "responsible" and they didn't have to bother trying to solve anything else by using me as a scapegoat. My only satisfaction rested in the fact that my little brother didn't have to face court and would be spared a criminal record.

Life really was like a game of poker, and I was glad I called its bluff and got away sometimes, but I also knew that I had to be extra careful from that moment on not to get too close to the heat, especially if I was still in the frying pan. I did not want to get out into the fire.

Bradford had become a very small place.

CHAPTER 15
Confronting Fear

Fear was something I didn't think too much about all too often, but when I did I realized I only ever really had two: Dad and Lateef, and after Dad left, just Lateef. The thing that gave my elder brother the edge, was more than fear, it was awe.

I always wondered what went on in that pea brain of his, how he felt about things, because he and I went through the same things, but whereas I only raised my fists to defend myself, or to react, he was cold and furious, in a way inhuman, and that's what got me.

I sat at the Olympus Café and reflected on the good old times my brother showed me exactly why I was afraid of him.

I had never been to one of those Spanish bullfighting events in my life, but I didn't need to because what I had seen was good enough. I remember one time in particular I saw that bull called Lateef being provoked, and it was nasty.

While fixing the old Robin Reliant, something that we did together in the good old days, his mate, Matti, came by. "There's some lad trying to check your lass," he said.

Lateef, with fire in his eyes, asked, "Where, mate?"

"It's some motorbike cunt on Moore Avenue.".

Lateef turned to me and said, "Get on the back of my scooter." By that time he was a Mod, the scooter was beautiful and he had done it all by himself.

We rode over to Moore Avenue and there outside the shops was his girlfriend. She was chatting with another lad. At that point the lad turned to walk to his bike while putting on his helmet, with a few of his mates standing by. Lateef stopped the scooter and said, "Wait here." He walked over to the motorbike guy.

Without warning, Lateef said, "Eh cunt," and as the guy turned round, he threw a punch, which went through the visor of the helmet and smashed into his face. His mates were stunned, and no one did anything as Lateef laid kick after kick on him.

There was blood on the streets and pavement and after finishing busting this guy up, with his helmet still on, Lateef walked calmly over to his girlfriend, who was screaming, and said to her, "Shut the fuck up and go home." She duly obliged.

Lateef then walked back to the carnage and said, "Anyone else want some?" All these so-called tough guys were quiet. He told me to get back on the scooter, and we left the utter devastation behind. We got back to the Robin Reliant and Lateef just carried on without a care in the world, like he smashed guys through visors every day.

I reckon the most telling situation, though, was on another occasion. While coming home from boxing we were all of a sudden surrounded by a group of white guys. It was typical during those times to be ganged up upon by one group or another.

Lateef turned to me and said, "Zahid, run." I ran. I expected Lateef to sprint past me while I was running, but I was alone. I turned back and saw my elder brother being confronted by those five white guys.

They jumped onto him, but he fought like a crazed man; a lion, his eyes wide, his head held high, a combination of punches and kicks hitting the right notes. One of the guys took a bottle and smashed it into his face, but rather than slow him down this only seemed to enrage him more, like the street kid version of the Hulk.

He went wild and all I saw was people and blood. I thought the bottle must have hit the "termination" switch, and I definitely did not want to join the heap of bodies all knocked out on the ground. I ran and ran, all the way home.

At the time, we were still living with our mother, and when I arrived back and out of breath my mother asked, "What happened?"

"Lateef's got into a fight." She didn't seem all that concerned, but I guess she felt that my brother could take care of himself. Sure enough, Lateef walked in through the door minutes later with a huge piece of glass sticking out of his head, as though it was a prop as part of a Halloween costume. My mother immediately stemmed the blood and asked him what happened, but Lateef didn't say anything.

It was just another day in his life, like taking a stroll in the park and obliterating five older, bigger guys with a shard of glass implanted into his head. My mother took him off to the hospital to have him cleaned up beyond her home nursing, even though he insisted he was fine.

It was thus my one and only fear was warranted. Lateef, naturally, could smell it from miles away, and I think it empowered him and that's why he took advantage of me whenever he wanted to, barging into my room at his convenience, and taking whatever he liked.

Meeting your fears head on is the best way to deal with them, and I found this out after having the last straw from my dear brother.

I was coming back home from boxing. We were going up a massive hill called Old Road, and as usual, for absolutely nothing, he was bullying me and picking on me. "You just a little pussy, you puff."

"Fuck off," I said.

Lateef froze and looked at me, his eyebrows raised. "Little cunt?"

"Fuck off." I repeated and without saying another word, I reacted fast and furious and put all my weight and sixteen years of frustration behind that punch. My fist seemed to travel in slow motion, as it gradually arrived to its target.

It knocked him to the ground, and he lay there for a moment, too shocked to react. I freaked out and ran back down the hill, as fast and as far away from him as I could. I knew it would only be a matter of time until the Hulk emerged, and old Pea brain would do me in for good.

I stayed away for a couple of nights, but after those two nights, I did meet Lateef again. It was a coincidence: I was on my way to the bedsit to get something I'd forgotten, when I found him walking in the opposite direction. We stopped and looked at each other, and for a second I didn't know what to expect, but he just came up to me and said, "Took balls to do what you did." That was the last of the bullying, and I knew I had earned Lateef's respect after what had happened.

I breathed a massive sigh of relief. If there was one thing that always weighed down on me, it was the sight of my elder brother sniffing around, looking for my loot and then torturing me until I gave him something.

I had waited years and years for that moment, and for me that was like defeating the darkest burden on my life until then. This triumph would have pragmatic benefits, but most importantly it would impact on my confidence and self-belief.

It took me a while to realize there'd be no more bullying, but after some time, I was home free and enjoying my days. I felt free as a bird; free to hustle away and sit comfortably at home.

It wasn't always the home comfort, however. I found myself locked up on a consistent basis for one or two days at the police station. It was all petty crimes; shoplifting and misdemeanours, that kind of thing. Those couple of days in the station cells was bearable enough for me to keep stealing, so that I could have enough money to get through the week and save something for the rent at the end of the month.

I knew how far I could go when it came to jail time, and would always avoid armed robberies, not just because those were a one-way ticket to the cells for a long time, but also because I would never fancy myself an armed robber.

The thought of taking an innocent person's life, rich or poor, black or white, was something I could not deal with, let alone holding somebody at gunpoint while asking them to fill my sack up with their money.

Still, whatever I'd done before, I was sure that life's got a sort of counter, where it marks up everything you do, and then it accumulates all the damage you've caused, and gives you the bill in full.

There was nothing to explain why, after everything I'd done, I was halted on a Saturday night on my way to 'Dollars and Dimes' night club. It was the very same cop that held my brother ransom so that I could testify to my own "crimes."

"You're under arrest for criminal damage, get in the fucking car." I was cuffed and taken away.

That wasn't something I'd gotten involved in, but there I was being escorted to the cells. I knew it wasn't a routine visit, because I was fully aware what being accused of criminal damage meant. They kept me there for a few days, and then I was bailed.

A few months later, I was summoned to the Magistrates court who in turn referred my case to the Crown Court. At one point I was minding my own business going for a night out, and the next thing, I was standing in front of a judge and a jury.

I got in there, and there was nobody to support me, let alone represent me. Not Mum, Dad, my brothers or sisters.

My court appointed barrister hadn't even bothered to read up on my case, and so I was representing myself. I stood alone, once again, and as the words, "The court hereby sentences you to eight months for criminal damage," reached my ears, I thought it was all just a bad dream that would eventually come to pass.

But the dream went on...and on...and on... I could see them all laughing at me; for the first time they'd solved a case using imaginary evidence, by setting me up.

I was not allowed to plead my own innocence and they took me downstairs to the cells beneath the courtrooms. I sat in the open cell, and that's when it hit me: I was going to jail for eight months for something I had not done. I had heard a lot about prison, and even though I used to laugh about it as I watched Porridge on the telly, it seemed as though British television had the last laugh.

"How long you got, mate?" I looked up and realised there was somebody else there.

"Eight months," I said, while trying to act tough.

He laughed and said, "That's nothin', mate, and if you can't do the time, don't do the crime pal! Fucking hell, mate. I got fifteen years, mate, now that's hard time." I guess somebody did have it worse than I did, but that didn't mean I was any less upset.

Prison was prison, after all. As I'd later hear the famous words, that everybody in prison is innocent, I would be able to relate to it, but at that point, I was standing on the edge of impending doom.

Before I knew I was on my way to prison. Where, I didn't know. I could do nothing, nothing but await my fate...

CHAPTER 16
The Long Walk

I used to watch movies about prison and think to myself, "Wow, must be hard in there." Sometimes I found it amusing seeing people going through difficulties there until the movie was over and what I got from that was the possibility of having an extraordinary experience, emerging with perks such as a heavy build, because there was plenty of time to work out, or that they ended up making life-long friends, or that they learned the most valuable lessons of their lives, receiving the education denied them.

Those movies make prison look like a luxurious five-star hotel.

I was put onto a coach, destination Armley Prison, which had a reputation for being one of the worst existing fortresses of pain, suffering and inevitable insanity. I was chained next to a stranger, at whom I did not even bother looking. As I could not do anything, I just sat and waited, perceiving my surroundings as the coach rolled on down the road.

It was a grey day as we left Leeds. The coach began to slow down, and I had my first sighting of my home for the next few months. It was a huge castle fortress that seemed impenetrable, even by the masters of prison breaks. The stone walls towered above me, warning me that beyond them, I would have no choice but to comply and do the time.

I was brought up to a holding area, where I had to await processing. At Armley Prison, there were different wings for the different degrees of the crimes committed. There was one section for the everyday criminals. That's where most the people who came to Armley went. Further up the crime charts, there was a wing for people involved in murders and armed robberies. It was intensified as there was one for child molesters, and there was a high-security wing for hardcore criminals, such as terrorists.

"Bit young to be here, lad, keep your head down and it will be quick and painless." The prison officer gave me my prison clothes, and said, "Sit there and wait." Ordinarily, I would have been too young to be placed in one of the cells at Armley, but as it turned out there were no places left at the youth prison, and they had no other choice.

As I sat there, another man sat next to me and said, "What are you in for?"

He had these small piercing eyes and was very creepy. I said, "Criminal damage."

He shrugged and said, "I'm here because the kid was too young to be with me but I thought he was older."

I ignored him and waited for my call. Finally, the screw, which was what we called prison guards, instructed me to stand up and said, "Right then, its simple here, lad. You answer the guards with Sir and end your sentences with Sir and if you don't do that, you'll be on report and would lose any privileges that you'd have gained." Oh yes, because I wouldn't want to give up my free spa session in the crap pit.

I was escorted to a cell. As I walked along the corridors, my footsteps echoing in the other pads, I saw most of the convicts. I tried to keep my gaze fixed forward, but my eyes continued to snap back to looking at the muttering lags in the cells. I witnessed a grey landscape of quasi-dementia, with an unruly strong stench. Most of them had blank looks on their faces, muttering to themselves, others just sat about, looking limp.

We arrived to my own pad, and it was torrid to say the least; dungeon-like with dismal walls and the hanging gloom of pending death, much like what I'd experienced as we drove into Armley.

Even though it was daylight outside, inside, it was dark and sullen and not because the sun didn't seep through gaps in the window. I recognized from where the stench was coming from. It was piss and shit like I'd never imagined.

I was sharing with two other men, and they sat there looking sombre and as though this was a stroll in the park for them. They both looked like ordinary, everyday lads, their prison outfits just as stained and dirtied as my own, and their matted hair limp and greasy after it had grown as the days ticked down. I did not acknowledge them, and they didn't bother me, and I sat perched on the edge of what you could call a bed.

The mattress was soft and reeked of urine as well. It seemed as though one of those two convicts had already done their business on that, marking his territory. He spared the sheets at least, which seemed clean, and there was a rag that I could only assume would be my blanket.

"We've got ourselves a sprog," one of the two finally said. A sprog was a new prisoner, and I sure hoped they had nothing against us "sprogs." He was blond and not so tall with decayed teeth. He looked like a badass, but his voice was surprisingly not menacing.

That wasn't the only thing that surprised me. I was psychologically prepared for the worst, and so I was somehow expecting my cellmates to rough me up, but I waited and waited and nothing happened.

"That bucket there, that's for 'slop out' meaning where you take a shit and piss, and you go dump it out in the morning. We take turns and tomorrow it's your turn mate. Best thing would be to do it in your sheets and chuck those out through the window, that way we won't have to smell it," he said laughing.

I wish I'd had some music with me, like The Specials for company, but the song was in my heart, and it sounded louder than ever in my ears as though a loud speakerphone were playing it. "*I walk and walk, do nothing...*" I felt that the song was speaking directly to me, describing my nature, my strategy. For the first time, I felt like I got it.

The first night, I fell asleep and woke up in the middle of the night and thought it was all a bad dream and I was back in my bedsit, but I gradually opened my eyes and at the same time could hear one of the guys snoring.

All around me, I could hear muffled tears being shed, words being whispered, and a subtle sound of something striking against the bars, the screws pacing up and down.

I didn't despair, because I had long since realized that life wasn't fair, but there was nothing for it except to accept the inevitabilities, shrug it off and get my head down and do my time.

Before prison, my favourite pastime was sitting about doing nothing, so at least I kept up with my hobby because that's all there was to do there. There was plenty of time to think about all sorts of things, like the practical side of all this: I wouldn't have to worry about paying my rent for a while.

I would have to worry about finding a new place after this was over. I thought about Nelson Mandela's time in prison that they used to teach us at school and the way he got inspired to fight for justice, or about how famous rap stars in the films wrote their jams on the walls, carving them onto there with a sharp nail filer. I didn't know too much about all those heroics.

I was wondering if Mandela's cell stunk worse than mine, because if it did, I respected how he'd managed to think anything constructive at all. I screwed my face up and tried to produce one credible thought, but there was nothing there, and so I didn't have anything else to think about.

It would take me a while more to start planning my thing. I just knew I needed to find the way to keep myself busy, because trying to think would have driven me nuts.

CHAPTER 17
HMP Armley

If there was one thing I'd learned at Armley, it was the power of obedience and discipline. This had more to do with the fact that messing about with the screws meant you got screwed. They were as strict as they came, like drill sergeants in the military, and just like any private, we'd have to stick to "Yes Sir" or "No Sir." Anything beyond that warranted serious trouble, and I'm not talking about what you see on television where they shout at you for a little while and leave you crying on the floor.

I'm talking about serious consequences, which would make time a lot harder in there. If you strayed a little out of line, you'd get obliterated to the point you'd have to be taken away, with the most likely destination being solitary confinement or even a transfer to another wing, maybe with the freaks, or the murderers, but I didn't want to find out, and so I stuck to the routine and as I was instructed to do so in the beginning, I kept my nose clean.

I recall overhearing one prisoner saying to another that many people had taken their own lives there, because they could not deal with it, even though a lot of them would not be there for all that long. I don't know what was creepier, the stories prisoners told you, or the horrors you saw with your own eyes.

The mantra "Things could be worse" gave me peace of mind. I could have been sharing a cell with bullies, but in my case my two companions didn't really get in my way at all. In fact, I'd say we got on fairly well and that was encouraging for me, because it meant I did not have to worry about putting up a fight at any point there.

Life really does play out its little ironies. It was a shocker that Lateef would ever be of any assistance to me, especially in a place like this. As it turned out, he was pretty well known, even in prison, and this was evident on the first day when I stepped out to catch myself a meal after doing my round of slopping.

As disgusting as it was, I just kept moving forwards, trying my best not to think about it, and then I'd empty the bucket and bring it back to my cell before heading down to the canteen in single file with every other lag.

"I wouldn't eat the soup if I were you," said a man who came up to me just as I was about to serve myself a bowl of soup.

"Why's that?" I asked.

"Well, you see these fuckers. They piss in there, you know. So stay away from that and you'll be fine." From that day forth I have never eaten soup anywhere and now you know why. I was surprised that somebody had thought of offering me that sort of advice, when everybody in there was just looking out for themselves. "Name's Jo-Jo. You Lateef Hameed's brother right?"

"Zahid, and yeah Lateef is my brother."

"Yeah I know your brother. Good lad. He's well known on the outside. Listen, don't worry about anything, I'll take care of you in here, just keep your head down."

"Thanks." I was truly grateful that somebody had my back, thanks to Lateef's reputation.

Jo-Jo turned out to be the daddy of the prison. He was a breed like me, half Jamaican, half English, mean-looking; a bodybuilder and boxer rolled into one. Still, he spoke about Lateef being top dog.

Nobody and I mean nobody crossed Jo-Jo's path. They respected and feared him. He had his own crew in there with him and it was clear that I was now part of that crew. He even got me my first job in prison. "Listen, I can hook you up with a job so that you don't have to be stuck in your cell all day."

"Okay, nice one, appreciate it," I said.

"No problem."

The following day I got up with a sharp pain in my back. I was still getting used to the mattress there, but I stretched and saw a ray of hope.

Jo-Jo had mentioned something about getting me a job, and that meant something to do.

I headed down for a shower on the landings, which was a communal showering area. I never experienced that whole "dropping the soap" myth, and maybe it was because everybody knew I was hanging with Jo-Jo, but no such thing ever came close to happening to me. There was no stress whatsoever, and I managed to wash up just fine.

After the shower, and putting on the starched jumpsuit that itched all over the place and dug into my skin, I went back to my cell. After about an hour, one of the screws appeared.

"You, get out, there's a job for you. You're starting straight away." I knew Jo-Jo had sorted it out for me, and I was grateful to him for that.

The screw led me down and out into the grounds, just beyond the walls. I wrinkled up my nose as I was met by a fresh wave of raw stink. Dotted all over were rolled up white sheets with shit inside.

The screw pointed out a shovel and a wheelbarrow and said, "Start cleaning it up."

"Yes, sir," I said.

It was impressive the way I took up the tool and started scooping the stuff up and piling it into the barrow. I let all the air out of my system, and tried to breathe through my mouth as much as I could to prevent the smell from reaching my nasal passages, but that meant I tasted the shit instead. I didn't want to look like I couldn't handle it in front of the screw, so I just kept it up, shovelling it bit by bit into the barrow, every last sheet, and sometimes there was no sheet!

"You're going to be doing this now," the screw said, giving me a twisted grin. I thought I'd never get used to it, but when you keep at something for long enough and it becomes part of your routine, you just go with it and you don't realize you're shovelling shit anymore.

Two weeks in, I was finally getting into my groove. I even managed to find a way to enjoy my meals. I'd always go for the duff and custard, which wasn't too bad to be honest. It was cake that fell to your stomach like a rock and stayed there, but the good thing was that it was filling and kept me going for most of the day.

One Sunday, I joined Jo-Jo and a few of his mates going to the prison's chapel, not because I was looking for a restoration of faith at that point, but specifically for the tea and biscuits they'd serve after the prayer session.

If there was one thing that the films and shows got half right, it was that the screws were mean, cold bastards. During searches of the cells, they'd bully us silly, with their outright condescension and their derogatory comments that made Beacher look like an angel. "Get your fucking shit together, you black cunt, and show me some respect!"

"Fucking Paki!"

"Cunt!"

"Bastard!"

"Degenerate!"

I heard all sorts of things, and for the first time, boxing didn't come in handy, as I would have expected. I did as Jo-Jo advised; kept my head down and just got on with it, watching them turn my mattress over, as careless as ever, and then running me down, searching every corner of the pad as though expecting to find anything there at all.

After six weeks, I was just about adjusting, getting into the rhythm of things, moving forward, not looking back and not really thinking. I was neither happy nor upset. Suddenly, just when everything was under control, I was disappointed when I was told that they were going to move me to the youth prison.

A screw appeared, as always, while I was in the cell. "You, out, they want a word with you."

I wondered what they wanted with me this time, when I was told, "You are being transferred to Borstal right away."

I did not even get to say thanks to Jo-Jo for helping me out while I was in there, and I knew he'd just say, "Fuck off out of here, boy," not in a rude way, but in a brotherly way.

And there I was on a bus again, to the next hellhole in my life. God knows what type of shit I was going to smell this time…

CHAPTER 18
Out of the Frying Pan into the Fire

The Borstal; a youth correctional facility in Hatfield, South Yorkshire, which to me was the middle of nowhere. A home for alienated kids, the buildings with a modern finish, but no less spooky than Armley.

Back into the itchy, nasty, jumpsuit it was, and this time I was tossed into a dormitory with twelve other young men, around my age. I felt a lot older in there, maybe because I was the youngest in the previous facility and could take the shit, and so these guys seemed like a bunch of babies in my eyes.

The screws weren't any friendlier, not that I was expecting a royal welcome, with one of them holding up a pineapple juice for me. It was boot camp; they'd wake us up early in the morning, screaming, "Get out of bed, you useless cunts!"

And it was "Yes Sir!" or "No Sir!" all over again.

It was not pleasant, but I sat tight and did what I was told. "What's that there, you Paki? I want a neat job! Smooth out those corners!" I redid the whole bed, making sure that the sheets were flat and smoothed out and the corners didn't stick out.

It was the screw's' world and their word against ours, and whatever they said, went. They'd take us up to the governor, like some kind of a kangaroo court. We would stand at attention facing the seated governor, while two screws would stand right in front of us, so close their noses would nearly be grazing your left and right cheeks and we could only speak in response to a question, but were not allowed to ask one.

A screw said to me, "You're in the kitchens doing kitchen duty! Get a move on!"

It was a fact of prison life that kitchen duty was the best kind of work you could get. I had to get up early, but I got the most food and I could use some of it as trade for other things.

Before we got to the meal preparation, we'd have to clean the surfaces and everything, until they were spotless.

"You missed a spot, this is not a holiday camp, do it properly!" the screws made sure I'd keep my head down and do a proper job, even though there was nothing more to scrub. I guess you could say I learned all about doing something until it was perfect.

In the bed next to me was a guy called Zanchetti. He was one of the few I got on really well with. It wasn't a formal introduction or anything, just a nod of the head, a "hey" and moving straight into conversing about this or that, about life in general and the music.

Night time was weird. I wasn't able to sleep straight away, and I'd just stare up at the ceiling, counting dollar signs. All throughout, I'd hear pages rustling and I'd think: wow, has somebody got exams when they get out, or what? Looking about me, I saw several pairs of legs facing upwards. I'd heard about people having bizarre studying habits, but I'd never seen it for myself.

"What do these guys do every night?" I asked Zanchetti one day.

He laughed loud and explained, "They are wanking mate!" Sure enough, I saw a magazine and tried to open it, but the pages were stuck together by a mysterious white glue.

I really had to figure out what the deal with the little ironies was, because at Borstal, I'd spot another one. Sometime before prison, I had heard about Caleb being bullied by a fat Pakistani boy called Zayshar. I didn't like to be provocative and start a fight, but Caleb was my mate at the time, and I wanted Zayshar to stop picking on him.

I waited until after school and went to Caleb's school and jumped the fat lug. I beat him up, and left him messed up on the ground. I thought that was the last I'd seen of him.

As I headed back to my dorm, seeing those wankers and putting a face to the legs, I recognized a fat kid across the yard. It was Zayshar, and in his eyes I saw that he recognized me, too. There was something steely about the way he glared at me, with a slight smirk on his face.

I didn't know what to expect; that he'd have me jumped unexpectedly while I was in my dorm perhaps? I didn't know anything about him, whether he was stupid like Lateef and liked direct confrontation, or perhaps he was more strategic, and would bring me down slowly and more discretely.

What I definitely did not see coming was a fellow inmate coming up to me during kitchen duty one day, saying, "It's been agreed that you and Zanchetti will fight at the toilets by the kitchen, if you don't then you're gonna have some trouble mate."

I definitely wasn't afraid of Zayshar, but the thought of expending energy to keep fighting those wankers off night after night made me realise it was not worth backing out of. Zanchetti and I were friends, but I was being forced to fight him and he me. I just hoped we could get it over and done with, and not cause one another too much damage.

I headed off to the kitchen toilets. The door opened and in walked my mate that I was about to pound. He said, "Mate this is not what I want but no choice."

I agreed, "Yeah, looks like we've got no choice."

I was squaring him up, but the anger I needed to punch him wasn't there because I counted him as a friend. "Look, I guess we-" The rest of my sentence was cut out by the most deranged head butt I had ever received. I felt my nose break as he rammed into it with his skull. I keeled over and blood poured out my nose in good measure. He followed up with jab after hook, right on the nose, and he sure was strong!

I needed to find a way in and pull back, but it was difficult as he was well on top. I found an entrance when he was regaining for another punch. I somehow grabbed his hair out of sheer desperation and dragged his head down and smashed his mouth on the toilet rim, knocking out a few teeth.

I held him there against the toilet rim and with my other fist punched him as hard as I could. He kicked out and threw me back, his rage turned on by my attack. He came in with a flurry of blows right to the nose. I couldn't breathe, and my nostrils were bubbling with fresh blood. My nose, mouth and jaw were completely damaged.

Then as fast it started, it ended, as two screws barged in and pulled us apart. "You idiots, you are on report now!"

I was numb from the pain, and could only breathe through my mouth because it was as though I had no nose. On the bright side, I would be taken to see the doctor, which had to be better than the wankfest of a dorm.

I was brought to the treatment centre, which was actually near the gates. The doctor broke my nose back, which was even more painful. I was right, it wasn't as bad a place as the prison, but I couldn't see out the night. My smashed-up nose was back in place and as I left to head back to the dorm, the screw told me that I was on report and would have to see the governor.

It was a quick sentence, I went in to see him and all he said was, "Solitary confinement, fourteen days!"

All alone, isolated from the rest of the world, I knew why it was said that no person was an island. Even if I didn't really talk much to other people, hated them even, being separated from civilization was a horrific grievance.

I was nothing in there. I couldn't hide behind my routine, for two whole weeks. I understood why it was that people were driven insane by being in solitary confinement because there was nothing to do, without a notion of time and the silence became so loud, they'd do anything to stop it. I was used to doing nothing, but I was wrong. This was different.

When I returned from solitary confinement, I was told that Zanchetti had been transferred to Everthorpe Youth Prison in Hull, which was one of the toughest Borstals. It was because he was a troubled kid, who was violent and had a record of physical assaults. I wasn't sure if it was GBH he was in for, but what I was sure of was that I was lucky to have survived. Not just that, I'd given him a good beating as well.

I lost my job in the kitchens, and was told that I would be shovelling coal instead. I was lucky to get another job so soon. I thought shovelling coal wouldn't be so bad, considering I had shovelled worse, but I was wrong.

As I stood outside scooping sooty black coal into a hole in the wall all day, the black soot got everywhere: in my hair, my eyes, my finger nails and my teeth. It was a miracle I didn't die of cancer because the poison I was breathing in was lethal.

I used to cough myself to sleep; it was like something out a scene from Oliver in the Victorian times, and the stuff would take forever to come out from underneath my finger nails.

I'd learnt nothing from being incarcerated, but on my own I'd learnt just when you think you can deal with things, there's another hurdle to jump and then another and another....it just doesn't stop...but there's nothing you can do but to keep jumping.

CHAPTER 19
Monday August 16th

Borstal did get lonely from time to time. I only ever had two visitors on the same day, while I was in there. I was surprised when a screw came up to me and said, "You've got visitors!" And sure enough, there stood Caleb and Zaker. My little brother was terribly upset seeing my face in a mess.

Caleb spoke very little and was more in awe of the place and only asked how things were, to which I responded, "What do you think, this isn't Butlins holiday camp." I told them about my altercation with another lag, but that I was surviving.

Zaker told me that my mother had gone back to Holland and the house she fought so hard to keep was up for sale. I also understood that my eldest sister was trying to get the house sold for my mother. Later I would find out that my mother had suffered a nervous breakdown and had just freaked out and left.

Most people dig for gold, but I was too busy gazing upwards, finding silver linings in every cloud. There really always is a hint of silver, if you keep looking for it.

I'd worked the coal-shovelling job for quite some time, and I think the governor agreed that I deserved a reprieve. I don't know what the deal was with these people handing me a shovel, but I was back to shovelling shit, this time cleaning out the drains outside.

The weather was great as it was summer and I'd much rather the stink than inhaling coal. I was actually glad to be able to walk outside and take in some of the sun.

Before I knew it, the countdown started. "Twenty-one and a break." That meant twenty-one days and a breakfast the next day before being set free. It wasn't half bad getting up in the morning and saying to myself, "twenty days and a break," knocking one more day off until I'd reach freedom.

As I got to the final four and a break, they were frustrating. Time passed so slowly and the days were so long, you'd think it had been stopped by a miraculous universal force. Still, it was not too long before I got out, and I hung onto that. As I sat having my usual meal, one of the lads came to me and said, "Four and a break eh?"

"Yep," I said.

"Got any outstanding charges or cases against you mate? 'Cause if you have you better be prepared, 'cause they won't let you go and once you get to the gates, the police will be waiting and you get gate arrest. And it all starts again, you're brought to the police station, you're charged, brought to court, you're sentenced again and then end up back here. They never leave you alone mate, I know loads of lads that have been through it."

I was unsettled by the news, and was not really looking forward to my release anymore.

Day and a break. I was ready for whatever awaited me the following day, which was Monday the sixteenth of August. I consoled myself with the thought that it didn't matter if I got gate arrest or not, because life outside my pad was like prison anyway.

A break. Time was up. The ritual on the last day or last breakfast is to give everything away including your last breakfast and that's what I did. I just hoped I wouldn't live to regret that, because if I got gate arrest, I'd not only be miserable, but starved too.

I waited to be called and then proceeded to the guardhouse for checkout. I was instructed to get out of my prison clothes, and was handed back my grey jeans, t-shirt and jacket.

I looked at the disgusting starched clothing I had worn for eight months in prison and in Borstal. I realized just how terrible those clothes were once I put my own jeans on. It was like wrapping my legs in silk; the texture was smooth as a baby's backside, and it just caressed my skin. My t-shirt as well felt cool against my chest and back. It was just a bit tighter as I had gotten bigger due to all that shovelling of the coal and shit, which was like a work out in the gym.

The moment of truth had finally come. I marched up to the gates and as I had expected, there was nobody to receive me, except from a representative from the social security. He handed me some money saying, "Sign here, it's dole for two weeks." I signed and took it without saying anything.

The screws scrutinized me, and one of them said, "See you again, boy."

I puffed my chest out and said, "You won't see me again, Sir."

The screw scoffed. "They all say that, lad, but you will be back!"

What mattered most for me was that I was out and free, free from shovelling shit and coal, free from sharing a dorm with a group of wankers, free from the stink. I think I could say that I was proud of myself, even if nobody else was. I didn't care anyway, what they thought about me, I was glad that I'd made it through and still kept sane. If I were a professional boxer and the amount of times I was knocked down and beaten up but still kept going, I think my hero Muhammad Ali would be proud of me.

It was the summer holidays, and that meant all the kids from school, my age, would be out and about, throwing daddy's money on booze and having a great time. I wasn't afforded those same luxuries, but I didn't need them. I got on a bus that wound up in a village called Mexborough. I paid for the ticket using some of the money the dole had given me, and sure enough there I was, without having planned it.

I went straight to a nightclub and got myself my favourite drink: a Bacardi cola, and hung back in a corner. I spotted a girl that met my fancy and I laughed to myself as I thought of Zaker and how he would just walk up to her and start dancing with her. He always had a way with it, and even though I was made to think that I was the ugly one, I had been to prison, and my kid brother hadn't, and that had to count for something.

"How ya doing?" I asked as I chilled to the music, held my drink in one hand and tried to act cool.

"Good, how about you?" she replied. She did reply!

"What's your name?"

"Janet, you're not from round here are you?"

I stuck my hand out and said, "Zid, nice to meet you, yeah from Bradford."

"Oh, okay, wanna dance?"

"Nah, tell me about yourself."

As she was talking I wasn't listening and had one thing on my mind. The booze was getting to me a little, but I didn't have a care in the world, and her lips were tantalising.

I asked her, "You got a place we can crash at?"

She laughed and said, "I thought you'd never ask."

The next thing I knew, she and I were in some room, and enjoying a very pleasurable moment together, and at the pinnacle, I felt relief like never before.

It was the sixteenth of August and after eight months of shit, what did I learn…absolutely nothing!

CHAPTER 20
Rebirth

It wasn't as though it made any difference while she was actually around, but the fact that Mum had run off to Holland unnerved me slightly, as I tried to regain my old self, and get back into peak action with the hustles.

This time, however, I wanted to do things differently. I wanted to do what any other seventeen year old did, and not always worry about things like staying alive. In fact, outside the hustling, I sometimes actually did feel like a normal kid and that was going out to night clubs and partying all night long. This time I was craving for a little more.

Roger and I would still keep our Friday nights at Checkpoint and Saturday nights for Dollars and Dimes. Prison had made me a lot more confident as well, and that meant I could approach girls without a problem, but I was still no competition for the boy wonder, Zaker.

He couldn't get enough of the girls until he met one called Angela. She was your proper English rose, creamy white with a red neck racist father to boot, but she and my brother were inseparable. Literally. I remember, vividly, after coming out of prison, that summer my brother was doing her the whole time.

Since my mother's nervous breakdown and with her travelling between England and Holland and my sister helping pay the bills, Zaker had managed to stay on at the house. Once, I'd gone up there while Mum was away. As I stood there with Roger, calling for Zaker, he came out of the bedroom and stood at the top of the stairs with just his underpants on.

"Zaker, you using a condom?" I asked.

"Nah I don't need it, pulling out before it happens," he said.

"You nuts or what, you're gonna get her pregnant!"

Angela and he had no idea of the consequences, so in fact she was as dumb as he was. When he found out that she was pregnant he freaked out about being a father at sixteen. It was worse that Angela was a mum at fourteen and even worse that her father had zero tolerance for unwanted pregnancies. If we were in the United States of America, he would have been the 'Grand Wizard.' If only that idiot kid brother of mine thought more without his penis at that age, things wouldn't have gotten so complicated for him.

One Saturday night, while I was hanging out with the usual suspects, something had to happen to that ladies' man. We'd seen that the Skinheads we knew were the National Front had infiltrated the club. They had only one thing on their mind: giving hell to anyone who wasn't white, meaning us.

It was pure mayhem as we fought them in the club. It spilled over outside and before we knew it, a coach load of these parasites pulled up. Roger was slow in terms of intelligence, but one thing he was great at was fighting and boy could he knock a man out. I once witnessed him completely spark out a club bouncer who was at least twice his age.

One thing about Rudeboys, we always stuck together when it came to fights. As we fought outside Dollars & Dimes, Roger jumped on the coach and dragged those assholes out one after the other. Gaffa, Jacko, Wendall, Mallet, Sykes and the rest of the Rudeboys entered the coach to help him out.

As I was charging in as well, someone shouted out, "Zid, help me!" it was my brother Zaker. I spun around and saw that my little brother was taking a pounding on a car bonnet. I ran over and with a flying kick that Bruce Lee would have been proud of, I floored the aggressor. He tried to react, but I had him, the rage was there as I rearranged his face.

He lay in the gutter bleeding profusely, but I didn't care. I ran up to him and for good measure stamped on his face. I think after years of racial abuse, that split second brought it all out. You could say at that moment I was Lateef; all fury and no space for intelligence.

I felt absolutely no remorse for what I had done. These National Front gang were a disaster. They would invade the place and pick on people all the time. They attacked older people in the streets. For the first time violence felt right because it tasted like justice.

As I stood back, I heard police sirens in the distance and that was my cue to get out of there. I told my brother to make a break for it. Roger and

131

I ran too; we just kept on running before crashing out to catch our breaths. We went back to Roger's house and celebrated our victory over the racist National Front. "Fuckin' cunts, loved how you knocked out that guy Roger," I said, and we sank into the sofas and laughed.

My mother was highly unsettled and without a clue as to what she wanted to do. I wasn't paying much attention to her at all, but she had flicked on the light switch in my brain that made me realize that there was more out there. There had to be.

I had been to Holland before, to Paris, which was a nutty adventure, but I'd seen what it was like out there. I liked Paris at the time, and even though I hadn't had the best experience in Amsterdam, it definitely had to give me something more than Bradford. It would have to be Amsterdam, because I didn't have family in Paris.

It seemed appropriate for me, especially after prison. I saw that I just did not have anything in common with anybody in Bradford, that I had a bad enough reputation without the fresh hustles to come, because that's what I would have to work with since I definitely did not want to fall victim to the typical circle of life.

It was not who I wanted to be. You couldn't really take the hustler out of me, but I needed to leave those Bradford stunts behind, and find a new me, with a new beginning. I went with my gut instinct, and decided it was time for me to head back out to Holland, and give myself another shot at finding something.

My mother had an uncle, named Frans, who had a daughter, Linda that lived in Amsterdam. The few times we actually saw them, they were probably the only ones that treated us normally and Uncle Frans seemed to really think I was a cool kid. Anyway his kids, who were actually my mum's cousins, were cool too and I thought it be a good idea to contact the eldest Linda.

Linda Merkx was working in the fashion industry as a super model and I knew that she had done shows all over the world. She lived in the chic part of Amsterdam Central, sharing an apartment with her boyfriend, Henni, who was a bit of a shady character; a smooth customer, but that was fine with me.

Linda was also fine with me and she let me stay on with her, which was great because Mum had clearly not shown any interest in having me close anytime soon, after making a clear statement in letting social services take me away.

My cousin was a true gem of a person; respectful, courteous and kind towards me, which was the bare minimum when it came to treating a fellow human being, let alone a relative, and I was grateful to her.

I thought maybe I could hustle myself into a job and then get my own place, and that's where I'd start. I hadn't really developed a plan, and after spending enough time without finding a job, or making any progress in getting my own place, I'd decided to call it time.

I headed back to Bradford, but this time, things would be different. One day while I was talking to my sister, she mentioned that she had changed her second name to Beacher. When I asked her why, she did not give me an answer, and she did not need to.

She only said, "Once you hit eighteen, you can change the family name too."

"Well I won't choose Beacher, are you mad, why that freak, why would you do that?"

"Who else could I choose Zahid? I thought it the best option, everyone else has done the same except you and Zaker."

"Well I'm not choosing Beacher, I ain't white and he ain't my dad and to hell with Daddy I don't want anything to do with him or his Pakistani culture."

"What name you taking then?"

"I don't know."

I loved and admired my oldest sister for the fight she put up against her sickle cell, but at that moment I was disappointed in her. I felt betrayed that they had all chosen Beacher's name, including Yasmeen, my favourite. At least I could safely say that I was the ultimate black sheep of the family, as I would not follow suit.

"When did you change your name?" I asked.

"We did it while you were locked up," she said.

It was clearer to me how I had nothing in common with my own brothers and sisters and this was my chance to finally break free from my father's roots, Beacher's nonsense and all the negativity, which surrounded me because I was an ex-con.

While I was staying at Linda's, I realized I really needed to leave my past behind. I was on the lookout for the new me, and it had to be a smooth transition. I couldn't move on until I had completely gotten over what I used to be. Changing my name definitely sounded like the perfect start.

I was about to hit eighteen, and I wanted to enter my eighteenth year a new man, with a new plan and, a new name.

"Where can I do this name changing thing, then?" I asked. She explained that once I turned eighteen I could, through a solicitor, officially change my name. She also told me how much it would cost and where she had done it.

I honoured my hustling days one last time by doing a couple more rounds to pay for a new identity. It didn't take me long to get it all together and just like I did in prison, I was counting down the time to my eighteenth birthday.

My birthday, which was never any different from another day, was on a Sunday. The following Monday I would be heading to the solicitors, ready and willing, but I still had no idea what name I would use.

As I stood in front of the solicitor it suddenly came to me. I was going to be called Merkx. That was my mother's family name from her mother's side, so it was a blood line within my family tree. My first name would be Frans, because my Uncle Frans had always treated me well and his daughter Linda had also been good to me when she allowed me to stay at her place without even really knowing me.

I also didn't want to be called Zahid anymore, but I didn't want to leave the good things of the past behind and I wasn't exactly the regular Dutch boy with blonde hair and blue eyes. I decided my new name would be Frans Merkx. It was unusual, but unique and that's how I felt about myself.

I stood outside the office, having just received my official notification and certificate of registering a new name, and breathed in deeply. I looked about me and realized that I was going to leave everything behind. All the shit that Bradford had put me through, and all the shit that I had put Bradford through, it was all about to finally be called even.

The companionship would change, the situation would change, and so I didn't feel the need to say goodbye or anything. I just wanted out, and I got myself a brand-new passport, with my new name on there, and traipsed off to Holland.

CHAPTER 21
Same Old Trouble

I had to start from scratch; from the very bottom, and work my way up, and that meant either homelessness or persuading my mother to give up her attic. It was quite the dilemma, but in the end I sucked up my pride and succumbed to the latter. I thought, if I wound up in my mother's attic, she wouldn't have to see me and I wouldn't have to see her, which was perfect.

She answered the door, and I didn't give her a chance to exchange unpleasantries. "I need a place to stay," I said immediately. I wondered whether or not she would accept my proposal, when she walked back inside, leaving the door open. I took that as a sign that I could go in.

As it turned out, Mum had finally sold her beloved house back in Bradford, and she'd actually made a profit. I guess it runs in the family, but it seemed as though she really wanted to put all the Bradford nonsense aside, and start over, and hence why she jumped shipped and had found a nursing job in Amsterdam.

The first thing I had to do was get myself a job, any kind of job; it didn't matter to me. I had no qualifications in terms of a formal education, but I did have an impressive resume, which boasted clicking credits, fishing the fruit machines, running my own mobile toy shop and generating two hundred per cent profits and starting my own line of low-budget fashion designs, with cardboard and Morrison's plastic bags. I was also handy with a shovel, something I'd picked up from a recognized institution, and I was sure I could get Jo-Jo to write me a letter of recommendation from his prison cell. I just wasn't sure this would be recognized in Holland, so it left me no choice, but to take the lowest form of work.

First up was working for a cleaning company sweeping railway platforms. Luckily, the only thing they asked for was a low life out there ready to do that work. The only people who worked it were idiots or asylum seekers, and I saw myself a part of the former.

The manager was condescending and bore down on me all the time and within no time at all, I was fired. I then applied at a warehouse and once again got the job. The work was just as shit as the previous one, but it was still a job, and I couldn't complain.

One day I was working in the yard, and one of the Moroccan guys who I got on well with, Mustafa, was messing around in the forklift, which accidently ran over my foot and crushed it. It was excruciating, and I was granted leave from work as my foot was busted and broken. I don't think the warehouse was ever going to get a Corporate Responsibility certification, because rather than call in on me to check I was alright, and ready to work, the owners tried to have me fired.

Fortunately, I had Mustafa looking out for me, and he asked me to make an official complaint, which I did and won. I ended up losing my job, but I still received some money, which at least bought me time while I looked for another loser job.

I thought I deserved a reprieve after the yard and the train station, and so I tried at a hotel. Again it was cleaning, but this time cleaning hotel rooms. I enjoyed the perks of having a warm working environment, with surprise bonuses for my hard work, such as unused breakfast meals, jewellery and clothing. The guests tipped pretty well too, in a strange way though as many a time I'd find loose change in gaps in the sofas, under the carpets and behind the bed's headboard.

It wasn't the best work, but it was a one-way ticket to getting a work stamp by the immigration police, and that was the light at the end of the tunnel. In those days there was no European Union or Euro, and so I was a foreigner that needed a work stamp.

After some time, I started to doubt my decision, because there seemed to be no end to it. I sure didn't want to clean rooms forever, and my pockets were filling up too slowly. But there was always the dark side; so easy, so quick, my pockets would replenish themselves in no time. The profits were tasty, the working hours were flexible, and I was my own boss. I was appreciated in that world, they'd welcome me back like a hero.

I was hungry, I needed to eat; my stomach was very much for the dark side. All I needed were my sticky fingers, my quick wit, and my fearlessness, and I could have it all, just like before...

And there I was at the local McDonalds, wearing the uniform, which included the frown, ready to serve fries and nuggets to brats and workaholics. I think I did the right thing, closing my mind to hustling. It wasn't exactly a step up in the world, but McDonalds was a permanent job, and that meant stability.

At first it was great, I must say, and flipping burgers was both stupid and easy. I also got on well, *really* well with the manager, as our one-to-ones in the storage room would testify and because of that, she'd never bother me at all, but picked on the others, which meant I was free to flip burgers the way I wanted, and spend as much time in the storage area as I liked.

Apart from being an expert in burger flipping, it forced me into learning Dutch, not the usual broken Dutch, but to master Dutch where I would speak like a real Amsterdammer. At night I'd watch movies and teach myself to read and write by looking at the subtitles.

After flipping my umpteenth burger that week, however, I was overcome by that familiar feeling of dissatisfaction. There were only so many burgers you could turn over, before you realize that there really isn't much of a future in the job. I remembered Hughie and his mates, how all they'd do was work the same meaningless jobs all week, and then end up in the pub after work. I reminded myself that I had gone clean, that I would not go back to my old ways, and reluctantly put another lot of chicken nuggets in the tray, ready to be served.

I did not last as long as I thought I would and after some time the situation became far too boring, as did the manager, and I couldn't keep it up any longer. I handed in my resignation, and left.

I thought about giving up and picking up on my old habits, but I pulled myself together and applied to the McDonalds in the city centre, which I succeeded in getting. My mind was still fixated upon that work stamp, and I decided that boring or not I was going to stick with it. What's more was that it was in the centre, where there was more life with the tourists coming round, and that meant it would be more interesting.

I had to pass through one final obstacle course, before I got the stamp: the immigration office. I sat there for hours on end, only to finally walk in and have one of those assholes stare me down with a sceptical eye; an expression I had seen only too often. I didn't buckle, and stared right back, it was like one of those Clint Eastwood style duels. Neither of us blinked. Which one of us was going to draw first? At long last, and after a tiring stare-off, he took the permit and stamped it. I had won the duel.

I kept up my job at McDonalds, but with the added confidence of having finally been stamped. I was motivated by the money and was free to do my thing.

I would see my sister from time to time, and on one occasion she came up to me after work and said she wanted a word.

"You know, you can get a Dutch passport, because Mum's Dutch." It was mixed news for me. On the one hand, I was relieved to know that it was possible for me to cement my status and not worry about renewing the work stamp, but on the other hand I was livid that I had visited the immigration office several times, and they knew full well that I had a right to citizenship, but never bothered to tell me.

I ended up applying for the passport, citing all the details I knew, and quoting my mother's name on the forms. It took a week to arrive, but there she was, finally, my brand new Dutch passport, and that meant no more immigration police.

Even though I had used my mother's address to apply for it, I knew that I was not wanted there. I had to think and move fast, before mum had a change of heart and kicked me out again.

Luckily, the perfect situation presented itself to me. Mum had a friend that visited sometimes, and one day while she was visiting, and I happened to walk in while she was there, she approached me about renting an apartment she had. She had decided to move to her other apartment and by law was supposed to give the smaller one away, and I was ready to bet that my mother had asked because she wanted to get rid of me.

"...so you have the place, and have to give me something every month as a, sort of, thank you fee," she said, and then asked, "are you interested?"

I would have to double check that thing about a thank you fee, but I was definitely interested and I went in for the kill. "I definitely am."

"Come tomorrow to take the keys, I've written the address down."

"Great, I'll be there."

I kept my word and found the place without too much difficulty. It wasn't that far from where my mum was living and that was probably the only negative. The apartment was situated in the Pijp, and right in front of the place was the world-famous Heineken brewery, on a street called Quellijnstraat.

"Good, you're here!" she said. She showed me around the place. It wasn't much; a bathroom, kitchen, hallway and living room that was also the bedroom, but it beat an attic in a clueless mother's house and it would be my own place.

"The rent is Seventy-Five Guilders per month. Gas and electricity are separate bills, and there's that Fifty Guilders on top as a thank you."

I had a place to stay, but it would be of no use to me if I couldn't feed myself to survive and live there.

As I tightened my belt, I told Mum's friend, "You'll have to wait until the end of the year, so I can pay you the difference once I receive my Christmas bonus." I had no idea thanking somebody would actually cost me so much, and I knew she was taking advantage of me, but I had a plan.

The house was rather ancient, with peeling wallpaper and grimy ceilings, and one day the housing authority paid me a visit there.

"We want to carry out some renovations," a gentleman representative said. "You are the rent payer?"

"Correct," I said.

"Right, because rent is automatically taken off your bank account, we will be sending you a tenant agreement in your name."

"Okay."

"After the renovation, all the tenants receive five thousand guilders, to redecorate their apartments." I was definitely not going to tell mum's friend anything about the five thousand Guilders, and that was enough retribution for me.

Not only was the place legally mine, but I'd also hit the jackpot and was getting money to decorate. I thought the wall paint looked alright, the tiles were my colour, and the furnishing was not half bad and the black and white TV worked so I guess I could save that money up and put it to better use.

Unfortunately Mum's friend heard about the money from one of the neighbours and came to see me.

"I want half of the money," she said. I refused outright. "Okay. I will have to go to the housing authority and complain to them that you acquired the apartment illegally, then."

I have to admit I was worried, because I did not want to end up in trouble again, although I still refused to give up half the money. In the end, justice was served and it backfired on her because the housing authority explained to her that due to the fact that I was paying the rent, gas and electric, the apartment had legally reverted to my name.

I guess the swindler got swindled in the end, that too by the Ultimate Swindling Champion.

It was satisfying dipping my hands into murky waters, although I hadn't dirtied them nearly half as bad as I used to in Bradford, because I still went through with all the legal procedures and proved that I wasn't a hustler for hustling's sake.

Those five thousand Guilders sure gave me some relief, and I was able to take a dip in the social scene as well. I was hanging out with one, Bryan, whom I'd met when I boxed at the Albert Cuijp Boxing School. We got on well, and in no time I found that I could trust him implicitly to be my reference point in my new surroundings. He was my number one confidant, and we'd go all over the place together.

I still had a blast from the past, as my old school mate Roger would pay me a visit whenever he had the money. He'd stay over at my place, and we'd always catch up on what we were doing with our lives, and what we used to do, that being Roger getting fatter and smoking too much weed and having far too good a time with the girls than was actually good for him, and it felt just like we were sitting on those low Yorkshire brick walls, chilling to some great Ska music and having a great time together.

And when I wasn't hanging out with Bryan, or with Roger, I was up and about with a fellow co-worker at McDonald's Amsterdam City Centre; a total nutty psycho called Pierre. To say he was off his rocker would be an understatement. I wondered where he'd get all his psyche from, when I uncovered the mystery as I found out he was on Crystal Meth all the time.

Somehow, we breeds always come together, and Pierre, just like Bryan, was yet another mix I'd added to my friend circle. His dad was from Surinam and his mother was from Holland. He was actually smooth looking, with a short haircut and a defined jawline and thick-set brows over sharp eyes.

While I did get along with him because I could relate to his background, I felt quite alienated from his favourite past time. I used to walk around with him, in the centre, on the subways, and he'd be doing meth, while all these other junkies sat with him. It was like some sort of meth club, and I was the plus one he was allowed to bring to those junkie conventions.

I also went out at night a couple of times with him, because I did enjoy his company. It was a way to pass time, and a sure way out of boredom, because even though I never got high on Meth, it was amusing watching the others do it.

One night, however, things were suddenly not so amusing. I had had a few close shaves with trouble, but trouble finally found me in my new surroundings. Pierre, the lunatic, said to me, "Meet me in Amsterdam north near my place, got a few things to do and then we can go out for a few drinks, the address is on there."

I headed up to the place that he had jotted down on a napkin. When I got there, Pierre said, "Wait here on the side of the street." He vanished for a whole half hour, and then came back and just said, "Run!" I didn't need telling twice, the look on his face said it all. I turned and bailed on him.

I could hear the police in the distance, and I also heard the dogs, and I didn't know where I was running to. All of a sudden I was standing in front of a canal. Amsterdam was not like Bradford; the coppers could shoot whenever they thought you were in possession of any kind of weapon, and one look at me would say I was probably concealing an AK-

47; they'd find any excuse to have a go at me. I jumped into the canal and began to swim to the other side, thinking the dogs would lose my scent if I'm in the water.

Waiting for me on the other side were the police and their damned dogs as I resurfaced. The game was up. I was hanging around with a robber, a meth addict and who knew what else, and there I was getting arrested. It was all too familiar, the cuffs placed over my wrists, they asking me to get in the car, I just could not believe it was all happening again, not since I'd done my level best to stay out of trouble.

At the police station, I was brought into the interview room for questioning. This is where my lack of speaking Dutch came in useful. The officer started off, in broken English, "Do you know about house breaking here in North?" It was not like in Bradford. Here, they were careful because they were trying to get a confession out of me, and had to be extra sure they didn't get anything wrong, because of the language barrier. "Do you know anything?"

I played the innocent one, which in fact I was, and said, "I don't know anything, sir."

"You are sure?" I was sure, sure about not grassing on a mate.

I briefly explained to them that I had met some guy in the city centre a few times and chilled out with him. I told them his name was Mike and he had blond hair and blue eyes, and he had told me to meet him in Amsterdam North and that we would be going out for drinks at his local pub. "…when I saw him he asked me to wait on the corner of the street as he had forgotten his wallet from home." Damn, even I started to believe my story. "So I did and the next thing he came back and told me to run. So I ran and the next thing I knew was that I'd been arrested for burglary."

"Okay but do you know where he live?"

"I don't mate."

"We appreciate your help Mr. Merkx and will investigate further, are you hungry we can get McDonald's for you and then drop you off in the centre if you like?"

The 'Keystone Cops' believed every word and on top of that I was getting free Micky D's, must have been the hard work I was doing there.

And there I was finishing my free burger, fries and a delicious cola, with my ride waiting for me outside. I got up, they thanked me and dropped me at Central Station, and from there I got on the tram back to Amsterdam South, and home.

On my way home, I thought about what had happened, and the temptations from the dark side started to elude me. The last thing I wanted and needed was to attract such company. I did not want to have anything to do with a junkie and his band of troublemakers.

I went back to work the following day, and as usual found Pierre there. He acted like it was all nothing, and that it hadn't even happened. "I can't and won't get involved in that kind of crap again, Pierre," I said to him.

"Thanks for not telling the police anything, bro. I appreciate it."

"No sweat, but never again, bro," I said.

I might have overreacted when I thought about not hanging out with Pierre ever. Somehow, we had a mutual understanding that we would not get into the criminal life, but that didn't stop us from going out and causing other kinds of trouble. Just like in Bradford, he and I got into fights, usually over women or because of the remarks about our backgrounds, but one thing was for sure, Pierre sure could take care of himself!

He could also take care of his mates. Things weren't going so well for me at McDonalds, and it culminated in me having an argument with the manager. "I told you, Frans for the thousandth time, mop the floor properly, you idiot!"

"Don't call me an idiot, jackass, I already did it and I'm not doing it again!" I replied.

"I am sick of you and that other loser Pierre speaking to me in this way, you are both fired!"

My hands curled up into balls, and I was on the brink of knocking his teeth out, but Pierre beat me to it. "Fuck you and your shit job."

"Get out or I'm calling the police."

"Fuck you and the police...!" Pierre turned the rage on, grabbed the manager by the hand, and stuck it in the fryer where we made the chicken

McNuggets. I was awestruck, and wondered who had placed an order for hand McNuggets.

The manager screamed as he watched his hand boil and bubble in the hot oil. It was nuts. "I'll be back if you decide to report us, you understand?" Pierre said, as he prepared to leave. One thing was picking a fight with a few street hooligans, but sticking your manager's hand in hot oil was way off my grid.

I had to get away from it, before I turned into a crazy hand-frying psycho, but I thought I'd bide my time. The strangest part in all this was Pierre's father Mr. Dubois was one of the richest people in Surinam, but it just goes to show money can't cure the crazy.

In the end, that was life's full circle. There's the ups and the downs, and the manager's hand that came as part of a special meal deal, but it was all a part of the game…

CHAPTER 22
Queen & Country?

One day, as I sat at home, an official-looking letter arrived in the post, addressed, surprisingly, to me. Great, this must be a court summons or something, I thought to myself. I tore open the envelope, and unfolded the letter inside, and go figure; I could not understand a word of what was written there.

It was not street Dutch, it was a formal, very official looking letter. If it was something serious, I did not want anybody else to get involved. I did not want to ask Bryan, just in case it was something embarrassing, and I was ready to bet Pierre wouldn't be able to read it either. The only person I could actually ask at the time was my mother, which was not a great choice, but I needed to know what this letter was.

I paid her an unexpected visit, and she was as uninterested as ever as she nodded for me to come inside. I sat down in her living room and I held the envelope out to her. She unfolded the sheet of paper, scanned the words briefly and then said, in a monotone, "Military service. You've been enlisted. They say that you're my middle son, and have been chosen for this." She handed me the paper in a manner that suggested our meeting had been adjourned, and I duly sodded off from the house.

I knew from other people I had met that the Dutch got enlisted, but I was from England, so how did that make sense? It was all so bizarre, the way I had been dragged on to the side of upholding the law by being enlisted, whereas not so long ago I was sitting in the interview room being asked for information about Pierre the Burgling Menace.

I had once wanted to join the Foreign Legion, and maybe this wouldn't be exactly the same, but it served a similar purpose, and that's what prompted me to go on ahead, and see what it was all about.

And there I was, standing in line waiting for a medical to see whoever was responsible for this military service. My first impression was that it was nothing like the Foreign Legion, with those impressive quarters, the mean-looking friendly recruitment officer and those men of steel that waited to get in. In this place, there was a line of guys speaking Dutch, but I didn't speak to any of them; they all looked like complete idiots to me and sounded like it too, giggling away and fidgeting about with their noodle arms flailing all over the place.

I did not want to be a part of this military service, and I honestly thought I could get out of it. I thought that they might have made a mistake in thinking I had been raised in Holland because I had a Dutch name, but once they saw my brown face and heard my Yorkshire accent they'd surely know otherwise. For the first time, I was banking on my breed status to come through, and bail me out.

Finally, they called, "Merkx! Merkx." I went forward to answer the call and entered the room. There are two types of army in Holland: the professional army, which is the same as the British or US Army, professional and correct, and then there's the Military Service Army, which was full of young guys like me who never signed up for it and didn't want to do it, but had no choice. It reminded more of the television series called 'Dad's Army', with a bunch of comedians posing as military recruits.

I stepped up to answer the call, and they asked me a few questions, but I just ignored the officer and I sat there looking blankly at the wall. Finally he asked me in English, "You understand what is happening?"

My answer was, "No don't speak Dutch, but I guess you idiots want me in your poxy army. I am English, mate, fuck your army and your country."

I wanted any way to get out of it, even if they had to shoot me. I was not going to be spending time with stoned losers. They reminded me of the lads in the Borstal; little kids that had no idea what they were doing. I anticipated an angry reaction, and a direct order to leave the premise and I was ready for it, eager to not get enlisted. "We are passing you fit, you will receive your call up papers to report to the barracks."

Within a few weeks, I was called up and had to go to Hilversum to join the Medical Corps. I had no idea what it was all about, and I feared replacing somebody's bladder with a skittle.

It turned out to be a sordid and monotonous base camp. There was a building with the dorms, and stretches of grassland, where we'd carry out drills and undergo training.

I froze as I looked over the premise. It might have been a different setting, and a different location, but a beast that had been awoken during my prison days was poked awake, and was prowling about, hissing and grinding its teeth.

It was familiar territory, going away with a bunch of wankers, and I knew exactly how to deal with wankers by now. It went against my principles, but the iron fist ruled the camp.

As soon as I got into my dorm, I sized up the toughest-looking guy among the members of the crew. I had to show them that I was not to be messed around with, and that they should all know to back off. I was going to be the daddy at this place, just like I'd seen Jo-Jo was at Armley.

While the other soldiers were all getting settled down, I caught them unawares. I found my target, grabbed him and grappled him to the floor before he could do anything. I rained down some blows for good measure and said, "Any one starts shit with me, I will mess them up, you hear me you cheese heads!" Everyone around me froze and looked on. I recognized the fear in their eyes, a look I'd seen in Lateef's victims when he went in for the kill. That's all it took.

My psycho rant paid off, and I became the unofficial daddy of the place. I was running things once more, just like I did in the Bradford streets. I figured as the daddy, I needed my own office space. Everybody had their own cupboard there, and I saw the opportunity and told everyone to take their steel cupboards and place them around my bed.

I also wanted to make money, and I pounced at the chance when it came. "I want everyone's meal tickets now! All three meals, breakfast, lunch and dinner, if I'm missing yours, you're a dead man." We were all given meal tickets, as well as a salary and so once I had taken the tickets, the new recruits would have to buy them back from me so they could go to eat.

The beast purred satisfactorily, as I ran the dorm. What had to be done had to be done, and even though there was no justification in the use of my fists, it was a silent justice in itself that I could sleep at night without worrying about any of them sneaking up on me, that I had my pockets full again so when I did get away eventually, I'd be able to finally get a leg up on life, and make my fresh start.

My Sergeant, Pluim, pronounced Ploum, was strict as they came, but he didn't say much to me as he too found it odd and stupid having a English man in the Dutch Army. He also thought of me as some kind of a psycho, because of the way I did things, but I didn't care and neither did he.

Around that time, the IRA's activities in the UK were at their peak. Explosives went off every now and again and this meant that the heat was up everywhere. Even though we were in Holland, British Army boys would visit from time to time and that meant we had to make double sure we knew who came into the facility and who went out. Sergeant Pluim called me up one day and told me, "I'm putting you on guard duty."

Every week there were deliveries being made to the barracks. There was everything from food to supplies to big trucks full of milk. I wanted to do guard duty right, and I was specifically told under any circumstances not to let anyone in who didn't have the correct documentation and ID.

One day, one of the milk trucks appeared. I motioned for him to slow down and asked him to put his window down too. "Can I see your papers, please, sir?" I turned around and told my mate, "Stand on guard, and put your gun like you're supposed to."

The driver replied in broken English. "Hello, no paper sir, you ask for me they know me ja? I just want to go straight through, is no problem."

I asked him again, "Sir, I am asking you again and for the last time, where are your papers?"

He said, "Ja ja, no paper, you open gate now."

I calmly pointed the gun in his face and said, "Please step out of your vehicle now." He did not budge. "I said get out now!" The milk man did not need to be told again.

It was a complete role reversal; I was now the arresting officer. I said, "Hands above your head and against the wall now, spread your arms and legs out, you are under arrest you asshole for failing to produce the correct documentation and not properly identifying yourself, boy!" I cuffed him, slapped him around on the head and then brought him to the holding area by our guard house.

I returned to my guard duties, waiting, and soon the sergeant was marching down from the main building, looking outright furious. "What's going on, what happened! What you doing? Let him go you idiot!"

"This man refused to identify himself properly," I said.

He replied, "He's here every week! He delivers milk! I'm taking you off guard duty. The commandant is on his way and you are in big trouble Merkx."

The commandant arrived, and I stood at attention in front of him. He knew I was the English speaker in the Dutch army, and what he said couldn't be clearer in any other language. After I explained to him what had happened, he said, "Well done, Merkx, for following orders correctly. He didn't show you papers, and you didn't let him go through. Well done, back to guard duty." I was proud of myself.

As Private Merkx, I finally saw the perks of being enlisted, and it was not so bad after all.

CHAPTER 23
Do Something?

At Hilversum, there was a lot going on to keep me busy. There was training, hiking with boots, crawling through marshes and going through obstacle courses to name a few. I even had fun doing the assault course by running around and beating everyone up. It even brought a smile to Sergeant Pluim.

I also had my guard duty, which was boring because after that first incident, the milk man returned with every single document he owned, and made sure he identified himself correctly and nobody else caused any more trouble.

On the other hand, business was booming with these kids getting hungrier each time, and more so because they smoked pot, and were starving the following day. One such stoner was an Indonesian-Dutch kid named Danny, who came from a village called Weesp near Amsterdam. He was actually one of the few in my good books.

Unfortunately, I wouldn't really get to know Danny all that well. The commandant called me to his office, and said, "You are being transferred to Johannes Post Kazerne in Steenwijk. You will receive official papers and are required to report there for duty, you will be stationed there as there are Americans at the base, so the language barrier won't be a problem."

I went back and collected my things, including all the new acquisitions. As the other kids saw me packing, I could actually see some of them looked relieved. I was ready to leave and found Sergeant Pluim standing outside my dorm. He said, "All the best, Merkx. Be true to yourself and just do your best." I shrugged, saluted and left.

I was actually tempted to ask Pluim what the real reason for my transfer was, but I really already knew. I was becoming too powerful at

Hilversum. Soon, even Pluim would have to buy his lunch from me, so before it came to that, they relocated me. Or so I'd like to think.

The main problem was that they had no idea what to do with me. I was a Brit in the Dutch army, and they were confused as to why I was there. For me it was just another case of belonging nowhere, like at one point when I was Jamaican eating Jamaican food and listening to Jamaican music, and at another point, I was being fostered by English folk, and there I was, a mix of everything with a Dutch name to add to it all.

As I boarded the train to Zwolle, I prepared for the next stupid adventure. I had no idea where in hell Steenwijk was and what it would be like. If it weren't for the old couple conversing next to me, from which I caught "Steenwijk" I would probably have ended up on an island, somewhere out at sea, but I eventually arrived to my destination, and it was an even smaller village than Hilversum.

The worst part was that it was more than two hours away from Amsterdam whereas Hilversum was only fifteen minutes away. It was in the middle of nowhere, with more cows than people, quite similar to Haworth.

I was determined to keep working my newfound formula, that had done brilliantly for me at the previous barracks, and that was to take over the dormitory before anybody else could.

I arrived in the room, which I would share with the other soldiers, and directly opposite me was a lad called Henk. He was as white and Dutch as they come. He asked me something in Dutch and I told him in English I didn't understand him. "Wow, an English guy in the Dutch army, that's something I didn't hear about before," he said.

I immediately warmed up to him, which was bizarre because he was Dutch and white, and he told me he was from Amsterdam North. He also said there was a big contingent of young men from Rotterdam. People from Amsterdam disliked the people from Rotterdam and vice versa. Amsterdam had Ajax football club and Rotterdam had Feyenoord and the rivalry between the two teams was fierce, and it went far beyond the pitch and the contest over ninety minutes. It was nothing compared to the Leeds United versus Manchester United rivalry, which was hardcore, but I suppose for Holland it was just as sour. As far as football was concerned, my club was Leeds United and so I didn't give a damn about Ajax or Feyenoord, but like I said to Henk if I had to choose it would be Ajax.

On my first night out, Henk and I headed to the barracks bar, which was a sort of pub with the high seats that swivelled around. The beer was mega cheap so most of the lads were already drunk by the time we got there.

I received the usual stares, this time not for the colour of my skin as there were plenty of brothers there, but more so because I was new and English. They had all already heard about me coming; I was famous.

I was minding my own business when a massive Dutch bloke, at least a foot taller than me, and that was saying something because by that time I was rather tall myself, came and sat next to me.

He turned and stared at me, which made me uncomfortable. "What's up?" I asked. I knew trouble was coming and I was more than prepared.

He smiled cruelly and turned to his friends, saying in English, "Oh this boy needs to know who runs things here." He then turned his seat back in my direction and said, "Listen, English boy, I'm the boss here and you do wha..." before he could finish his sentence I had hooked him straight in his nose.

It was an ace in the hole as I sat there and made use of my seat, spinning to my left and hooking him beautifully on his nose with my right fist. The force of the punch was devastating and he went flying off his stool. I didn't give him a chance to come back, I got right on top of him and while I pinned him down I head butted him clean on his nose Zanchetti style. I kept pounding him for good measure and he screamed for me to stop.

All around us, the cheers erupted. 'Lurch' was the classic bully from Rotterdam and the boys from Amsterdam jeered him. Even his own crew were loving watching him getting ravaged.

I knew that if I had sat there, and done nothing, he'd take it as a sign of surrender and that would be my ass on the line. It made sense that I absolutely had to do something. It seemed as though the new me was actually keen on doing something more than doing nothing these days, like I'd developed some sort of an alter ego that was a hybrid of Lateef and Machiavelli's Prince, and I reacted spontaneously.

Once again, I'd gone and proven I was top dog, and I became the daddy of this place as well. I started running things, with my Lieutenant: Henk.

In the mornings everyone had to stand outside at a half past seven, ready for inspection, which they called 'Appel'. I was always tired and came late and the sergeant would always shout me down, which would make me and everyone else laugh because I simply didn't understand him and he refused to speak English. It was like Mexican stand-off.

Everyone was immaculately dressed in uniform except me. They all had their shiny boots on, and it was true: I could see my reflection in them. On the other hand, I was a complete slob. I couldn't be bothered with them, and they couldn't be bothered with me, it was an even game in the end.

I just could not take those stoner soldiers seriously, not even the senior officers, because they did not have my respect, and that was why I played by my own rules and did whatever I wanted to do. I also did not appreciate the way they treated the Surinam and Antillean boys.

I'd use a lighter and burn the tip of my boots and then shine them, which always worked and they looked great. Still, I had done it so many times to the point I managed to burn a hole in the shoes. One morning I turned up for Apell, with my clothes a mess, my beret on all wrong and my burnt shoes with holes in them.

The sergeant came up to me, screaming in Dutch. I was so sick of it and screamed back at him, "I don't understand you, you wanker!" All the lads stood there stunned. I was arrested by the military police and they threw me into the guard house, which was a cell for them.

When I was looking at the hopeless barred windows at Armley or the police station, I truly felt that there was no escape. This was not like that at all. It was such a jest; there was an open window there, and it was so easy for me to just crawl out and escape the place. I ran into the village and got onto the train to Amsterdam and returned to the city.

The military police re-arrested me and brought me back. This became a part of my new routine there, and I got creative finding new ways to get into the cell, so that I could escape, have fun and then be recaptured and brought back. It was almost like a play in the end.

At the camp, I had set up a terrific neat operation. There were many fairly geeky guys doing the service, from all over the country. In the end, I spoke with one of the resident geeks called Friso from Arnhem. He was such an idiot and loved the fact that we were from Amsterdam and was always asking if he could visit me there. The worst thing though was that he was a total junkie.

I absolutely detested drugs such as cocaine and heroin. I'd seen in Bradford what it did with people. I'd seen what it had done to Pierre and his mates. So in my eyes anyone who used it was scum. Friso approached me in the dorm one evening and asked, "Hey Frans, do you think you can get me cocaine?" I was taken aback: just because I was not white, it did not mean I was a drug dealer. I nearly raised my fists at him, but instead of getting on the defensive, I thought I could use the situation to my advantage and make money from those rich kids.

I had absolutely no intention of endangering myself by going and finding an actual cocaine dealer, but I was innovative and I knew how to turn lemons into gold. I would take paracetamol pills and crush them into powder and Henk and I would sell them to those suckers.

I was surprised at how stupid those idiots were; they'd just take the stuff, sniff it all night, and the following weeks actually ask for more! Word spread that I was dealing some "seriously good stuff" and I even managed to take my operation out into the village.

Friso was still insisting on coming to Amsterdam when we were free at the weekends so I decided to give him the time of his life, something he would never forget. One weekend I told him to come back with me and that he could stay at my place. As we headed out to Amsterdam all I heard was his bullshit about how he was excited to hang out with real street guys. I had informed Bryan that I would be bringing the resident geek with me and we would need to take him out.

We arrived in Amsterdam and went to my place so I could change. When I asked Friso if he wanted anything, he asked for weed and space cakes.

Bryan and I took him to a coffee shop and bought three pieces of cake filled with LSD and hash resin. Friso sure was greedy, and he nearly swallowed all three cakes whole. I had warned him to eat slowly and not the entire piece in one and I told him to take the other two pieces back home, but the geek did not listen.

Bryan and I agreed that we'd take the train to The Hague and go out there. It turned out to be the funniest train ride I had in my life. As we sat on the train, I looked at Friso and his eyes were unfocused, his jaw hung low and he was shouting things like "Can you see the twits twooo, I can see flying heads." I told him to calm down, but only half-heartedly as my eyes were streaming with tears from the laughter.

We got to the club and while Bryan and I stood around, chatting with some girls good old Friso was completely spaced out standing there like a statue. We decided to cut the night short and told him he'd best go home. I'm not sure how he managed, but he did and after that never asked me again about going to Amsterdam. I actually think I saved his life from drugs because he would never ask for anything and said to me that he didn't want to experience that ever again.

While going to the village, however, I had to put up with more scum, because the people there were nasty and loathed us. Well, I couldn't really blame them as we'd go there and sleep with their women, but after a while I got sick of the place and I, in spite of my grand money-making scheme, didn't want to keep coming back.

That was when I'd decided to stay home and report sick. Once they grew suspicious with how often I called in with diarrhoea or the flu, they sent the military doctor to come check up on me. He was a black guy, a brother, and took one good look at me, saying, "Yeah you don't want to go back there, eh?" I nodded, and he wrote me a letter confirming my medical condition. I kept this up for a long time, and sooner or later, I had my own routine going again, escaping the day cells, hustling in the nights, escaping during the weekends after reporting sick, and only coming back to get my salary and money from Henk.

After several weeks, however, they sent a different doctor; a white guy. He knew I wasn't sick and ordered me back to the barracks, "Merkx, you must go back, you are not sick." I refused. "I'm warning you, I'll send the MPs to come and collect you!" I didn't actually think he would, but he proved me wrong and when they came it took four of those boys to arrest me.

In the end, it was just a game of cat and mouse, either the mouse gets away or is caught by the cat, and then it escapes and the game starts all over...

CHAPTER 24
Back to Bradford

It was only a matter of time until the sergeant just gave up on me, and stopped trying to get me back to the barracks.

I was having a real laugh at it, until I received another rude awakening: a phone call from my sister Yasmeen. "Daddy is sick. He's not doing too well, you should go back and see him," she said.

"What's going on with him?" I asked.

"He is going to be having a very big and serious operation soon, and I think it is a good idea for you to go and visit him before that."

"Oh okay." I hung up before she could say anything else.

I paused for a moment to think about the conversation. To be honest, I didn't really care much about it at all, that my father was sick, but there was that inexplicable nag, just above the naval, around the sacrum, that prodded me, probing me to consider heading out to visit him. I had relied on that twinge, which later on I would discover was my intuition, for most of my life. I heeded its call once again, and decided that I would fly out to visit him.

By now, I was sick of the ferry, and flying was my best choice and cheaper. I had gone back a few times by then to hang out with Roger, but this time I was headed out for a mission.

More than just to see my ailing old man, I wanted to strut in there, looking sharp in my uniform and to tell him that I was in the army. I wanted to do this before I was dismissed, because the commandant had informed me that they were on the verge of processing an early release for me, which was terribly ungrateful of him considering he was buying dope from me and Henk.

When it really counts, a man knows who his true family is. I couldn't agree more with this. I marched up the steps to my father's home and knocked upon the infamously familiar door. I was wearing my military outfit, and as my father's Pakistani wife answered it, it was evident in her widened eyes that she was impressed by what she saw.

I had not seen her ever since I'd been sent down, but she had seen more than enough of my face invading my father's sweet shop and snatching a fistful of notes to make off with. She was familiar with that glowering look I gave her; loathing etched all over my face, my eyes narrow and fiery, and she only half-matched my disdain this time. She recoiled slightly under my imposing image as I marched through the doorway, and into the entrance hall.

It was 1985, and that meant several hospitals were attempting to experiment with serious advancements in modern surgery. My father was to be one of those test patients for a triple bypass, and I did not need a medical expert to tell me that there were immense risks involved with that sort of a procedure, considering it was relatively new to medics worldwide. He must have been terrified, but I'd have thought he had no other choice, because nobody in their right minds would take that sort of a gamble with their own recovery.

My father was nowhere to be seen as I scanned the silent faces staring in my direction. If that Pakistani lady had not answered the door, I would never have known that my father even lived there. As I had walked in, everybody was chatting merrily to one another, exchanging irrelevant news and gossiping to no end and it was only when they saw me, and felt my hate, that they fell silent at once and did not dare to flinch.

At that moment, it was as though I had turned into my father, with his powerful aura and fearsome demeanour that made people shake and shiver as he proceeded through. I stared down at one old man, who was sat on the floor, and I demanded, "Where's my dad?" He pointed nervously to the ceiling, indicating the man was upstairs.

My half-brother stepped forward to greet me, but I gave him an irreproachable look and said, "Don't come near me, I'm not your brother." He stumbled backwards, looking away from me and his sisters did not dare to attempt the same.

I climbed up the creaking staircase. The house still reeked of curry, which meant that they were cooking to add spice to their mindless chatter, while my father was stuck upstairs and desperately unwell. "Fuck them and their food," I thought as I reached the landing and saw a door left slightly ajar.

I paused outside it, and closed my eyes. I had a speech ready. I wanted to tell him what I thought of him, without remorse and filled with regret. This was it, finally, after all those years, it was my turn to get the record straight with him, to unleash the angst and to make it clear that I hated his ways. I pushed the door open.

I froze. There, on the bed, to my utter shock and horror, lay my father. I could not believe this was once a man that I feared more than anyone or anything else in the world, even more than Lateef. He was meagre and sunken, his eyes blackened and his bony jaw half open as he gaped at the ceiling like a mite-ridden skeleton. His wrists were thin, and his fragile face was lined prematurely, even though he was still relatively young.

He was tucked beneath a musty blanket and wearing what seemed like a pair of pyjamas that had not been changed for days, weeks even. He was unkempt, shabby, the complete antithesis of what I knew him to be. I still recalled how he left home, standing in front of the mirror and combing his hair with the comb he'd carried around everywhere, in the top pocket of his thousand-pound suit.

This was a man respected by all of Bradford and not just the Asian community. All the respectable leaders from the Tories, Labour and those snobbish white politicians, the businessmen and even the common folk, because Dad was a true gentleman with them. This was Councilman Hameed, the original Godfather, to me the hardest man in the country, but seeing him right there and then, looking pathetic and vulnerable, it broke my heart into a million pieces.

All the hate, the rage, the anguish, the frustration that I held for him, bottled up for so many years, all of that vanished in a flash as I looked into his unrecognizable face; the face that had tormented me for years, that I cursed and despised, that same face was the most pitiable and least doling face and I consoled with the man. For the first time, I consoled with him.

I looked away from him, and the room came into focus again. It was dark; the curtains were drawn, dispelling even the tiniest ray of hope for my old man. It was a reflection of what they thought of him; they had already shoved him into the shadows, to the irreconcilable place we all knew was dark and grim, and to compliment this horror show, it stunk of decay as though the sheets of the bed had not been changed for months.

I spotted a cup of cold tea on the bedside cabinet beside him. The contents were mouldy and grimy, as though it had been placed there a few days ago. That was what my father meant to his family; cold, spoiled tea.

I wanted to yell at him, to shake him up, to tell him that he was the stupidest son of a bitch alive. I recalled my speech, which had been pushed aside by shock, but now I wanted to show him, clearly, that the people he had chosen had spat right in his face. They were like vultures, circling him, waiting for him to kick the bucket so that they could feed off his remnants; his property, his financial wealth, his assets, everything.

It was all paradoxical, and that's when I realized that life just doesn't make any sense. It is no wonder that half the philosophers went their whole lives in search of the answer, but just couldn't find it, because every answer to the question is a question in itself, so what was the point?

My father had wasted his time with those people, wasted his precious moments when he could have had so much more had he chosen better, and the same could be said for us.

I felt tears burn in my eyes, how could life be this unfair? That one of the most powerful Asian men in the country was lying there with mouldy coffee, or tea, or whatever it was for company, and not even his so-called wife checking up on him? If it had been my mother, she would not have left his side. If she wasn't so lost in her own world, she'd probably have marched in there and slept right there with him, comforting him!

In the end it was us half-breeds that turned up when it mattered most while the rest of those slobs sat around and went about their lives.

Dad opened his eyes at last and took a good look at me. At first, it was as though he couldn't recognize me. Maybe it was the unfamiliarity of the uniform I was wearing, all cleaned up with shining boots, but once the recognition kicked, I saw something in his face that would empower me for the rest of my life. Right there and then, that look in his eyes said how proud he was of me, and it made up for all the years he'd neglected me.

He mustered a smile, and said in a faint voice that was not typical of him whatsoever. "Cookie, why are you wearing uniform?" Cookie was my dad's nickname for me because I looked so sweet when I was little.

I lifted my chin up, and said, "I'm in the army, Dad." I didn't specify which one. He needn't know it was the Dutch Military Service. For him, army would mean just one: the British Army. And being from the old school the British Army was honourable and respected, everything my father sought.

Another smile flickered on his lips, and he said, beaming, "You've done well. I'm proud of you, my son." If the proud look in his eyes wasn't enough, those words were. They echoed powerfully in my ears and in the walls of my heart. I had never gotten emotional about anything anybody said to me, but at that very point, something hit home, and those words felt just about right.

To be honest, those were the times that really did count, and everything else was a filler, and I could have waited a lifetime to hear my dad telling me that he was proud of me.

I spent a little more time with him. We didn't really talk much, but we were both at ease and it was fitting because I actually felt like he was my dad and not some Pakistani man who cared more about his community and power.

Finally, after a long, long time, I saw that he wanted to rest. He needed it to recuperate any strength at all that he'd need to stay alive and wholesome. I got up, kissed his brow, thanked him, smiled and left his room.

I went back downstairs and immediately confronted his disgusting wife. "You better get those sheets cleaned and look after him properly, if I hear you haven't I will be back for you and the rest of you cunts."

On the way back, I tried to not think about Dad or his messed-up family. I closed my eyes, and the thought of a hot cup of fresh tea by my deathbed empowered me greatly.

And it did turn out to be a couple of days of sheer empowerment. When I got back to the barracks, the commandant asked to see me. "Well, Merkx, I think you've had your time here. I'm giving you your release letters; you're ready to go home."

I was actually disappointed to be leaving the army, not because I was having a great time there, but because I'd actually had something going for me again. Still, I accepted the papers, and turned to leave, but the commandant interrupted me. "Just want to say, Merkx, it's guys like you that win wars."

I looked back and saw him standing looking at me. "Sir?"

"I know you act crazy but you are a good man, you've got balls, you're fearless, and you just get on with it and don't complain. You couldn't speak the language, it didn't matter you just got on with it. Good on you, Merkx."

I saluted him, thanked him and left feeling as though that was possibly the best send-off anybody in the history of the army could have received, and all because he'd highlighted the one thing I always did: nothing.

CHAPTER 25
The King is Dead, Long Live the King!

It was a good thing that I had saved up enough money from selling crushed tablets, meal coupons, having had a salary from the army and other side jobs with Henk, and that meant I was not in desperate need of a job to sustain myself.

Since I had nothing to do, I picked up the pen and started writing my music. I had done it as a hobby to pass time and with my fellow Rudeboy Wendal as well, I had joined forces and had a go on the trumpet and keyboards, but now there was no Wendal, and there was no trumpet or keyboards, and so I had to adapt and take what I had, and that was a pen and a blank sheet and words to be scribbled down.

I had not really explored this side of me much, but because I had so much time to spare, I let myself go and jotted bits and pieces down. It was nothing serious, like I had mentioned I was not aspiring to be an artist or anything, I just noted a punch line here, a rhyme there and that was what kept me occupied and out of trouble.

It started off like that, one or two lines, but I actually found myself enjoying it. I kept it up, writing about what I knew, about what I had seen up until then in my life. I told a story just to amuse myself, and I did not care if nobody else in the world paid attention to it or listened.

For just about everybody else that shared my year of birth, they had their parents planning out their lives. They were studying to become something, they were doing internships to make headway and they were courting compatible partners to spend the rest of their lives with. I heard it on the streets all the time, the threat of social security running out and being left to liquidate assets, and all that kind of nonsense, or not being able to pay off credit cards.

I could not care less about having a plan, or having one drafted for me. I had seen my father have his entire empire brought down as he lay in bed waiting to die, and that warranted my cynicism about life. Did he have that in his plans? Lying around with cold tea on his bedside?

A few months after I'd gone to see Dad, the apartment's phone rang. It took a while for the person on the other end to respond, and when I finally heard Yasmeen's voice, I knew it couldn't be good. "Dad's gone, Zahid..." she said. Her voice trailed off at the end. I knew it would have hit her hardest because she'd never quite forgiven him for abandoning us. Even though she did go to see him when he was sick and claimed she did it out of respect, we knew she always loved my dad the most and that's why she was hurt the most.

I did not know how to respond. I did not feel upset or saddened. I did not freak out and become exasperated, or fall to my knees and sob. My heart did not beat any faster, or any slower, it was just like Yasmeen had given me any other news of the inevitabilities of life. I stayed firm and I said, "I'll...I'll see you soon." I couldn't manage anything else.

One thing was for sure, and that was that I could not gather that Dad was gone. The one real head of this dysfunctional family, the King, was dead. For the second time in the space of a few months, I was back in familiar surroundings.

There was a gathering at the house before the final send off. I was expecting a morbid atmosphere, where everybody would be crying their lungs out, and nobody could really utter more than a few indiscernible words. I had not really attended a funeral before, but I had the gist of it from the movies and television shows, and from what I saw, it was awful. Being there, at the house, and seeing it for what it really was, however, you lift that veil of ignorance an inch further, and those movies don't mean a dime when you see what really goes on.

At first I thought the murmuring was the voice of the spirits that had passed, after all somebody had just died, his body erased from the world, his physical being never to be encountered once again, the photographs the only recollection of a smile, or the ghost thereof, and his legacy his true worth. I could not believe the rest of the family, all these brothers and sisters of mine, all my father's relatives, they all just sat there and chatted away.

I was dumbfounded, and could not bear to eavesdrop any further. It left a sickly feeling in the pit of my stomach, the sort of thing that would make me knock them all out. I had figured that that was how the world worked, that a person's material possessions mattered more than the person him or herself, and it was the most deranged, the ugliest truth I had to face.

I was not sure how many of these people knew my father, but I could damn well be certain that they had all appeared to see what they could squeeze from his loss.

I decided I did not want anything to do with it. I had come to pay my final respects to the man responsible for me being alive, and that was where I drew the line.

Lateef came up to me, nodded and looked away. We had nothing to say to each other. It was the first time I was seeing him in a long time, and that's all he could muster.

"Zahid, Lateef and Zaker, come. You have to wash Daddy now." It was the Iman; a priest like figure that supervised the rites. I was angered at the way he scrutinized us. Even the holy man, preacher of truth and equality, was a prick.

I followed him through to another room, and there was dad, his head slightly raised. He would have been sleeping, possibly in hibernation for a long time, had a ray of sun not bathed his face entirely, and he did not crease his forehead nor squeeze his eyes shut to filter out the light. His body was draped in white sheets, but his face, expressionless, clearly visible.

I did feel a tinge of regret that I had not told him what I needed to tell him. I had held back when I visited him while he was still alive, because I took pity on him, and now it was too late.

His hands lay resting on the top of the sheets, and I noticed he had a scar on his left ring finger. I would later come to learn that the moronic assholes that were my uncles actually cut that golden piece of jewellery off and kept it for themselves.

In the room, there stood my father's brother, my two brothers, two half-brothers and myself, aside from a few other men that I vaguely recognized. Of the two half-brothers, one of them was an out and out asshole; Mahmood, Dad's eldest son from his first marriage. I guess the crooked nose was a mark of House Hameed.

166

My brothers and I held him in the highest contempt, and he loathed us back. I could never forgive him for bullying and beating me up when I was little. I was never afraid of him, like I had been of Lateef, because he was not tough like my brother, he was just a lousy bully that thought he could do whatever he wanted to me because I was younger.

The hate bubbled in my stomach like boiling acid, and I wanted to do something. I wanted to lash out, to turn into a monster, a berserker and smash all of them up. I could hear his brothers in the corner of the room babbling away in Urdu with a piece of paper between them, clearly arguing about who would get what.

Later on, they would conspire and have the will altered, each one getting something from my deceased father. My brothers and sisters would want to fight it legally, but I never got involved in that, as I made my own money.

The Iman said, "Now, put these gloves on and take a sponge and wash the body and say *Bismillah*, which means in the name of Allah."

I gently lay the sponge down on my father's motionless chest, and said, "*Bismillah*." I kept my hand still, and felt older than my twenty years. My hands acted on their own accord, and before I could fully register the situation, we were finished.

I looked down into his face and saw my own reflected there. It was the inescapable truth that he was my father, that I was a part of him and that he was a part of me. I connected with my own mortality that someday I would be there, and who knows who would turn up at my funeral, or if I would ever have somebody to wash my body, or if I even wanted that in the first place.

I kissed my own fingers and then rested them gently over his mouth, and simply said, "Love you, Daddy."

His body was sent off to Pakistan, where he'd be buried beside his father, and his father's father, and so on.

There was a massive commemoration for him, which I didn't bother to attend. I did not see the use of it, because people there would be talking about him, and those were people that knew him. I did not know him, and I did not want to answer questions about his personal life.

From what I heard, thousands of people turned up, and the political leaders spoke about Dad. They mentioned that he was a trendsetter that he had broken free from the bounds of race and creed and had risen to prominence in Bradford and in Britain in general. They talked about how he handled his tasks in an accomplished manner, they talked about his straightforward demeanour, and his blunt conduct when it came to getting things done. He always wanted more, and this was clear when they talked about his ambitions and about going three steps beyond everyone else to ensure he'd fulfilled his portfolio requirements and done everything to the best of his abilities.

I had just one good memory with him; when he took my brother and I to the circus. It was the first time I saw that he had teeth, because he laughed so hard, but I had not shared any other laughs with him, nor tears. All this meant that he meant nothing for me, nothing more than the man who was potent enough to get me born, and then to leave me to raise myself.

The common folk said that he was a genuine man with a big heart. When had I ever gotten to meet this man? He'd been brutal, cold-hearted and stony, and had never given me more than free sweets as a consolation prize for keeping my nose out of his business.

I was finally on my way back to Amsterdam after a heavy couple of days. My dad came in the papers, with the subheading, "Councillor leaves widow and three children behind." Widow and three children? That was another blow to the gut. I felt nauseated because nobody knew and nobody would know that I am actually Councillor Hameed's son.

Did I dwell on my father, and how unfairly he had treated me, and that he hadn't mentioned me to the press? No. Did I have any bad feelings for him? No. Did I feel sorry for him, the way his life had ended just like that, when the people he had chosen, the people he had worked desperately to win over, when they failed to turn up when he was needed most? Yes, I did feel sorry for him, but that was all. Apparently Dad had died on the operating table, having bled after complications with heart surgery.

Yasmeen did tell me that one day, before Dad died, he informed her that he regretted his decision; leaving us and marrying that horrible Pakistani lady. He regretted leaving my mother, who loved him no matter what, even to this day. When you connect to your mortality, you begin to see things clearly.

I wanted to make the most of it after seeing Dad go like that, but I did not want to plan anything. I wanted life to give me what it had in store for me and I wanted to embrace it and follow through.

After all, I still shared DNA with Councillor Hameed, and if he always wanted more from life, well, the same went for me. His mistake was he did something and ended up with nothing and I was going to try and not make that same mistake.

CHAPTER 26
A New Birth

It was as though my life up until then had two parts: before and after Dad's funeral. Before, I was selling crushed tablets to idiots in the Army. I was hanging around with a Meth junkie. I had to get away from that. The new me was all about getting serious, and part of the epiphany was that I needed to rally an onslaught and push harder than ever before to get it right.

I hardly slept and was working day and night. By night, I'd landed myself a job at a change bureau, which meant buying and selling currencies. It was mostly honest work, but being the rebel and always wanting more, and never passing up the opportunity, I'd managed to find a way to squeeze some extra dough from the tills.

There was a nine percent commission charged on small amounts being exchanged, and this went to the company. For larger amounts, they either paid a lesser commission or no commission depending on the amount. How it worked was that I'd have to take the money from the client and pay them out minus the commission and then I'd hoodwink the system and without putting it through the computer, I'd gather the loot. Then I'd add up all the money and put it through as one big deal and take the nine percent for myself. This way, I was earning huge amounts every week, more than what I knew any kid my age was making. Mr. Thompson could sod off after all, I didn't need his school, I was solving algorithms on a whole new level.

This financial liberation made me keen on getting my career as an artist together. My inspiration for music was not just drawn from my youth, but from my experiences at the change bureau. I saw a lot from there; from the junkies that wandered by the offices looking like zombies to other hooligans that were up to no good.

They never caused me trouble. It was like we had this telepathic understanding with one another; they knew I was from the street. Once a street guy, always a street guy, and it was a good thing because those junkies respected that code.

Many times the other change bureaus were robbed and most of the time at gun point, but somehow they just left me alone. In a way, it felt like I was my father, walking past people, and receiving nods in salutation, not head jerks, but courteous nods, and for a moment, I had stepped into his shoes.

Things at the bureau were going so well, mostly because we'd somehow retained our money, that the manager, Derek, came up to me one evening and said, "Frans, things are going great. We would like to offer you a managerial position in London. We have an office there and need somebody to run it, and we believe you're the man for the job. You can go for a trial to see how it works for you." I didn't fancy going back to England, but thought I might as well check it out. It's not every day you get offered a managerial position, I thought.

Once I arrived, it was well and truly dreadful. The office was situated by the underground. It was dark and far from inspirational. I played like I was interested and stayed for two days and when I went back to Amsterdam, I told my superiors that I would think over their offer, but I already knew I didn't want the job and was happy to get back to Amsterdam. I told Derek, "I won't be taking the job in London, Derek."

He understood and said, "I'm actually glad you are back."

During the day, I was inspired to take ideas for my music, jotting things down and then going around to different recording studios and asking for time. Seeing as how I'd been rejected most of my life, I couldn't care less when I was turned down by studio after studio. Still, I kept it up, it never bothered me, and I'd pop in every day and ask and it all became a part of my new routine.

It was 1989 and my routine was once again interrupted. This time it was my old friend, Javaid. I'm guessing one of my mates back home had given him my number, but somehow he managed to reach me. I hadn't seen him ever since the arson episode, so for me that was the last person I expected to dial my number. "Hey mate, I'm coming to Amsterdam, and I was wondering if you could put me up for a few nights?" I played it down, and didn't directly respond to his request, but he turned up anyway.

By this time Jav was a dancer or at least he thought he was. He always reminded me of being a second hand Asian John Travolta. We went out a few times and most nights he was either stoned on weed or high on magic mushrooms. After a few weeks he came to me and said, "Zid you got a nice job at the change place, can you sort a brother out?" I really didn't want him on my patch, but agreed that he needed a job so he could get his own place.

The next day I went to my manager and asked, "Derek, are there any vacancies here? I've got a mate who's looking for a job."

Two days later, Derek came to me and said, "Frans, I need a new cashier, would your friend be interested? Since you've referred him, I trust your judgment."

Javaid was a smooth talker so the interview went well and the training was minimal. Derek offered him the job as night-time cashier, which he eagerly accepted.

That Tuesday night was Javaid's first night shift. At eight in the morning, it was a bit like déjà vu: there was banging on my door and I answered and sure enough it was the police. "Can we come in? We want to talk with you."

I said, "No, talk to me here, what's up?"

I would never allow coppers in my place, but the next thing the copper said was, "It's about your friend Javaid."

I was still in my boxer shorts and I asked them what they wanted from me. "The morning shift started, and your friend Javaid wasn't there, but the main safe and all the tills were completely empty. We suspect that he's gone with all the money, we know it's nothing to do with you but we'd like any information you might have on him," the copper said. I had only myself to blame, I knew Javaid and if I was honest I had always suspected something would go wrong, but I just didn't do anything.

I chatted with the police, but didn't give a statement and they left as they knew I had nothing to do with it and I guess the look on my face convinced them that I too was angry about what Jav had done.

Later in life I would come across some people I know and they would tell me how Javaid would brag about stealing over two hundred thousand pounds and that it was the easiest job ever for him. It seems in the weeks he had stayed with me he had planned it with one of his uncles to rob the place at gun point and would have shot me dead to get it done, but because he got a job there, it was made even easier for him and at the same time probably saved my life.

His uncle drove a van from England, they loaded up the van with the loot at one in the morning and drove off to the Hook of Holland port and on to England, and seven hours later when the next shift came he was long gone.

The police explained to me that because he worked at the place the crime was classed as theft because the owner wouldn't disclose how much money was taken. That was not much of a crime, so Javaid got away with it because he never returned to Holland.

The good thing about this brand new Jav adventure, was that it made me focus more on my path. I realized what a loser he was, and there was no way I was ending up like him.

I decided to focus even more on my music and during this time I befriended a lad from London called Mark or as he would say, "Call me, Mistri Shine Love one," to my amusement. He, like me, was writing songs and we decided to combine our work and we called ourselves 'Two of a Kind.' God knows why we called ourselves that because we didn't look like each other; he was full on Jamaican and from London and I was a breed from the North of England, Bradford.

There we were, writing songs and discussing ideas and, boy, we had some great ideas. What I didn't know was good old Mark was taking my ideas and putting them down in another studio.

One day he turned up and said to me, "Bruv, I think it's best we go our separate ways." I was extremely disappointed and thought, how will I do this by myself? Then again whenever I was successful it was always when I was alone.

I agreed and we went our separate ways. I'd heard from others that Mark was recording in a studio called Tink Productions, so one day out of curiosity I decided to check out what exactly he was doing. To my dismay, as I listened in the corridor of the studio, he was recording tracks that we had written together and telling those jerks that he had done it all himself. I was livid, but decided against making a scene and instead was determined to show that I could also make it.

173

I'd kept it up: going into studios, asking them for a shot to show them what I'd got, they'd refuse and I would march on to the next studio. Money wasn't an issue for me, and my motivation to establish myself in music spurred me into action. The rejection I would get would perhaps break most, but not me as I just prodded on and on.

My musical roots were in Jamaican and British Ska, Hip Hop, Reggae, Blues, RnB, and I thought about introducing a blend of hip hop, R n B and Soul, but the Dutch entertainment industry was not buying it, even though the public wanted it especially after I'd talked to a few people about it and gotten them excited.

The industry was so backward and actually still is in Holland, being run by suits and the radio DJ's were a complete bunch of nerds. All in all, it was stiff guys who had no idea what the youth wanted or what it was like growing up on the streets.

Back then, you didn't have the N Syncs or Justin Timberlakes of today, where you've got white kids doing R n B or the Eminems rapping, all acting black. You had breeds like me and black kids trying to do it, but it was still something they were not keen on and especially in such a small country as Holland. To many others and I, it seemed as though we just didn't fit the profile. We had the music, the talent, the lyrics, everything, but not the white skin that would certify us and open those doors.

I was still eager to learn and I did get to learn a lot from going into all those studios. I got to see some real talent. I once watched a group, with a combination of whites and blacks. One particular guy, called Sander, would actually become a good friend later on. He, like me, played trumpet and he had actually played in a Surinam group called 'Young Sound.' Sander was a rare breed; a typical looking Dutch white boy with blond hair and blues eyes, but he loved everything that was "black," including the women.

I must say, there were some good singers involved in the industry. I remember a couple of strong vocalists; Berget, whose brother Dillan was the leader of the group and did his best to bring R n B about. At that time it was tough for anyone trying to break into the music industry doing 'Swingbeat,' which was a form of RnB. The other vocalist was Trijntje Oosterhuis, whom I found to be a fantastic singer, but her character was suspect. The former was a black girl, the latter was white, but they both sure could sing.

174

I kept it up, round after round, until one day my fate decided to turnaround, and hope had finally found me. I returned to the Polderweg Studios, as part of my custom rounds. The studio engineer and producer there was called Fred Thomas, and he was an arrogant prick, who thought he knew everything and stuck his nose up at anything that differed from his vision.

"Sorry, we are not interested," he said.

I turned away and made to leave. I was just about to exit when a guy came over to me and asked me what my ideas were and what thoughts I had on music. One thing I knew I could do if I was given the chance was to sell myself and that's exactly what I did.

The guy in question was called Carel Oohms. He was the weirdest looking guy I had ever seen, and that was saying something considering I'd seen Harry Beacher in my mum's clothes. Carel was tall, had buckteeth and spoke in a high-pitched voice. He was one of the partners at the studio and also an engineer.

"I've seen you here before," he said, in that trade-mark high voice. By this time, I could speak relatively good Dutch, and so communication was no longer an issue for me.

"That's right."

"What are you looking to do?"

"I have some great ideas and just need a break and time in the studio. I haven't got the money but will share my royalties."

He peered at me through his silly glasses, his friendly eyes scrutinizing my face. "You from England?"

"Yes, mate."

"Well one thing England has is great music."

"Yep."

"So what's your idea, what would you like to do?"

I did have something in mind. "Actually there's a song called *We Got the Funk* by Positive Force. You know it?"

"Yes, I do."

"Yeah, well I want to do a mix of that, with some rap and Chicago house style, that kind of thing. You know what I mean?"

"Sounds great, I'd like to ask a friend of mine Jerry van Beek to join us as he plays keyboards and we need that," Carel said.

At that moment Fred walked up to us and laughed, "Carel you are wasting your time and time is money here."

Carel seemed to be a little afraid of Fred even though he was joint owner, so I used what I knew on the streets and squared up to Fred and told him, "This ain't got fuck all to do with you mate." At that point I thought: *oh shit, what I have I done?* But Fred backed off immediately.

Carel turned to me and thanked me; it seemed that Fred was always bullying him, but now he had me to back him up and I had him to back me up: it was a perfect partnership.

"I'm looking forward to your material, Frans," he said.

All my painstaking effort had yielded this. I had finally gotten my shot, my one opportunity to get something out there, and I was going to give it my all to make sure I seized that chance.

I returned to Polderweg the following day, and met with Carel. "This way."

We walked through a set of doors and into the studio. I closed my eyes, rubbed them, and opened them again to make sure I was seeing right. It was like something out of a Star Trek movie, with all the lights and buttons, like I'd entered a space ship that was going to propel me to my dreams. I was home and I was ecstatic.

"This is Jerry, Frans." Jerry was like Carel, just a cool white dude, harmless but eager to hear my ideas.

I felt in my element, my space. It looked so funky, I was just mesmerized by the switchboard, the clear sound proof glass, through which I could see the mic, where the singer would do his or her thing. All I knew was that I was ready to get started, to put my material down.

I wanted to learn everything and explained to Carel that I could play a bit of piano and trumpet, but wanted to learn the technical side of things too. "Okay, I'll take you through the engineering and this and that, and then we can start getting your track together," he said.

"Right, this here is the switchboard. You see, you've got all sorts of effects and varieties for when you're recording. So if you flick this switch, for example," he put one of the switches up, "you'll get an echoing effect. Different types of music require different equalizing effects, and so you've got to keep working it, until you get the sound you're looking for. It's not easy, but with practice, you'll get used to the different switches and the overall engineering that goes behind producing. We work with Cue Base which helps us put the track down and mix and use different sounds." I never paid attention in school, but I hung on to every word that came from this weird, but cool, Carel guy. I could stay there forever.

"I'm a fast learner, so no problems there," I said.

"That's good, then. Now obviously you've got the recording room, this is where all the stuff goes down. Do you need a singer or is it just you?"

At the time, I was having a casual fling with a girl and she had a sister called Maureen, who turned out to be a singer. She popped up in my mind, and I mentally added her to my team. She wasn't the most dynamic person, but I'd work on that.

During my time in Amsterdam I had also befriended a music-oriented lad called Martin Meyers and he was completely different to Mark from London. I'd met him through Pierre, but he was quite the opposite of that psycho. They lived in the same area, and I'd gotten to know Martin after seeing him a few times.

He, like me, wanted to be in the music industry. The problem was unlike me he didn't know what to do about it. Martin was a level-headed kid, quiet but likeable, and whenever I'd pass by his house, his mum always made me food and was genuinely kind to me. She always made me laugh and said, "Make sure you look after my boy, Frans."

I suggested to Martin, "How about you being a DJ and getting me beats to work with?" Like me he was zealous and that's what he became; my DJ.

It was a dream come true. I spent the next few weeks working my way round the board. I was drawn to the science of production, because I could see where it was taking me; to creating something out of nothing.

Whenever I was free I was there at the studio even if I wasn't working there. I loved to listen to other bands good or bad. Gradually people knew me as the guy who was a fast learner, and I earned their respect.

"You really do learn fast!" Carel said, five weeks after I'd started working with him and Jerry. He'd allowed me to mix tracks with him for other artists.

I felt that I'd garnered enough practice that I had explored enough of my talents, and I told him, "I'm ready to get my own track down."

I got in touch with Martin and I laid the basics of the track, and then asked Jerry to add some piano pieces on there and together with Carel we fattened up the track. Then I brought in Maureen and directed her on how to sing the chorus and then instructed Martin on the kind of samples I wanted.

"Right, so the track's 'We Got the Funk' and we'll need a rapper to come in with that rawness." I actually never planned on rapping, but Martin explained he couldn't do it, which wasn't surprising, as he never really came off as the rapper type.

So out of nothing I rapped on the track. It came natural to me, I just let the words flow, I didn't think too much about how I sounded, I just felt the beat in my veins, and I followed up with my voice, and the two just got along.

"Let's do this..." We began recording, and got the gist and feel of the song by end of the day.

Carel and I returned to the studio every day for the rest of the week, and kept at it, tweaking it here and there, making sure it flowed. Carel was impressed by what I was doing, and I was impressed with the direction of our partnership.

It was the fruits of my hard labour that I was finally able to consume. I'd found my place, and Carel, and Polderweg Studios without good old Fred Thomas, had been my key.

By that time the word was out that the English guy in the studio was working on a great track. One day while discussing new tracks, a gentleman walked in. Carel immediately got up and greeted him: "Hello Ronald, how are you?"

He said, "I'm fine, but I'm hearing great things from other people about this guy." he pointed at me and then walked over. "Hello I'm Ronald owner of CNR records, heard great things about you."

I was stunned, but glad that a representative, someone that was objective, appreciated what I was doing. I didn't hesitate as I asked, "Wanna hear what we have done?"

He sat there and listened and after a minute said, "I'd like to sign you up." Next thing I knew, I was signed up and my song was being released on white label. Ronald was a great guy and I could honestly say one of the few Dutch guys who knew his music and tried to think out of the box.

Out of nothing, Infobeat was born and within just under a month, 'We've Got the Funk' had become a hit around the club scene in Holland and Scandinavia as well. It was the start of something, and the winds of change that would take place at Polderweg began with Fred Thomas coming up to me and saying, "That was some track! I knew it you'd be a hit!"

It was the end of 1989 and I was on and off with a girl called Jaqueline that I had met in the city on my nights out. She was attractive, from Aruba and used to hang out at the same places that I used to.

We ended up meeting a few times, but it didn't seem that serious. I didn't think she was really into me, but I did like her. One night while working the Christmas night shift, she called and said she wanted to meet up. When I finished I went out to see her and one thing led to another and it became more than a casual rendezvous.

After we'd spent time together, I would try and call her, but could never get a hold of her and I eventually lost contact with her, which was disappointing but I accepted that maybe she just wasn't interested.

1989 was coming to a close and as I was quietly celebrating my breakthrough in the music industry in my shitty apartment, the phone rang and on the other end was Jaqueline.

"Frans, I have to tell you something. I'm pregnant and the baby is due first week of August."

"What?"

As I sat there in shock, I asked to see her but before she could say anything the line went dead.

CHAPTER 27
Changes

It was 1990 and great things were happening with Infobeat but on the other hand my private life was a disaster. Somewhere in Amsterdam Jaqueline was walking around pregnant with my child. I went to the clubs where I'd seen her before but there was no sign of her. After quite some time I decided to let fate play its hand and do nothing in the hope she would contact me, so I buried myself into my music.

There comes a time when every kid dreams of being a superstar footballer or laying down a track and hearing it being played back on the radio. They're told that dreams are for rookies, and that they should focus on their studies. For one thing, I had nobody to tell me what to do, and for another I had no studies to focus on, and the result was hearing "We got the funk" blasting out of speakers everywhere. It wasn't really my dream, though.

Looking back my dream was and still is stability. I understood that hard work and luck brought me to where I was but on the other hand at the back of my mind was a terrible guilt knowing that soon a child of my own would walk the earth and I didn't want for him or her what I'd been through. I somehow knew what my mother might have gone through; how difficult things were for her.

I had to stay focused on what was at the time becoming quite successful for me. In what seemed like no time, the owner at CNR records rang me up and said, "On the club charts in Scandinavia."

I sat there with the receiver to my ear. I was on the Scandinavian club charts, which was quite something for a nobody like me from Bradford.

The hit single, the great synergy of Infobeat: everything was moving forwards. I found myself becoming one with the switchboard, and discovered I was actually a better producer, writer and mixer than I thought I'd be after being haphazardly tossed into doing it.

I definitely had the ear for music and I could identify what sounded good and what didn't, and tweak the tracks wherever I saw fit. Even Fred Thomas was suddenly very interested, as he so often came up to me, smiling and offering his advice, which I respectfully declined. Still, there was now a mutual respect and he even said to me, "Frans, I apologize for being a jerk, you've really shown that you have skills."

I had signed with CNR records, which was a great little independent company, and together we were growing in influence and hitting all the right notes. Since we were escalating in stature, I and they felt that we could do with a better female singer. I needed one with real scope, talent and star quality, and even though Maureen was a great person, I thought that maybe she didn't have pizzazz to be the lead vocalist.

I knew it wasn't going to be the best news for her, but I decided to do it quick and swiftly.

"Maureen, I'm sorry, but I think I've got to let you go," I told her as she came in for work on a new single.

"Why?" she stood there and raised her eyebrows.

"I'm afraid your voice is not quite up there with what I have in mind, so we're going to have to replace you with someone else." She was devastated, and became teary, but I did what was necessary.

I was writing new songs all the time, whether I was at work or not, in my broken-down apartment or hanging out with Bryan. Wherever it was; I was always writing. And when I was not writing, I had to move fast and find a new singer, so I decided to search the club scene and see if there was a singer out there with a voice, if possible, like Whitney Houston and with star qualities to match.

Martin had mentioned to me that there was a show at The Escape club in Amsterdam and there would be some live acts and he had heard about a great singer called Irma. We decided to pay her a visit to see what she was all about.

Irma came on stage with two other girls and they were doing covers of 'En Vogue's' songs. Her voice was tantalizing, the way she held a note, sending powerful vibrations all over the place. Not only was she an amazing vocalist, but she also knew how to control the crowd. She was a real entertainer, she had the pizzazz I was looking for. God had blessed this girl with the voice of an angel. I was impressed and wanted her in the group, which would not be difficult because by this time I was quite well known in the club music scene.

Sure enough, I managed to get her on board my project. The first day in the studio made it very clear that Irma would not be the easiest person to control. She arrived late and outside the studio with her boyfriend who she had been fighting with.

"Fucking stupid maniac, thinks he could get away with that, fucking..."

"Irma, calm down, what the fuck?" I felt like a bleeding social worker, but at least I tried unlike the Bradford social services. I eventually got her to settle down, and we got to work.

Personally, my best musical work was composed at that time. I had written a song called 'It's a Feeling," which was about the struggles I had been through in life and now looking back it was more about not seeing or knowing the situation regarding my soon to be born kid. It was slightly Gospel orientated because I always loved that style of music, not from a religious perspective, but more so because the songs were always sung from the heart. I had already pictured what I wanted.

"Get to the mic and read the lyrics. Listen to the music and then freestyle Irma, do what you feel, do what's in your heart sister," I said. She did, and guess what: it was absolutely phenomenal. She sang my song so effortlessly, exactly the way I had wanted it, with soul, passion and belief.

Right there and then I knew that I had found not only the newest member of Infobeat, but a real star as well.

Even though being famous didn't interest me, I had always hoped to do better things with my life than just hustling and stealing. Still, I never in a million years imagined I'd be behind a switchboard and a microphone, laying down hit singles.

There were a few usual hitches on the rise. The publishing of our tracks was done by EMI Holland, and at first they were great, but then things started to change, not with EMI itself, but the actual people who were running it. They tried to influence the way I was writing the songs, which was highly disconcerting.

182

I didn't care much for commercial music. I wanted to try and bring something new out; something fresh, a fusion of musical flavours. Sometimes in life you've got to fight for what you want.

At that moment things were heating up and I got a phone call from a promoter who worked for Euro Pop. "Is this Frans?"

"Yes it is, who this?"

"Hi I'm calling from Euro Pop and we promote shows all over Europe and the world and we'd like to arrange shows for you, can you come and see us?"

"Okay, I can come by tomorrow if that's okay, around one?"

"Great we'll see you then."

I arrived at their offices in Haarlem, which was near Amsterdam, without a clue of what to expect.

"We've heard good things about your group Infobeat and we are interested in promoting and arranging tours for you, Frans."

I shrugged and said, "Okay."

"You will need at least forty-five minutes of material. Think you can manage that?"

I had no problem doing that because I'd written so much that there was more than enough to produce, and I had already laid down tracks amounting to around sixty minutes. "Not a problem," I said.

"Great, we are looking forward to it, meanwhile we will be in touch about venues and events and that kind of thing."

"Sure."

At first, we did the small clubs, which weren't much in terms of audience and impact. The stages were small, and we were cramped up on there with our equipment and everything, but all in all it worked out alright.

During our first gig, I lost my voice because nobody had taught me anything about using vocals live. It was also surprisingly physically exhausting, not on the scale of what I did in boxing or in prison while shovelling coal and shit, but round after round, I grew wearisome.

We didn't exactly have rehearsals per se, that was more freestyling, but we had to get things right about who did what. As a group, we were tight and everyone knew his or her place. Irma's voice was mega and complimented the beats brilliantly and in the studio I would be improvising with a random drop here and there, and then fiddling with the mixing and various switches to create a sweet mix.

I'd mastered the technique of controlled mixing, which meant that I was not merely playing around with the switchboard, doing things without awareness, I was full-on conscious about which switch I hit, when and where.

Up on that stage, the audience roared their approval, and spurred us on to keep going. I noticed the increase in the volume, and I knew that I had found the place where I belonged, and my people welcomed me on board only too kindly.

We ended gigs with our club hit single, and I stood up and put my hands up in the air. I let the cheers and the whistles sweep over me, the crowd screaming for an encore. I could feel the vibrations coming from the noise below, which was chaotic, but melodic at the same time. I used to be at the centre of abuse and accusation, but now I was at the core of loud cheers and mad love from people I didn't even know, but that loved the music.

When they say sky's the limit, I say it ain't. There isn't a limit, you reach the sky, you go beyond it, you shoot out into space, and you keep going. On and on, there is no stopping it, when the wheels are in motion; it's an everlasting cycle of dynamism and non-stop action.

A few weeks after we toured around the club scene in Holland, I got another call from Euro Pop, the tour company. "Mr. Merkx? Would Infobeat be interested in signing up for the Marlboro tour?"

"What's that?"

"You know what a packet of cigarettes are don't you?" he laughed. "Well they are sponsoring a major summer tour throughout the country. We're getting together a number of groups to perform in a festival-type event. It will be a great way to promote your group, if that's okay with you we'd like to add you to the line-up."

"Sounds phat mate, count us in."

At the time, Holland was a haven for all these so-called man-made groups, where they put people together to perform in line with their synthetic visions. As a result, they had had great financial backing, something we never had. As always, we stood out as the rebels, the black sheep, and this was evident during the Marlboro tour. All the other groups had people dancing in sync, perfectly choreographed by professionals. I don't know much about that, but to me it looked bizarre. As they say, each to her own.

With Infobeat, on the other hand, we stuck to what we knew; pure and raw, and with just the three of us and our kit. We engaged the crowd and our tracks just seem to emerge from nowhere. I was an illusionist; pulling one trick out of the hat, another from up my sleeve. It was unpredictable, but always filled with excitement. We didn't even have a set that we would do, we just did what felt natural, improvised and somehow it worked great.

Those were outdoor festivals and people would just be walking around, but when we got on stage, the public were drawn to us, like filings to a magnet. Irma and I belted out verses of our choices, coordinating brilliantly to draw a fabulous reaction from all those hungry fans that were watching in earnest.

We were an unstoppable force, a class act that weaved the magic wand and enchanted watchers-on with our spell-binding music. I realized that it wasn't about just putting on a show; it was also about the music and the crowd, which together became the show. In the end, the people were the stars and we played for those stars.

Off the stage, I had employed Pedro Hoedraad as our road manager. He was kind and cheerful, always enthusiastic and just loved being involved. I actually hired him to keep an eye on Irma, and he stayed loyal to that task, watching her every move. He was from Surinam, and he was dedicated and always had our best interests at heart. I guess he also had his own interests at heart, because he was definitely living the dream.

Naturally, other groups had noticed our prominence. Whenever we went first, there was a huge contrast in the volume of the cheers we received, compared with the one or two whistles for the others, and they were not happy about that. They just could not understand how three low-maintenance rookies rocked the crowd day in, day out, while they put on elaborate and expensive shows for less than half the response.

By that time, my favourite sister Yasmeen had moved out to Holland and was living in a place called Heerhugowaard, which was close to the town of Alkmaar. She had married a man called Peter, whose character bore an uncanny resemblance to Beacher. I already knew the Beacher-type, and I never trusted Peter, whom I found to be every bit as weird as the Master himself, but I loved my sister and she said she loved him, so I decided not to interfere.

It just so happened that we were playing in Alkmaar, and my sister decided to come watch us. The show had just finished and as usual we had done an amazing set, when suddenly a member of a different group wanted to get on to the bus where we were chilling. Problem was Irma was changing into her everyday clothes.

"You'll have to wait, mate," I said.

"Listen, boy, I'm with the artist Tony Scott. I'm coming on the bus so move out of my way." Tony Scott was a rapper, who at that time had a huge hit and was headlining that day. I didn't have a problem with Tony; I didn't know him, but his entourage were a bunch of jerks.

I confronted him again and said, "Listen, mate, you ain't getting on, my singer is getting dressed; once she's done you can go on." He refused my request and decided he was going to force himself on to the bus. Before he could react, I had floored him and the next thing I knew the security were heading towards me.

There was one thing about my singer Irma, boy could she fight. She was having none of it and joined in to help me out. Martin, who was by no means a fighter, gave us a hand to drive off the scum. I was battling idiots, with my two sidekicks showing off some insane moves.

And then I heard something what I hadn't heard in a long time; a sweet voice that said, "Zid, I'm coming!" It was Yasmeen and she had been watching what had evolved. I knew she was tough as she was never afraid of my psycho brother Lateef, but I had definitely underestimated her. Here was a respected orthopaedic specialist for the elderly jumping in to help out her own brother. My favourite sister, my crazy talented singer, the timid Martin and I fighting the masses and we were not losing; it was a spectacle.

After it ended and everyone was dispersed I went over to my sister and thanked her. "I'm always here for you, Zid, wow and you guys were great on stage." I laughed and said little, but I did feel a rush of affection towards her. Even though we hadn't spoken in a while, she was still my favourite; the coolest and prettiest sister I had.

Word had reached the organizers about the fight, and we knew what was coming. Sure enough we were informed that we were being taken off the tour. I was pissed off and dissed those bastards for banning us.

The good thing was that Euro Pop had seen enough for them to want to work with my group and I, despite us getting into a fight.

"You guys were mega impressive and so you know you were voted the best group from the tour, but because they banned you they gave it to someone else."

The accolade didn't matter, but that the crowd had a great time; that did.

As I celebrated, I knew something was coming and then I got the call from Jaqueline;

"Frans, you are a father to a son, would you like to see him?"

It was the end of August, 1990 and my life would change in every which way...

CHAPTER 28
I'm Still Standing

We were getting calls from all kinds of representatives, all across Europe, but that was not the only kind of calls I was alerted to. Irma Derby was having regular meltdowns, and I could not tell whether or not it was that time of the month, or if it happened any time of the month, but she'd call in to the studio every other day, arriving late, or sometimes not arriving at all, with one thing or the other.

Good old reliable Pedro seemed to be having his hands full with her, but he grew increasingly frustrated and desperate, and I knew I'd have to step in and take the reigns.

"Irma, relax, we've got a whole week off before the French promotional tour," I said.

"I don't want to go there, why do we have to go there, are there even any black people there or mixed people like us?" she said.

Irma was from the ghetto, and I knew where she had come from. She hadn't ventured out of Holland before, and so the concept of cross-border travel was alien to her. She was a nervous wreck, and was wrecking my nerves as well, but I did know one thing, and that was that she was a great singer. In fact for me there was no one better in the country.

She had it all, the artistic looks and million-dollar voice, but her terrible temper and emotional instability could not be ignored. She really was a nutcase sometimes, with the emotional turmoil a week before we'd be performing live, or recording at the studio.

I was like a big brother to her, though; someone she could trust and confide in and I thought the world of her and knew if she could stay the course she'd go down as one of the most famous black singers in Holland, but, and that's a really big but, she'd have to stay on course.

I was still hanging with Bryan and he was undoubtedly my most trusted confidant and best friend. We were very much alike, he coming from a mixed background of Black and Chinese, which I called Blackinese, so he too understood that guys like he and I didn't really belong anywhere. The difference was that he did have a home life; his father was the spitting image of the boxer Evander Holyfield and his mother was the sweetest, tiny little Chinese lady.

Bryan had decided that he wanted to be a photographer and would become Holland's first black photographer, which he later did then quit because of the racism. It had actually worked out great for me as he took our pictures and if the record company or tour company needed photos, I insisted Bryan take them, which was great as it meant I kept the artistic control over everything.

Bryan always came across as the tough guy, the ex-kickboxer, the trusted one and it was inevitable that Irma would develop a soft spot for him, something I knew would only end in tears. Bryan was your everyday dog, sniffing butts and finding any opportunity to mount girls, and then trot away, but Irma was totally infatuated with him, and there was nothing I could say or do to change her mind.

It was a difficult situation and I was stuck right in the middle of it. In one corner, I had my best mate in Amsterdam and in the other my star singer. I warned them both not to continue with it, but they pursued it and eventually Bryan pulled off his famous act.

Two days later I got a call from Martin saying Irma had freaked out because Bryan had dumped her after a few days and she wanted to end her life. I called Bryan who laughed and said, "Fuck that bitch, she does my head in."

I was furious and told him, "Look you have to come with me and sort this out, she's my singer and a friend." At first he refused, but in the end after he saw that I was not happy at all, he agreed. We met with Irma and even though she was hysterical I managed to calm her down and make her realize she could do so much better than Bryan. It took her a moment to see what I was saying, but I could be fairly convincing, and after some time she accepted that she could do better.

We'd been invited to several gigs, and it was prime time for Infobeat. It was hard work, but I kept up with it.

There was friction between EMI and CNR. The former was nudging the latter out of the way, and I was having a problem agreeing to the direction they were taking with our music.

"Frans, this is all great, but we still want you to move into a more commercial direction. You can keep what you've got, just tweak it a little, you know, also we'd like to drop Carel and Jerry and bring in some other producers." I was furious and wanted to give them a piece of my mind, but there was nothing I could do, because EMI were paying for the studio time, which meant they had a major input in what happened with Infobeat.

I was devastated for Carel as he received the news from the representatives at EMI. He, on the other hand, as always, was the ultimate gentleman and he said to me, "Frans, I've enjoyed myself so much, but you've got to move on. Just remember that if there's anything you need, I'm always there for you."

"Thanks, Carel, appreciate it all, you really are a top man."

EMI called on us again and said, "The guys we want you to work with are Arthur and Kees. They are up and coming producers and will work well with you, just keep in mind what we are saying."

Luckily for them, working with their new producers turned out to be great. They were excellent guys and we did work well together. Even though they were stoned most of the time, there was no doubt that they were talented. The real problem was that those EMI Holland people had no idea how to promote us, because they didn't know the kind of music that we were endorsing and that was creating great difficulty with our publicity.

To make matters worse, they insisted on shooting an expensive video, which I thought was an absolute waste of time, but we went with it and got it done.

I felt that we could have put that money towards our sound productions. There was no essence to the video; no strong Infobeat vibe that we'd worked so hard to demonstrate during our shows, on tour and in the studio. The public loved us because we were real and not some made up group of mindless plastic puppets that did the biding of some enigmatic source, but the truth was, that was what we were becoming; slaves of the industry, and I would never forgive those people for destroying our raw image and music.

It was a real cut throat business, as I'd notice day after day. EMI kept insisting on having things done their way, and even though I was never about to step down for anybody, the friction was escalating to breaking point, and my rubbing shoulders with them was starting to produce fire. I cooled things down, however, for the sake of the group, and salvaged my pride in the studio, when it was just the switchboard, the mic and me.

We moved on to touring France, the northern and the southern parts, with Auxerre being our highlight. It was great being back in France, and listening to the enticing language, and smelling the fresh bread, and the French received us with as much fervour as anybody else had done.

We really had gone international, and actually performed an extended version of our hit single live on French TV. That was truly fulfilling, knowing thousands of viewers across the country were going to watch our performance.

And yet again, Irma just had to pull a class act of her own and cause us an embarrassment. As we sat at the restaurant in Auxerre, she asked the local promoter whether they had rice and chicken. At first Pedro, Martin and I laughed because we thought it was a joke, but Irma was dead serious. "I want rice and chicken! How can there be no rice and chicken, what kind of a restaurant is this and why does the burger have a fried egg on it?"

I pulled her to the side and straightened her out, "Fuck the rice and chicken and the fuckin burger, that's not what we're here for. Pull yourself together and either eat what you're given or leave it." I had burst her bubble, but by then she was used to that, and didn't get too sulky as we kept up the laughs and had a good time.

When we got back to the hotel, Irma dropped in on Martin and me. We were sharing a room, and she'd decided to swing by and chill. It wasn't turning out to be the best day for her, as she'd forgotten to turn the tap off while filling the bathtub up in her room. I could almost hear her shrieking that the hotel was sinking as she saw the devastation. The promoter was fuming as he had to arrange another room for her, but we laughed our heads off as it was an honest mistake.

Once we were back from tour, we returned to the studio to get to work on more tracks. I wasn't exactly sure why, but Irma started to talk less and less to Martin and I. She had always confided in us about everything that went on with her. We knew that something was up.

As the days progressed, she didn't turn up to sing, or sometimes she'd keep us waiting, or call in to cancel for no apparent reason. One thing led to another, and before I knew what was going on, she burst into the studio and said, "I don't need to do this anymore!" We were used to hearing that, and we merely shrugged it off and got on with doing our parts for laying down the next track.

I was receiving regular phone calls for various promotions, commercials, events, acts, all of it, but one call that stood out for me came later on that afternoon. "Frans Merkx? This is James Hyman, I work for MTV, and we met briefly at one of your gigs when I was in Amsterdam, remember at the Escape?"

"Yeah, bruv, I remember, how's things James?"

James Hyman was a passionate cinematographer, moving up the ladder just as I was. I was impressed with the way he did things, and always valued his advice. "I'm going to be honest, Frans. I can see what you guys are trying to do, and I can really appreciate that. I love it, actually, always known you to be different and ambitious."

"Cheers."

"Thing is, be careful of the music industry because others always seem to think they know more than you even though it's your baby."

"Yeah, it's not easy working in this industry, there's some real assholes mate."

"You've got a lot of talent and courage, Frans, and I think you should think about the original approach. It's not in my place to say, but if you ever have time come and see me in London."

"Appreciate it, James, thanks for that."

James' warning was a definite sign from the beyond as the people representing EMI were playing dirtier than ever. They were doing their best to prize Irma away from my grasp, and that's where it all added up.

Sure enough, she walked into the studio calmly one fine day, and announced, right before we were going to record another track, "Frans, this time I'm for real, I really can't do this. Sorry, I'm quitting the group."

There was something finite in her tone, and she hadn't come bursting in like she usually did. Irma Derby was history.

I found out a couple of days later, from an insider at EMI that they'd offered Irma hair extensions in exchange for her leaving the group to start a solo career with them. I couldn't help but laugh to myself. I had underestimated just how low they could stoop to break our group apart. They had done their homework well, and taken my star singer away in a move that was not only calculating, but tremendously funny as well. That was the beginning of the end with EMI.

I didn't complain, but went about my business, and I was rewarded with a phone call from my mates back home. Roger's voice said, "Zid, how's it going mate?"

"Fuckin' Roger! What gwan?"

"Nuttin', mate. Hey listen, Jacko and I thinking about coming to the Dam to visit you, can we manage that?"

"For sure."

"Thanks, bruv, we'll see you this weekend then?"

"Sounds good."

There they were, my two partners in crime, and they brought Bradford with them, with the memories and the good times we shared. "Zid! Can't believe it, mate, you in the music biz, funny but definitely cool," said Roger.

"Fuck off," I laughed.

"You've done well for yourself, Zid," he said again.

"Yeah, mate, me too, proud of you," Jacko said. They looked built as ever, Jacko looking muscular and wide from all the years working on construction sites. He told me about how he had his own company now. Roger was as huge as ever.

"It's good to see you guys again, how's things back in Blackistan?"

"Same old, bruv, same old," Roger said.

"You know how it is mate," Jacko affirmed.

"Glad to hear it," I said, grinning.

"Hey, so where we going tonight?"

"Leidseplein. We can check it out, it's early now so we can wander around a bit down there then come back here to go out later on?" I suggested.

"Yeah, we'll just freshen up, and be off, yeah?" Jacko said, turning away to use the bathroom.

"Left Bradford, became a star, like some kind of a movie," Roger said.

"Fuck off," I repeated, laughing.

"Nah man, it's no joke, bruv, you done summit ill man, guys back home still dreamin' about that shit, nobody done nuttin' about it, but you, bruv, you done it."

"I done nuttin', too, bruv. I just be hangin' around as usual. mate, but you know how these things go, eh?"

"Sure do, bruv, we do nuttin', we get somethin', s'all good bruv."

It was turning out to be a great day of reminiscing. We caught up on what had gone on since I left, and I filled them in on how it was with the music industry, and we laughed at Irma Derby's debacles, the best of the laughs coming from her getting hair extensions. Roger was bent over, clutching his stomach as his eyes welled up from laughing so hard, "What a cunt, but that shit's funny!"

"Mate, you have no idea, it's a dirty business, they so fake here," I said for what seemed like the thousandth time.

"Nah, bruv, I can imagine, we always hear shit, but now we really know what is like. Hair extensions? For real?" And he laughed again.

"Ey, Zid, think I can make a call mate? Need to ring home up, see how my missus is and the kids," Jacko said.

"Yeah, there are two pay phones up there, at the American Hotel," I said.

"Sweet, I won't be long."

"No problem." I watched as Jacko disappeared up the stairs and into the lobby.

"Eh, so you were on TV and shit, bruv? Tha's crazy man!"

I laughed and said, "Eh bruv, you have no idea-" I noticed Jacko coming back outside. "Great, there's Jacko..."

I watched as he walked back down, just as another black guy came out after him and said something. Jacko stopped in his tracks and turned around saying, "Sup bruv?"

The black guy replied, "Ma nigga keep walking..."

Jacko said, "What's up bruv, I didn't say anything."

"Shut the fuck up, boy."

Jacko was irritated, "Who you calling boy, I don't even know you, mate."

"What you say?"

"I said I don't fuckin' know you."

"You wanna go, ma nigga?"

"What you sayin'?"

"Yeah you tough now, I'll be back," the black guy said. Before I knew it, he disappeared and reappeared with a herd of more than twenty guys. I saw it happen in slow motion. I barely had time to react as they stampeded in our direction. It was three on twenty, and five of them were at my neck.

They pummelled my face; I received blows to the head, the jaw, everywhere. Multiple fists and legs lashed out at me, and I struggled to hold back against them. I tried to get up and hit back, but they kept it up, and blood poured out from everywhere. I was hit at so many points of contact; I had no idea where the pain was felt most. I was beginning to lose consciousness, as I got bashed up, ganged upon.

It was the least fair fight, I didn't do anything to warrant it in any case, and I found myself crumbling to the ground, still lashing out like a cobra, but there were too many of them.

And then it ended. I looked up and there was a huge black guy who shouted at me, "Hey, chocolate boy, better stay down or ya gonna get a beat down again..."

I refused and said, "Sod off, you bastard, what have we done to you?" and rose unsteadily to my feet. They were actually surprised and I sensed a touch of respect that this brown boy wouldn't stay down.

"Let's get outta here." The group of guys retreated back into the hotel. Amidst the chaos, I could have sworn I had seen MC Hammer, but I wasn't entirely sure. I was full blooded and messed up, but still standing.

Beaten, bruised and battered, we stumbled to the tram stop and got on the tram that would take us back home. I was nauseated, and the stifling blows caught up with me and I threw up all over the place. Everyone had shed their fair share of blood, which shone on our clothes, leaving bloodied footsteps everywhere we stepped. We got back home and slouched down into the sofas in pain, my eye was swollen and bust up, and Jacko had scratch marks everywhere on his neck.

"What the fuck, Jacko?" I asked in a mumble.

"Hey, I don't know what happened, the guy looked high on coke!"

"Shit, twenty on three, that's messed up," Roger said.

"Damn, my fucking gold chain," I said, noticing the piece was missing from around my neck.

"Yeah, my ring's gone too," Roger said.

"My wallet, those mother-," Jacko added.

"What should we do, go and get it back?" Roger asked.

"I'm not going back now, I'm cooked. Let's rest today, and go back tomorrow," I concluded wisely.

We rested and returned to the hotel the following day. As we stood in the lobby, I said to the duty manager, "Yesterday we had an altercation in front of your hotel with people we believe are guests at your hotel. We've not come here for any trouble we just want to know if anyone has found anything and handed it in. We're missing a gold chain, a wallet and a ring, and other valuables."

Suddenly, before the manager could respond, a man turned up in the lobby and shouted, "You mother fuckers here again, you come back for more?"

"We don't want any trouble; we just want our stuff, that's all," I said.

"Ey, who do you think you are?" he was joined by more guys, and we were surrounded again.

"We're not here for trouble"

"Listen to this guy, it's the chocolate mother fucker who took the beating, but he's come back for more!" I hadn't noticed there was someone standing right behind me. He grabbed me up and shoved me into a seat. In a flash the whole lobby was filled out with what we would soon discover was MC Hammer's entire entourage.

It was packed out, and one of the guys I recognized from an MC Hammer video, Frosty, stood in front of me and said, "We've gotta teach you brown niggas a lesson." He tried to grab me, but like a reflex I stood up while at the same time I used my well-versed uppercut to connect with his jaw, and sent him flying.

The retaliation was tenfold. I was getting knocked down again, just like the previous day, and I could see that Roger was getting nailed as well. I had to hand it to him, he was putting up a real fight, and I knew for certain that he was a brick wall.

I was deafened to all the sounds around me. I didn't panic and automatically went into fight mode to protect myself. The rush of adrenaline served as a painkiller, and I pulled every move I had learnt. I knew I could not win the fight, but I tried nonetheless, I reared like a bull, and fought back no matter how futile it all was.

It was a real blood bath, hardcore gladiator arena style combat. To make things worse, the elevator doors slid open and out walked MC Hammer himself. I hadn't imagined it; it was him after all, and it was weird, not because it was MC Hammer, but the fact that these were his people, and he was about to join in.

They had Roger pinned up by the lift. Meanwhile, I'd been drained of all energy. They'd stopped bashing me, but they held me up, and I watched as MC Hammer walked slowly up to Roger, pulling out a white glove from a back pocket and putting it on. One of his guys handed him a knuckle duster, and he looked at us and said, "You brown mother fuckers, let me teach you a lesson." MC Hammer took a swing, and connected with full force; the knuckleduster made contact with Roger's jaw, splitting it open. Blood spurted out everywhere, I thought they'd ended Roger, and I was shocked to see his bone protruding from his jaw.

What I could not believe, and not that it mattered as we were all being beaten up and then cast out of the hotel like a bunch of rag dolls, was that this was MC Hammer, a so-called good Christian and a God-fearing man, with a white wife and mixed kids, breeds like us, using that kind of racial slur against us, and subjecting us to that kind of battering, all for nothing.

Roger looked a complete mess and I was nearly in tears because this guy was like my own brother. We picked him up and carried him off to the police station. When we got there, the numb skulls began asking, "What happened, could you fill out a report please?"

"Fuck the report! This guy needs an ambulance!" I yelled into his face.

They didn't wait, but got hold of the ambulance.

All Roger could say then, that was something that would stick with me for the rest of my life was, "Ey, Zid, they didn't knock me out!"

Damn right, you do nothing, you get whacked, but as long as they don't knock you out, you keep on coming back for more, and not more violence, but more from life, and yet we were still standing.

I was still standing.

CHAPTER 29
Drifter

Inadvertently, the showdown with MC Hammer outside the American Hotel had reached the ears of millions of people. It was not the best way to have people talking about me, as the guy from Infobeat that had gotten into an altercation with MC Hammer, but it was all over the news and there was nothing I could do to stop it.

Jacko, Roger and I were in full accordance when we decided that we were going to file suit for assault and damages, even though I had long since known about the comedy justice system in Amsterdam that would not take up such a claim. Roger was insistent, and who could blame him with that swollen, bandaged face as he said, "We gotta sue that cunt, look what he did to my face!"

Through a Dutch lawyer, I was recommended a couple of lawyers based in New York, who knew how to handle high-profile cases. I wanted justice for my mates, for myself, how could that hypocrite get away with bits of Roger's face hanging off his knuckle duster?

We spoke over the phone to the recommended lawyers, who were both Jewish and world class, to explain what exactly had happened.

"What we can do, Mr. Merkx, is work the case on a 'no win, no pay' basis," one of the lawyers said.

MC Hammer carried on with his tour in Europe while at the same time denying all allegations against him. It was absolutely nauseating watching him on MTV and other news outlets, describing the altercation as something he knew very little about, when seated beside me watching the news and protesting incoherently with a fat lip and broken jaw, was the living proof of Hammer's nonsense.

I wouldn't stand for it, and I arranged to fly out to New York to officially lodge our complaint. Their offices were situated in one of the World Trade Centre buildings on eighty-eighth floor. It was dreamlike looking right up all the way, and realizing the incomprehensible truth about the city. I loved New York City. It was in a country built by immigrants, put together brick on brick by all races and creeds, by whites, by breeds, and they were a proud bunch too, unlike in Holland where immigrants were looked down on and never recognized for anything they built.

It was everything that I had imagined, and it boasted a particular confidence that stood out from other cities in the world. From the towering skyscrapers, to the thriving entertainment hubs all over the place, it was a city full of life and lights, and it was a pity that I had gone there strictly for business.

As I entered the lift to go up to the eighty-eighth floor, I felt a rush of blood to the stomach, as though I were falling from a great height. It was immense, and my ears were blocked when I arrived to the designated floor, and exited the elevator.

The lawyers explained, "Due to the fact that Hammer is wanted for another altercation, where another guy had his jaw broken, this is going to be a cat and mouse case, because firstly he's denying all charges and secondly he's on the verge of being broke. If you want compensation for the damages that he and his people inflicted, you will have to be patient while we pursue them."

I was not interested in the money. I honestly believed that they could lock him up for something like this, but thanks to the Dutch authorities, they hadn't bothered to pursue it as a criminal case.

In the end, it was up to us to follow it up as a civil case in the United States of America. It just proved to me without a shadow of doubt that the authorities in Holland didn't care about the everyday people.

What really was eating away at me was the fact that here was someone who claimed to be a God-fearing man, who claimed he respected all people of all colours and faiths, who at the end of the day would say what he did was unthinkable. He had shown himself to be a fraud that was even more racist than the white people who spat at my mother all those years ago, and for that he had to pay. A racist was a racist. It didn't matter if he or she was black, white or in between.

After quite some time, and a hell of a lot of 'Cat and Mouse' the lawyers managed to reach a settlement with Mr. Stanley Burrell, also known as MC Hammer. I wasn't happy about that; I had gone there to bring this menace to justice, to avenge Roger the legal way without harming anybody's reputation, but it had all been for nothing, nothing but a worthless settlement. To me Roger's jaw was worth more than what he offered to pay us in exchange for our cooperation.

I would have felt worse, had Roger not pointed out the simple truth, saying over the phone, "It's better than nothing, bruv." It still did not do much to make me feel better, because I was hell bent on having Hammer exposed. I wanted to show the world that he was not only a bully, but a racist bully.

I would have liked to have pursued the case further, but right then I knew that there was nothing more I could do, other than sit and watch as he would later on be ridiculed in the industry. Sure enough, it came right round to bite him because he was even declared bankrupt and his name would be used as the butt of all jokes, and all that happened while I sat around and did nothing. I suppose if there is a God, then he does work in mysterious ways, I laughed as I saw Hammer humiliated and become a nobody.

I returned to Holland and tried to work full-swing in the studio to keep the tempo up. Irma Derby's departure did not slow me down. I put new material down, laying the foundations for some more tracks, but things didn't seem right. Something was missing.

I wanted to keep up with the money and so I had landed myself a new job working in the administration and warehousing departments at a paper factory. It wasn't the greatest job in the world, but at least I got on with the people that worked there. It was back to the routine.

As the days passed me by, I was losing more and more interest in Infobeat. It was just disconcerting, watching EMI steal my star singer, and then Jaqueline doing the same with my son. All in all, there was just no inspiration, and it was just oh so bleak.

In all the bleakness, I started seeing a girl called Marsha. We had what could be called a boyfriend-girlfriend relationship. She being Jamaican meant we got along great, seeing as I had enough experience with her lot. In the end, we got on more as friends than anything else.

Marsha wasn't enough cover for me to still feel like I was drifting out in the ocean, without a goal in sight. Every now and again, I returned to

Bradford to touch base with some of my old friends. The usual suspect was Roger, of course, and we'd wind up at these so-called Blues Parties in Manningham, down in the centre of Bradford.

They had nothing to do with Blues music whatsoever. On the contrary, it was an occasion where we'd gather at someone's house, it would be pitch black and people would just mingle and chill while a 'sound system' would play 'Lovers' rock' in the background. This was the soul version of Reggae music.

I ended up meeting plenty of people, and not just my old friends. It seemed to me that Bradford had expanded in the years I'd been absent. Chilling in the darkness with total strangers felt like my thing in the end, because I still felt that I did not belong anywhere.

The months passed me by. Bradford, Bryan and the Studio became a part of my routine, and I stuck with it. It was nearly the end of 1991, when it all began to catch up with me. My life was at a standstill and I was as confused as ever. Should I just leave Amsterdam? Should I stick it out and see where it takes me? And if I do leave Amsterdam, should I go back to the shit hole that's Bradford?

As though it was reflecting what I was going through, my apartment was falling apart. Literally. There were cracks in the walls and the toilet continuously stunk because the drainage system was non-functional. In the end, it was all too much, and I approached the housing authority to come in and fix the problem.

They had the best solutions to everything, and they told me that unless the building was unsafe, I would have to continue living there and there was no chance for me to get somewhere else to stay.

I didn't know which way to look, and my former self, that I thought I'd escaped completely after changing my name, returned. I asked my neighbour to lend me some money, so that I could take care of things. I think he'd always taken a liking to me, and he did not hesitate in loaning it to me. After that, whenever he asked me to pay him back, I told him to "Fuck off," which I guess sent the correct message to him.

I'd also rented the attic out, and one of the occupants was a fellow Breed from Scotland. His name was Mark and he was one of the oddest people I'd ever met. One night Bryan and I were going out and he asked if could join us. We agreed and that was not all he asked for.

"Frans, bruv can you cut my hair for me?" Mark asked.

I was no expert with cutting hair, but I could get it done. "Yeah no problem, bruv, how do you want it?"

"Just get the clippers and give me a low cut and shave the sides."

That sounded simple enough. "I've only got this old razor for the side, is that alright?"

"Yeah just do it, bruv."

I proceeded to cut his hair, using my common sense to see how much to take off and even it out. In the end, it was quite good considering I had no idea what I was doing. I moved onto shaving the side of his head. The problem was the razor was blunt so I had to apply pressure, which in turn cut into his scalp. It was a bloodbath and his scalp was bright red.

"Bruv, I've cut into your scalp 'cause the blade was a bit blunt."

"No problem, bruv, hope it doesn't get infected." Mark didn't look in the least bothered that he was a bleeding mess.

It was anybody's guess that Mark wasn't the brightest guy around. It was a good thing he looked mean. Bryan was pissing himself laughing and suggested I apply aftershave to the cuts on Mark's head.

"What do you think Mark, want me to add some aftershave just to make sure there's no infection?" I asked, trying my best not to laugh as well.

"If you think it will help, bruv, then yeah throw some on."

I wet my hands and threw what seemed like half a bottle of aftershave onto Mark's head. He screamed with pain and Bryan screamed with laughter, but after a moment, Mark turned to me and said, "That should do the job, bruv, that will kill any infection." Mark sure was a nutter and he had the psycho look to go with it.

It didn't help that his clothes were much too small for him, and seeing as he had a hefty build, he looked outright terrifying. My eyes streamed with tears as I laughed and laughed and laughed some more.

I'm not sure why, but Bryan and I followed up with our plans for the night, and took the maniac along with us. Before we left, however, I had one more thing that would really make it an epic night. I exchanged one knowing look with Bryan, and offered Mark a drink before leaving. I had some laxatives as part of my collection of medicine, and I dropped some into his drink and handed it to him.

As we sat on the train heading to Rotterdam, Mark turned round and said, "Bruv, I really need to go for a shit." I had to keep a straight face and looked at Bryan.

Bryan responded with the most stupid answer, "You have to pay on the train to go to the toilet, bruv."

Mark believed every word and just said, "Okay I will hold it till we get to the club." I think it was all a stretch, but then again I thought a bit of a laugh wouldn't hurt anyone.

We arrived at the club, with Mark looking thoroughly stressed out. He wanted to shit so badly, he kept exhaling strongly and closing his eyes. As we stood there in queue, Mark said to Bryan and I, "I can't wait in line guys, I need to fuckin shit now or I will shit my pants, fuck this." He pushed his way to the front of the queue and I followed. There were two huge, mean bouncers in front, one of whom we knew very well because he'd always refuse to let us in. He hated blacks, breeds anything that wasn't white.

I stood in front of Mark and said, "Let me deal with this, bruv."

"Stop there, where do you think you are going, boy?" the bouncer said.

"We wanna go in, what's the problem, mate?" I asked.

"Wrong dress code, mate, you can't come in."

I was furious and was just about to walk away when Mark confronted the bouncer with a combination of his insane look and a powerful smell that was certainly not aftershave.

"I need to go in NOW! We are coming in, don't fuckin try and stop me." The bouncer froze and he didn't even need the elementary Math he obviously didn't know to tell him not to mess with this massive Mohican breed, who not only took shit, but literally smelt like it too.

"Err yes, mate, no problem, come right in," the bouncer said.

"These two are with me," Mark said pointing Bryan and I out.

"Yeah, mate, no problem come in."

"Thanks, mate, thought you'd see our side," I said sneering at the bouncer.

We entered the club and Mark said quickly, "Lads I will be back I'm going for a quick shit," before running off into the distance.

Bryan and I were sat at the bar chatting up a couple of girls, when Mark reappeared. He was completely tactless in front of women, and this time was no exception.

"Fuckin 'ell lads, I shit up the whole wall of the toilet, sprayed out everywhere," he said laughing his head off. I shrugged at the girl I was talking to, who looked Mark up and down, cringing.

The idiot still had toilet roll attached to his pants and it wasn't white. We decided there and then to get out of the club and head back home. Mark was disappointed. He'd actually been having a good time and insisted we go out a lot more. We insisted he go get a shower.

Going out wasn't always a laugh, though. Once, Bryan and I made a big mistake going to a nightclub in a village called 'Kijkduin' located just outside The Hague. We had decided to check it out as we were bored of doing the rounds in Amsterdam.

This time we were with another bloke we'd called 'Curly Romeo.' Reason why we called him that is because this brother never had an afro, but always had a perm with tons of greasy gel in it.

The three of us arrived at 'Kijkduin.' It was a hick country with real rednecks, and we saw this for ourselves as we entered the club. One look around the place told me that there were no Black, Asian or brown people around. The way those guys in there looked at us made sure that we were not welcome in this part of Holland.

I used my wisdom and said to Bryan, "Bruv, I think it's best we leave, they don't look too friendly here."

He agreed, and the three of us headed for the exit. By the door stood the club bouncers. We had only been in there for thirty minutes when the bouncer stopped me from going outside by aggressively putting his arm across the door.

"Waar is mijn fooie," which meant where is my tip. If I was to give him a tip, it would be never to ask for one, but I was so angry that I reached inside my pocket and handed him five cents.

"That's all I've got, mate, don't spend it too quickly," I said, glaring at him.

"Think you are funny, boy?" he said, pushing me away.

"Don't touch me, you fat cunt, we just want to get out of here."

The switch flicked on, and before he had the chance to have a go at me, I slammed a right hook full on his jaw, knocking him out cold and that was the start of the commotion. Bryan ran up to me, looked from the floored bouncer to me, and without warning ran out the door, grabbing my shirt as he did. 'Curly Romeo' who screamed for us to keep running followed us outside.

We sprinted and ran straight over what seemed like a bridge an, just like in the movies, I fell over. As I was getting up, I felt a fist on the back of my head, which was then followed up by some tasty blows. The bouncers had arrived, and they were trying to toss me into the water. I held the railings for dear life.

I looked up and shouted, "Bryan, help me!"

He shouted to Curly Romeo to come back, and he replied, "Fuck him I'm out of here."

Bryan screamed back before running to me, "I won't forget this!" In a flash, Curly Romeo was gone.

I have no idea how he managed it, but I guess with a combination of luck and adrenaline, Bryan freed me from that tight spot and we ran off bruised, but again, not beaten. I owed Bryan; he'd done a David Mallet and saved me.

CHAPTER 30
The Transition

It was December 1991 and I was still seeing Marsha. We got on really well, but somehow I just had the feeling that she wasn't the one, the love of my life. Intimate or not, for the second time, a girl I was involved with told me she was pregnant. This time, however, I was pleased, and determined to not let what happened to my first son occur again.

To raise this kid and my long lost one properly, I had to make sure he wasn't brought up in a dump. For that's what my apartment had become. The switch was flicked and I remembered what the housing authority said about offering me an alternative place if the apartment wasn't liveable. I consulted with my neighbours to work something out.

And we sure had ourselves a case. On the staircase going up to each apartment there were cracks in the wall because the house was actually sinking on one side. The housing authority concluded that we could still live another ten years in the dump before they'd move us. There was no way that I was going to wait another ten years in that death trap.

I got together with the neighbours once more. Our verdict was to collectively acquire a pneumatic drill to speed up the process slightly. I was the real "Demolition Man" with that drill in my hands, and I monumentally increased the size of those cracks.

The housing authority finally agreed that we had to be re-housed. It was a victory for the 'Neighbours Union.' This was my chance to get a decent apartment, but at the same time remain in the South of Amsterdam, which was an area I knew and wanted to stay in.

Moving day arrived and I relocated to my new apartment. At last, I was on for a new beginning, and it sure was one without the carpets, wallpaper, furniture and bed. Yet, it was a palace compared to the shit hole I was living in before. I wanted to buy everything new and even though we were confident that we could win our case; MC Hammer, the settlement and payout would be a long way off.

I had to find a way to get money to kit out my new apartment. I was once again in that familiar territory: to hustle or not. Bryan told me about how he'd scammed a company that gave credit and suggested I do the same and ask for credit under my British passport. I was reluctant, but I was running out of options and in the end I bought everything on credit. I was highly unfamiliar with the word "debt." It was alien to me, but there I was neck-deep in it.

Now that I had the place set up, I approached Marsha about coming to live with me. She would be able to register and reside at my address, which was beneficial on two fronts. On the one hand, it gave her a chance to acquire a Dutch passport, and on the other hand, I would be able to live with my child.

My resolve was strengthened with the arrival of the pregnant Marsha. I wanted to do everything right, and I worked harder than ever with my music and everyday job. She, too, got herself a job and took good care of the apartment.

I was still paying Jaqueline's mother visits, to try and get information on whether or not the mother of my son, Carlton, would be coming back to Holland with him. Jaqueline's mother was a gem. She understood my desperation and that I needed to see my son and promised me that if she knew anything, she would inform me right away.

I also kept up with my own family, every now and again. My mum and I didn't share the greatest relationship, but I'd see her from time to time. She'd moved to The Hague, where she had bought herself an apartment and was working at a home for the elderly.

I discovered, too, that my younger brother, Zak, had gotten himself a job at the Change Bureau. He'd followed me right down that path, the only difference was that he didn't have the knowhow to make the money I once had made. All the same, he was happy there. My suspicions about his crumbling relationship where confirmed, after his wife took their baby back to Bradford.

1992 was becoming a year of transition for me. I was preparing to be a father again, only this time it would be for real.

That's when I got the call.

"Hi Frans, it's Frida, Jaqueline's mother. She's coming back with Carlton soon, I will let you know when."

I felt a rush of excitement, but that was short lived because there was one major problem. I hadn't told Marsha about Carlton. It was stupid and selfish, but I thought that it was my business and I would have to deal with it and there was no need to involve anybody else in that.

The days turned to weeks, turned to months, and before I knew it the year had gone by without anything really happening for me. That would all change in August, when I was at work.

The office manager called me in and said, "Think you better get over to the hospital, looks like your kid ain't waiting anymore."

I jumped into a taxi and went straight to the 'Prinsengracht Hospital' in the centre of Amsterdam. I was directed to the room, and as I entered there was a lot of commotion as my son was being born and placed in the cot.

I looked at him, and felt my chest swell. Just like his older brother, he was beautiful and when he opened his eyes, I was the first person he saw. I had already known what I wanted to name him: Ryan, after my two best friends Bryan and Roger.

I was spurred on by the arrival of Ryan, and I was adamant that by hook or by crook, I was going to be successful and give my boys everything I possibly could, and not just materially.

News finally came from Jaqueline's mother that Carlton was back with his mum, and I went straight to the house and demanded to see my boy. Jaqueline was reluctant, but her mother mediated and said that Carlton needed to see and be with me. In the end, she agreed and I was able to spend time with my first born.

It was hard for Carlton because he had to get used to me, but he was a little charmer and I had always been fond of him. With Ryan, it was easier; he'd see me most of the time and we had always been close, but I wanted to show him that he had an older brother. I vowed to do that when the time was right.

It turned out to be a pretty good year in the end. I had a new son and chilled with Carlton as well. Leeds United were crowned champions of

England and, even though I thought about giving up, I was still in with my music. I wondered what 1993 would bring for me.

One phone call answered that question.

"Hello, can I speak to Frans Merkx?"

"Yup, who's this?"

"This is Wessel Van Diepen from Veronica TV. Is it possible for you and I to meet up, I'd like to discuss a music project we'd like to do with you. My partner is in Leidschendam and if it's okay with you, I can come and pick you up and we can go down there together?"

It sounded interesting, but I didn't get excited too quickly. "I have a work meeting at eleven until twelve noon then I'm free."

"No problem, will pick you tomorrow."

"Sure."

"See you soon."

Wessel was quite well known in Holland and worked for a large independent television station called Veronica. It could not have been clearer that my musical prowess was valued somewhere.

He arrived at my work place at exactly one, as though he was oh so eager to land a deal with me. I found his promptness amusing, and also found him to be very arrogant as he marched up to me, sticking his hand out, wearing his high-end sunglasses and bobbing his head in a very cocky manner, as though to say, that's right, I'm 'The Man.' To me he was another 'Dutch white middle class' geek who had the look of a saccharine suburban white kid.

"Hi, Frans, pleasure to meet you. Wessel Van Diepen, we spoke over the phone?"

"Yeah nice to meet you, mate," I said, shaking his hand.

"You ready to go?"

"Yeah," I said.

On the way to Leidsedam, Wessel told me about how he was close with a guy called Mr. Lex Harding. "I'm telling you, Frans, this guy's going to make it for me. You know, I just…I gonna be a radio DJ on

Radio 538, which as you know Mr. Harding owns, so I'm trying to…you know…get in well with the man..." Radio 538 was one of the newest radio stations in Holland, and I'll give Wessel this: the man was ruthless in his pursuit of the good life, and he didn't care about anybody or anything as he climbed.

He drove quite a flashy car; it was a black BMW convertible and he revved it up like he was taking part in a Formula One race.

We arrived to Leidsedam in no time, which was not surprising considering how fast we were going. He introduced me to his confidant, Michiel, who had a studio there, and that's where we headed to next.

From the introduction, I gathered that he was a genius geek on the keyboards, and Wessel was sort of his sidekick. I didn't really think anything else of Michiel; he was alright. I was laughing to myself when Wessel said, "Yeah, I call myself Max Mondino and Michiel calls himself Denzil Slamming, pretty cool eh Frans," They'd ask me the most ridiculous questions, like how it was growing up with nothing or whether or not England was rough.

I tried to explain to them that I wasn't proud of the fact that I had a rough upbringing, but more of the fact that I worked my way out of it. They didn't listen; I think that they were more turned on thinking how it would be to come from the streets.

They told me how they'd made a few hits and used some dancer as a rapper, but it hadn't worked out and they thought he wasn't street enough or cool enough, whatever that was supposed to mean.

Wessel explained that they wanted to do house music, but to rough it up a bit and that they had heard my old Infobeat single, 'Are U Ready' and felt that was more in line with what they were doing. I found that to be an insult, because what I'd done with Infobeat wasn't some shoddy handcrafted bullshit, it was real, but I said nothing of the sort to these guys.

Wessel told me about an additional producer called Fonny de Wulf, who was in Belgium and I would need to go there to meet him, but more importantly said that I needed to acquaint myself with the owner of the project and record label Raymond Muylle.

It was clear to me that the biggest jerk was good old Wessel. He excused himself and left Michiel and I to go somewhere and when I asked Michiel where he had disappeared off to, he said that he was probably in the back watching some real hardcore porn. What a sick loser, I thought.

Michiel had a demo of a track he was working on. He let me listen to it and all it had was a sample of a voice singing "Oh neh neh, Oh neh neh." He asked me to add rap lyrics and words in different sections. That sounded easy enough; I let Michiel know that and by the time Wessel came back to the studio, I had already demonstrated where I thought the rap lyrics should go and suggested the title be "I'm Raving," which was agreed upon unanimously. I then put down some lyrics, while Wessel sat there acting like a producer.

What he lacked in musical knowledge, he more than made up with his contacts in the pop world because like everything else in life it was about 'Who you know' not 'What you know.' I worked out his role as the person that would get our music out there to the public; something EMI Holland just could not do with Infobeat.

After completing our session, Wessel drove me back to Amsterdam. On the way, he was hyped up and said, "We are gonna be famous, Frans, and we'll make a lot of money."

"And great music, mate," I said.

"Fuck that, Frans, the public just take what's given to them, whether it's good or not."

That's where I knew that this project wouldn't last. The only reason I was a moderate success with Infobeat was because the public were the stars and we played for them and that's why they loved us. Here I was with guys who looked at making music like a donut factory; just churning out crap after crap without a care in the world for what the listeners thought of them. I spared a thought for the everyday person, the broke teenager in the street who would spend her last penny buying this crap.

At that time, I wasn't in a position to be the philanthropist. I had to work towards something, so that I could be there for my sons. Wessel dropped me off home and I thanked him and told him I'd see him down in Belgium and that I would drive there myself. He shook my hand and claimed great things would happen for him and everyone else.

A couple of weeks later I arrived in Belgium to meet with Fonny and Raymond and as I approached former he said, "Nice to meet you, Frans, I'm Fonny."

"Frans." I shook his hand.

"I'm sure Wessel and Michiel have filled you in a bit about what we'd like to do and from what I heard you already get it," Fonny said.

"Yeah it's pretty basic and simple, mate," I said.

"Well, that's good because I really want something harder, musically speaking, you see. We know what you can do, and I think we've found what we are looking for."

It was a good concept, I had to admit, and that's when the real L.A. Style was officially born. Fonny was a classically trained pianist that had then branched off and developed his own unique style, mixing it up, playing around with the minor chords. I respected him immensely as he was trained at the Conservatorium; an academy for very talented musicians.

Michiel, or Denzil as he would call himself, was the man with the natural ability to turn a track into something commercial that everyone wanted to hear. He waved his wand, and suddenly, it all somehow pieced together and came out fluently.

Wessel was the talker with the contacts in big places that would help us bring the music to the masses.

I was the final cog in the L.A. Style juggernaut. I had the lyrics, the street credit, and the raw, hard creativity to keep everything real. It seemed on the outside like the perfect recipe.

Later on, I would meet Raymond and he was the so-called money man who controlled the finances and made the deals in other countries for distribution. He was very polite and courteous with me and spoke with a thick French accent because he was from the French speaking side of Belgium, but there was something about him that made me wary.

My time with Infobeat had come to an end. I dropped the project and decided to go with this larger scale group. At the time, I didn't realize it, but I would discover that it was probably my biggest musical mistake. I was not to blame for the shortcoming, which would later appear in the form of an epiphany, because I did feel that I was on the verge of having a serious break and I just had to get a way to move forward and actually see something in return instead of being continuously let down by everyone.

I travelled back and forth between Leidsedam and Belgium, working on tracks. It didn't feel the same, to be brutally honest. It was everything that I loathed; a man-made group with no soul. The beats were bland and uninspiring, and even though I tried to give it my best, it just felt empty.

Whereas with Infobeat, each track was an original, beautiful, one-of-a-kind, once-in-a-lifetime masterpiece, here I was mass producing and fooling the public. I guess Wessel knew what he was doing, because I sure as hell wasn't buying into the whole commercial deal. I looked at it like this, I needed money and if I wasn't doing this what would I be doing?

It really was a small world, and this was confirmed to me yet again when I returned to the studio one afternoon to complete some vocals. I arrived and Fonny asked me to wait as they were busy with some session singers.

I felt bad for those Session musicians that hadn't managed to get their careers off the runway and most of the time session singers were older and this was a way for them to make ends meet. I was preparing myself to go into the studio to work my magic, when out walked Irma Derby. She was stunned and embarrassed to see me standing there.

I, on the other hand, was taken aback, and even though I knew exactly what she was doing there, I asked, "Irma, what you doing here?"

She cleared her throat and tried to avoid making eye contact with me as she said, "Doing some session work for extra money. EMI arranged it for me."

I looked at her in disbelief and followed up, "What happened to the solo career they promised you?"

Again, she kept her eyes lowered as she responded in a slightly faint voice. "They are working on it..." there was a momentary pause, and to cover up she said, "I see you are doing great, you now a star, Frans."

"Fuck that crap, you should have stuck with me, sister, they done nothing for you and now you've missed the chance. Those cunts ruined everything for us all, we had a great thing going now look at you."

She shrugged her shoulders not knowing what to say. What an absolute waste; she was without a shadow of a doubt the most talented soul singer Holland had ever had or will have and now she was scratching around trying to raise money through session work. I didn't laugh at her, but felt sorry for her and angry and bitter that EMI would ruin such a great artist and what could have been with Infobeat.

It was an enjoyable time for me, working in Fonny's studio in Waasmunster, Belgium. He had a wonderful family; three great kids and a lovely wife. He thoroughly despised Wessel and Michiel and told me how he felt always left out even though he was the one with the original idea for L.A. Style.

I took a fancy to the country as well. The main cities were just like any other post-war European city, but I did love the unique characteristics of the village of Waasmunster, where Fonny lived.

The people that lived there were generally very helpful, and lacked that pompous, "city" nose-in-the-air trait that I disliked so much. They were a tight-knit community, and because it was a small settlement, they all knew each other and got along with one another and worked together, sharing the communitarian spirit, rather than stepping on each other's shoulders to get to the bone.

It was an upscale village, and the inhabitants were extraordinarily well-off financially, but they were wealthy in other ways as well. I also felt that Waasmunster had that soul-filled rural culture that gave it its own humble, precious identity that you wouldn't really find in Brussels.

As I continued working with LA Style, I began to feel disenfranchised by the whole process. To begin with, I wrote all the rap lyrics and hooks, and I was also a major contributor in the actual productions of the songs, but I was never given due credit from anyone for my efforts, not from Michiel, Wessel, Fonny and especially not Raymond.

They were all ripping me off. It was irritating when after I'd laid down my lyrics, they'd find a way to chop and change them, and when I saw what they'd done with them, I felt as though that wasn't what I really wanted. To me it sounded robotic, and demoralizing, and it wasn't my truth. I wanted to spit out fire and have people hear what I had to say, I wanted to let the world know how shit really was, but every time I wrote down something direct and daring, they'd say it wasn't commercial and ask me to write childish lyrics instead.

I wasn't the only one that wasn't impressed by the whole deal either. The singer was in full accordance with me. One day, she turned to me and said, "It's not you, Frans, it's just that this kind of music is not meant for me. I have no appetite to work with these people, I don't trust them and I certainly don't trust Raymond, and we just don't have any artistic freedom like they promised we would. You've got talent, Frans, and I really hope things work out for you." She hit the nail on the head and vocalised what I'd been thinking all along.

She even took it a step further, and after singing on a few tracks, she announced that she would not be pursuing the project any further.

The others didn't care a damn that she was leaving. They thought they were the real deal, that everyone else needed them and that they didn't need anyone.

To be honest, I wasn't surprised at all that she felt that way. She and I got along fantastically, and there was a deep mutual respect we shared for one another. She was originally from the United States of America and actually the real McCoy; a Red Indian and like all large women she could sing.

What she'd done was confirm to me that this wasn't for me either. I didn't feel in control, even though I was spearheading the project, all those behind-my-back deals, the restructuring of my material, the decisions without first consulting me, all of that just pissed me off. In the end of it all, I'd given them gold, and they'd turned it to bronze, and always with the same reasoning, "It's what we want, we know what will sell."

Unlike the singer, I didn't end up leaving the group. I wanted to stick around and see where it took me, and more importantly how much money I could make before walking away. I also used it as a testing ground, to see how different audiences reacted to what we played.

They were fortunate to have my creative talents and dynamism on their team, because the tracks that didn't involve me didn't sound as great.

It was getting hectic because we were expected to tour and do the promotions for TV, but we had no singer. After our lead female vocalist left, I was introduced to our new manager Mr. Dirk Paternoster. I was taken aback, because even though I had never signed anything with him, he was introduced as our manager. He whipped up a contract for me to

216

sign, but I kept delaying it because it didn't take a legal expert to understand how rubbish his agreement was.

Dirk Paternoster was actually a great guy. I had no issues with him personally and even professionally. It was clear to me that Raymond and his band of merry men were all working together and ripping me off. The hilarious part was the amount of sheer backstabbing on their part. Fonny would say to me how much he hated Wessel and Michiel, and that they had stolen his ideas and that Raymond still owed him money. He would tell me how Dirk was Raymond's spy and all that.

Wessel would be full of himself and say Michiel was nothing without him and that Raymond was a terrible person. He would claim that he had no idea why Fonny and Dirk were involved in the project.

Michiel would play the innocent guy who just wanted what was best for the group, but self-victimised by saying he was undervalued by everyone.

And at the head of the bullshit was Raymond himself. He lived like a Don in a mansion and wrote himself down as an Executive Producer, even though he did absolutely nothing at all.

With all the ruckus, in walked the so-called "new manager," accompanied by the group's brand new female vocalist. Once more they'd gone behind my back and found a singer without first consulting me. I had actually been thinking about bringing Irma in; even though she was difficult I knew she the best of the lot, and because I'd even worked with her before I'd know how to handle her, but I was not consulted at all and this made me realize that I, too, was becoming some kind of puppet for Raymond.

The new singer's name was Bibi and she was a breed. A half-African, half-White singer from Belgium. I had to say that she was talented. She was also a pleasant person, and in the end I did not mind her at all.

I was, however, deeply confused about her role in the group because she was not allowed to actually sing on any of the tracks, and was told that for the album we were working on at the time, she'd have to mime.

We went on to make our first TV appearance, which was on a show in Holland called the 'Countdown.' This was the Dutch version of 'Top of the Pops' in the UK. It was quite an experience, mostly because I'd met some great artists, particularly one group from the United States of America, comprising three girls, called TLC. They were wonderful personalities and if I was not mistaken a member of their family managed them.

It was not until we actually put Bibi to work that I realized how truly fake everything was becoming. To add to the stupid alterations on the tracks, the miming looked pathetic and impure. At least my voice remained on all the tracks as the lead artist, but poor Bibi's was nowhere to be heard. It was a kind of semi 'Milli Vanilli' scenario, and boy it was shit.

When I could no longer stand it, I tried my best to convince them that we were going the wrong way about things, but they were never bothered, and never even listened to me as I said over and over, "Look, we are fooling people by letting Bibi mime." It was to no avail. It was not just Wessel; it was the entire Dutch scene. They just didn't value real entertainers, and in my eyes they were all a bunch of cons and frauds.

The L.A. Style current carried us to the Swedish Music Awards and we went to Stockholm. That city looked exactly like Amsterdam to me, only I found that the people were less judgmental, probably because they were reserved and just minded their own businesses.

At the awards I met with other artists, one called Dr. Alban. He considered himself a top rapper a 'Toaster, Jamaican style' original. He made me laugh when he said in his African accent, "Ahhh I am big now Frans and people know me, if you want to learn, learn from me."

"Nah bruv all good, you do it your way and I will do it mine," I replied. Overall, there were several genteel artists, but when we got to talking, plenty of them voiced the same frustrations that they were doing tracks that were not from their hearts, that just filled their pockets.

After the awards, we hit the clubs in Holland and Belgium. It was good fun, but nothing like the times with Infobeat. I laughed to myself as I remembered Irma's antics and Martin's shyness. It was all so enriching.

In between all that we were nominated for a Belgian award and played for twenty five thousand people in a sort of stadium live on TV. Even though our music really sucked, I enjoyed entertaining the crowd. I think they felt my vibe, and knew I was real, and when I received the 'Gold Mic' as my award, I took it thinking this is for all the shit I've put up with.

I didn't even want to celebrate L.A. Style's successes. I remember when Infobeat's track got on the Scandinavian charts, I was so thrilled, and I basked in that glory for sure. I could not say the same for "I'm Raving" when it became a chart topper in seventeen countries. I wasn't feeling it, but the others jumped up and down, and why wouldn't they? After all they were being duly paid.

Bibi joined me in the misery corner. I could tell that she hadn't put her heart into the project at all and like me she just did it for the money. She had a spectacular voice and dynamic stage presence, the only thing was they stopped her from doing what she did best: sing.

Bibi and I got on very well as a result of the "us against them" bond we shared. While Raymond and his boys were raving about how great L.A. Style was doing, she and I would stand to one side and discuss how frustrating it was that we were not able to tell the public the truth.

During our tour in Holland I decided that enough was enough and made sure she would sing live. I asked Fonny and he agreed, but asked me to keep it quiet and changed the tapes around so that Bibi could sing live. I told her to give it her best, and boy she sounded good live and I bet she felt great, being able to express herself and be in her element.

It was the end of 1994, and it was announced that we would tour the United States of America. We hit the United States of America, which was phenomenal. The people there were so laid back and an absolute pleasure to get to know. I had always loved the country, and this time I got to actually enjoy it.

Being in the States, in that environment with that whole "American Dream" idea, I was motivated to do my best. We played at an old Church in New York called 'The Limelight' on New Year's Eve. It was an exciting way to usher in the New Year.

I put aside my contempt for the commercial crap that was L.A. Style and focused on making my best effort to acquaint myself with the fans there. Performing live meant I had a lot more freedom than when I was in the studio, and I took advantage of that to strut my stuff, and throw in a little bit more of an original verse, the uncut version, while hitting a couple more drops at appropriate times, so that it would still flow with the rest of the track, but sound phat for the fans.

We played all over the States from festivals to shady clubs. There we were in 'rainy' Seattle, to sunny Florida in Boca Raton playing for a rich guy at his private club and then onto Sunset Boulevard at the Florentine Gardens club in California.

We played for service men and women, we were down in Texas playing Houston and Dallas, which always reminded me of my mum and the way she loved that TV series with good ole JR Ewing. We even played Corpus Christi watching the tumbleweeds like an old school Western. It was superb.

I opened the new 'Tower Records' store in Hawaii, which was an honour. Atlanta, Georgia was one of my favourite places, with the famous Fox Theater and the flashy people there.

I felt large, larger than life, the cities bustling with a rich vibrancy that I just could not explain. The people felt proud to call themselves "Americans," but like every other damned country in the world, they had their problems.

In between all this I was sending money back home so that Marsha had enough to feed my son. With Carlton I would have to wait until I got back and then personally sort that out as Jaqueline refused any contact with me.

It was 1995 and the tour was going great, better than I expected.

I decided one day to make my usual call home to check on my son.

"Hello?"

"Ja hallo, who is this?" said a man's voice on the other end.

"Pardon, who is this?" I asked.

"Oh sorry, ja this is Rogier."

"Who the fuck are you and what you answering my phone in my house for?"

The line went dead. I know my best friend's style of humour and Roger would never pull off a Dutch accent like that, but more importantly would never call himself Rogier. I was fuming; Marsha had some random guy in my apartment where my son was.

I tabled my speculations and stayed focused on the tour. The ensuing week was a very important one for us, in terms of promotion, because we were playing on MTV's 'The Grind.' I did the show, but the real highlight from that was me giving the makeup artist a little private sideshow. She was a beautiful Puerto Rican girl, and I just had to know which mascara she used, and I suppose she liked the fact that I paid her that much attention.

I loved going up to New Jersey, and sitting in a bar where I didn't even have to perform for the people to like me, because all they wanted was for me to say something in my English accent. The Puerto Rican girls, in particular, went crazy over it and found it unusual that I was a guy who was brown and had an English accent.

And after a hard night of performing, I savoured the enormously delicious and thoroughly filling real American breakfasts at Denny's. One of those could keep me going for a whole day. I went to 'All you can Eat' diners as well and saw the largest people I had ever seen, but as they say when in Rome do as the Romans do and I gorged myself on the food.

I touched base with some extraordinary people, like the singer Robin S who called me good looking 'Brownie' and just hugged me all the time. But the highlight was when I sat in BMG Arista Records' office, and a legend walked by and greeted me with a dazzling smile and terrific confidence. The legend was Whitney Houston herself. I think that's the first time in my life I would be star struck. She looked amazing, an angel and I felt lucky.

While in Atlanta, I was even offered a Junior A&R Position by the legendary producer Babyface at his record company, La Face Records. I never really followed up on that, which in hindsight was another mistake there.

I had some funny times too. While we were in Los Angeles, I was walking along Rodeo Drive, which I'm sure every tourist has done. The problem for me was that I really needed to piss and I just couldn't hold it anymore. I found the perfect spot; a palm tree right there, smack in the middle of the road, and I decided to go for it. I glanced this way and that, unzipped my jeans and relieved myself by the palm tree.

Suddenly, there was a shout from behind, saying, "Hold it right there!"

"Could you please refrain from doing that?" the police officer told me.

"I couldn't wait anymore, and really had to go," I said.

For a second, I thought that he was going to take me to the station and it would be back to the usual routine, but to my shock, his lips cracked into a smile, and he said, "Alright, but don't do it again otherwise I'll have to arrest you for disorderly conduct."

"Yeah, sorry," I said, but he just laughed.

He asked, "Where are you from?" And I told him that I was on tour with my group called L.A. Style, and that I was from England. "England, well I'm sure they wouldn't like you pissing on streets?" he said with a smile.

We even went further up, right into the neighbouring Canada and got to play on their music channel, called, "Much Music." I relished Canada and the Canadians. It was a clean and well-organized country. I saw a lot of Asians and Jamaicans and so I felt at home. They even had a Jamaican Jerk Chicken place. It was a beautiful country, and I particularly liked Vancouver and the 'Falls' was just wicked.

A memorable show I remember performing was on "Vancouver Island" where we played with different acts including 2 Unlimited. After the show, Ray, the rapper from 2 Unlimited, and I would drive through the city in his limo with bottles of champagne acting like nutters, but we certainly had an entertaining time.

I felt like I could live out there if I had the chance, but I knew I had to stick with the group. I could not ignore the fact that being involved with L.A. Style was special because we went to prodigious places and met fanciful people from all walks of life, with so many tales to tell, and so much to share.

As the tour ended, I prepared to head back to Amsterdam and I had not forgotten the phone call where this mysterious guy called Rogier had answered my home phone. I arrived unexpectedly at home.

The place was empty; she was out with my son. As I sat there contemplating what I was going to say or do I noticed a stack of photos on the coffee table. I picked them up. The first photo was a beautiful one of my son Ryan playing on the beach, but what came next wasn't beautiful.

There was photo after photo of my son, some white guy and Marsha enjoying the beach.

I was livid. I sat there and waited for her to come home. With each passing minute I grew angrier and angrier, and it wasn't because she was seeing someone else, we never really had a tight relationship, it was because my son was hanging around with somebody I didn't know and it looked like he was trying to play the dad, but my boy had a daddy: me.

She arrived home at last and once she came through the door my boy ran to me. I felt a swooping sensation of pure joy as I lifted him up and peered into his face. My face quickly formed a scowl and I confronted Marsha about the phone call and the photos.

She stammered as she said, "It's nothing, Frans, he's just a friend, nothing more."

"You are a liar, why did he panic and hang up, why are you playing happy families at the beach with this cunt."

"Look, Frans, I told you it's nothing, ask my mother she knows him too, he's a friend of my family."

"I don't care, and he's a friend of your family eh, funny how I've never heard of him or seen him before, you are a liar."

"Fuck you, Frans, I suppose you didn't do anything in the States right, don't make out something about me when nothing happened!" I stared daggers at her, and then put on a wide smile for Ryan.

It was over with Marsha. The year was 1995, the month was June and I prepared for what would be my last tour, which was scheduled to be in Japan. She eventually left and took my son and stayed with her mother.

As a father I was failing. I was unable to stop her from storming out on me, and I knew that if anything really disturbing happened, it would be all over the news and the last thing I needed was the media trying to bring me down as well.

Still, I would never give up on my sons, and from that point and for the rest of my life, I was going to make sure that I was there for them no matter what.

The transition had happened. I'd become an idiot pop star with two failed relationships behind me, but what the transition did do was make me focus even more on my sons and career.

CHAPTER 31
Japan

I stole the headlines in the States, but I could never forget those that helped me along the way, that gave me a place to stay when I had nothing, that stole rice pudding and baked beans so I could eat, or that convinced their mum to let me stay at their house and cook for me. Who fought with me in trenches when a maniac wannabe 'Gangster Rapper' assaulted us. I could never forget my brother from another mother, and that was Roger.

I had a plan to get my best mate involved. I wanted him to taste the life of being an artist and see the positive side and not what MC Hammer had portrayed. Before we headed out to Japan, and just as the tour was being finalised, I instructed Jan Maarten from Euro Pop and Dirk our so-called manager that we would need a dancer to spice up the live act for our shows, which we didn't actually need. They agreed to that, and said there was enough in the budget to pay for it.

Roger was no artist and certainly not a dancer. Still, he jumped at the opportunity to leave that dump Bradford behind and come with me on tour in Japan. He would be in costume so no one would know it was him.

Off we went, straight from Amsterdam to Tokyo. We flew business class, which was one of the perks of being an international star. Roger and I must have looked like two of the dumbest breeds on the planet because the stewardess served us sushi on the way. The problem was that neither Roger nor I had ever seen what sushi looked like before, let alone tried it, unless you count the time I ate poisonous fish from a canal in Amsterdam.

The flight attendant arrived to our seats with the meal trolley, and said, "Sir, your meal."

She placed a tray on our tables, and Roger turned to me saying, "What's that, Zid?"

I shrugged my shoulders and replied, "I dunno."

Roger bent over his dish and took a whiff of the food. "Eh, they've forgot to cook the food, thought this was the snobby business class?"

I shrugged again, "Dunno mate, best ask the stewardess."

Roger called the stewardess and politely said, "Miss I think your cooker or something is broken 'cause the food is cold and not cooked. You think you can warm it up a bit or something?"

The stewardess did her best to keep a straight face, but I know that look of disbelief when I see it, and it probably hadn't dawned on her what these two crazy guys, fresh off the street were doing in a plane, let alone business class. "Sir, this is sushi and it is supposed to be like this."

Roger said, "Oh sorry, miss, any chance we can have some English food?"

She smiled and said, "Absolutely, no problem sir, I will be back soon. We have steak is that okay?"

We both said, "Yes please!"

Later on in life I'd realize how wonderful sushi was, but at that moment in time the most exotic food I'd ever had was either Pakistani curries or Jamaican rice and peas.

We arrived in Tokyo, and I was mesmerized by the Technicolor, supersonic speed, and highly developed technology of the place. It was, as well, extraordinarily clean, cleaner than the States by far. Roger and I tried to keep up to speed with it; everything passed us by in a whir of hue. Roger, in particular, ogled at everything we passed by, this being a total contrast to what he'd seen before.

We were signed to Avex records and met with our Japanese promoter whose name still makes me laugh to this day: Sony. Roger thought he was literally the Sony Company. We arrived at the hotel, which was another part of the perks, and Sony explained that he would be taking us out around the town in an area called Roppongi. Off we went, and it was one wild area to hang out in. The women were beautiful and the people in general were polite and stylish.

The next day we went out on our own and decided to hit a record store. We went inside and as I was browsing the records Roger looked up and laughed.

"Look at that, you are on a big poster, you ugly cunt," he said laughing.

"Damn they must really like us here, Roger."

At that moment we noticed that there was a bit of a commotion by the entrance and before we knew it the whole place was packed out with screaming girls. They grabbed at my clothes, my hair and even tried to rip my gold dollar ring from my hand. We were like the Beatles, it was pandemonium and we had to get out.

We managed to get to the doors and just ran, it was like something out of a 'Benny Hill' sketch, but boy was it fun. I realised then and there that we were really big in Japan.

We toured extensively like in the States. We went everywhere, from the island of Okinawa in the south, which was warm and tropical, to Sapporo in the north, which was cold and wintery. The country was beautiful, and my only problem was travelling in the 'Bullet Train.' The ceiling was so low I used to always bang my head and have cuts in my scalp, which entertained Roger at least.

Tokyo Dome for sixty thousand screaming fans. I don't think there were too many people that could say that. It was colossal: a mammoth showpiece for a highly-energized crowd. The fans circled the stage, which rotated so we'd get to see them all.

As I stood there I realized that I would never in my life time be able to top this. I was standing on the edge of mega-superstardom. To say it was amazing would be the understatement of the year. I knew in my heart that I had to enjoy the moment because this wouldn't last a lifetime. If there was one thing I knew, I had gotten lucky.

In the hullaballoo, I even met a sweet girl called Rumiko. She said her dad was an executive at Mitsubishi. She was more infatuated with the fact that I was a pop star, but I didn't mind because either way we sure had fun.

In the end, I really was grateful that I got to travel and meet people, but I couldn't run away from the fact that this was just another phase, another part of my life's story. I had always felt that way, from the moment I discovered the devils beneath the smiles at the studio that played around with my lyrics and tracks and disregarded me completely.

I still hated the music we made and even though we were hailed the 'Godfathers of Techno' or as they called me in the States 'Mr. Styles,' it was all just a means to making money, and looking after my kids and myself, and nothing more.

Once again, doing nothing paid off. I did absolutely nothing, I didn't leave the group, even though I should have, but when I connected the dots, it just made perfect sense.

CHAPTER 32
It Ain't Over 'til It's Over

I arrived back in Holland and was determined to straighten things out with Raymond. I wanted answers as to why I wasn't being given credit for the songs I had written. A few days later, I headed straight down to Belgium to confront him.

By that time I had seen little of Wessel or Michiel. Ever since they had heard that I was on the war path, they just kept out of my way. I knew to slay the snake I would need to cut the head right off. I arrived at the studio and was informed that Raymond was busy.

"You tell Raymond I am here to see him," I said.

"He informed us that he didn't want to be disturbed as they are recording in the studio," the secretary said.

"I'm not going to ask again, get Raymond here please."

Noticing that there was no use arguing with me, she said, "Okay please wait."

She disappeared behind a door that led to the studio booths and moments later returned with Raymond.

"Yes, Frans, what can I do for you, how was Japan?" he asked.

"Tour was good, I'm sure you'll make a lot of money mate, but I'm here for something else."

He suddenly became nervous and started shifting his feet uncomfortably. "Well it's good that you came, Frans, err, I wanted to inform you that we will be dropping Bibi from the line up and I will need you to sign a new contract."

"What do you mean she's dropped and what new contract? Hang on, let's first talk about the money I am owed."

"Money you are owed? Frans, you have been paid everything you were owed. Now look here, if you are not satisfied I'm sure we can find someone else who would love to do this."

Not only was he dropping Bibi, he was also trying to get out of paying me my royalties by inadvertently saying that if I don't sign I won't get anything and I would be out. That's when my mind, body and soul hit the roof.

"You fuckin wanker, you wanna kick me out after the work I put in to make this successful?" I said while holding his nice new shirt.

"Frans, you earned money from the shows, isn't that enough?"

"And what about the lyrics I wrote? What about the productions I did? What, I don't get credit for any of that? You are just going to steal my work and not even pay me? I don't think so, you fuckin asshole." My face was mere inches from his as I stared him down.

As if it would do him any good, he tried to act tough with me and said, "What lyrics, Frans? What work? Wessel and Michiel said they did it all?"

"That's a fuckin lie and you know it. How come they couldn't do it before, and now with me on the scene they can? That's my shit and you are going to pay for it."

"Frans, Wessel is the lowest you should go to him, you know how he treats Michiel, he told me you just did vocals that's all, I swear."

"You and the rest are a bunch of criminals, I want my money now otherwise I'm not leaving and neither are you."

"Okay, okay, Frans, let me write a cheque out."

"Yeah and it better not bounce, you fuck. And you know what, asshole? I quit."

I didn't want to give him the pleasure of dropping me like he did with Bibi. My last words to Raymond were, "You'd better pay me...or else..." I walked out with my pride, and my soul.

It was September, 1995 and I was living alone and decided to go out with Bryan, not to drown my sorrows, but to contemplate my disappointment with everything that had happened. We decided to go to a familiar place, that being the Escape club.

My eyes scanned the club, and I saw the clubbers laughing and dancing, some of them had already started to get frisky, with the gropes and the pulling, but I wasn't really paying much attention to any of it.

Suddenly, I doubled back as something did catch my attention. There she was, leaning over the balcony, and damn she had the most sumptuous…you know, that I'd ever seen. It was as though she'd given me CPR or something and I was suddenly aware of my breathing and the stifling heat.

I saw that she had noticed me after she'd turned in my direction, while also scanning the place, and her eyes lingered over me for a fraction of a second longer, but I didn't have the guts to make a move.

Bryan and I stood by the dance floor, he babbling on about who knows what, while I nodded my head and tried to figure out a way to get to that girl. Eventually, I noticed another girl checking me out. I thought, she isn't as pretty as the girl leaning over the railing, and in any case I didn't think someone that pretty would be interested in me. I smiled and shuffled my feet, ready to head over to this other girl, when the stunner who had stolen my voice, mind and heart suddenly intercepted me.

She stood in front of me holding a broken cig out to me, with one hand on her hips. "You have a spare cig?"

She smiled and I felt the butterflies fluttering about in my stomach. I said, "Yeah sure." I pulled out a working cig from my pocket and handed it to her.

I knew right there and then that she was something special. It was something I'd never experienced before, because all the other girls I'd been with, they were, well just girlfriends that amounted to nothing in the end.

Later on Nadia confessed that she broke her cig on purpose as I had done nothing to talk with her. Boy she sure had moves and I did nothing, and out of nothing, I got the most beautiful girl in that club.

L.A. Style fell apart with Wessel going on to spread his bullshit and ego with another project called the 'Vengaboys' where he did very well and I suppose for his massive ego that's what he wanted. Michiel worked on aerobics tracks for Raymond who would sell them on to Japan. I guess he would never learn because he still did his thing and was used by

Wessel. Fonny went back to what he knew best and that was actually composing and producing for TV productions.

Even with all that nonsense, I still got on quite well with Fonny. I happened to know that he had earned some serious money with L.A. Style. Fonny hated Raymond, Wessel and Michiel probably more than I did, but I guess he just didn't have the balls to march up to any of them and say what he really thought. Instead, he used to tell me stories how before L.A Style, Raymond was a nobody and ever since the success, he had become arrogant and dishonest.

"That Wessel has no skills and still he thinks he knows it all," he would say to me. I couldn't agree more, and after quitting L.A. Style Fonny insisted we stay in contact; "Let's stay in touch, Frans."

Whether or not we got along alright, I wanted to give him a piece of my mind, too, "Mate, the money you earned is also my money, that fuckin Raymond, Wessel and Michiel....and even you ripped me off, you owe me, mate."

Unlike Raymond, he didn't even try to act the tough guy, but said, "Okay, okay I tell you what I've got a few projects coming up and we can work them together, and you'll make something off them."

"Okay mate, let's do that."

I travelled to and from Belgium doing all kinds of productions with Fonny. I wrote songs with him for a Belgian TV series called 'Windkracht 10' and helped him on his Disney projects, but I still never got the proper recognition.

I would have liked some recognition and even though I stupidly trusted Fonny when he said, "I can't let people know we are working together, especially Raymond, because he won't pay me what he owes me," he promised to pay me. He ended up keeping that promise, and gave me some, if not all of it.

I wanted to make a mark in the music industry and explained my frustration to Fonny and that I didn't care about Raymond and all that had happened. I said to him that I didn't need to be the centre of attention, the lead artist, all I wanted was to be behind the scenes doing the productions and A&R because they were on top of my skills as a producer.

Fonny had just signed a deal with a record label to start a new music production and suggested;

"Frans, we can't do the productions ourselves that would be too much. Let's use your production company, the one you were thinking of officiating and get some artists signed. Do you know of any other producers we can work with?"

I thought about it for a second and remembered the two guys I'd worked with on Infobeat, Cees Scholten and Arther Bronkhorst. I couldn't approach Carel as he had stopped making music and had sold his share in the Polderweg studios. It was a gamble because the other two were good, but always high on weed.

I went back to where it all started: Polderweg Studios. Hoping for a new beginning, and a chance to enrich my being again, I teamed up with an engineer called Mathew and because of my reputation as an international pop star, I was able to bullshit my way into using the studio again whenever I wanted.

I thought I could start over, that I could take full and complete control of what went on the tracks, and as a result I set up my new production and Management Company, which I called Da Klik, which was slang for family or posse, in association with Fonny.

The hard work began. We all worked every single night, putting different productions together, from hardcore techno to hip hop and from soul to R n B. I even called back my old singer, Maureen, to cover a track. I recalled Irma Derby's fate, and when another talented, down-to-Earth black singer called Edsillia Rombley came by to have a go, I gave her a try.

She would eventually represent Holland at the crappy and whacky Eurovision song contest, something that I guess meant the world to her, but which I felt was a huge waste of her natural talent. She truly was the sweetest girl and that's probably why she made it in the Dutch scene, unlike Irma who was just as good if not more talented, but her character let her down.

Apart from all the productions I was doing with Arthur, Cees, Matthew and Fonny, things just didn't seem right. I knew it would take one more throw of the dice to see if I still had it in me. I was approached by two famous Dutch producers to restart Infobeat and I made a single, which they thought was outstanding and I thought was shit.

I decided Infobeat was dead, if I couldn't do it the way it was supposed to be done then there was no point to it. The situation regarding my collaboration with Arthur, Cees and Mathew wasn't working; in fact I even caught Matthew stealing my material, so I ended it.

I kept cool with Fonny as he kept up the money I was owed for the work I did with him, but I was running out of steam and becoming more and more disenchanted about everything. I never really had anyone to confide in and let them know my real frustrations so I carried it all around and it was weighing me down.

I had become friends again with someone I had met in the early days of Infobeat, his name being Sander.

We'd hang out and grab a drink in the Leidseplein, more so because he lived in the area. It was with Sander I decided that I would lay down my last track and if it didn't work then I'd walk away. At that time Ray Slijngaard from 2 Unlimited had started his own label and was eager to work with me. I found Ray to be a breath of fresh air.

It was interesting because the people from the industry had the nastiest things to say about 2 Unlimited, but I thought the complete opposite. It just goes to show how those assholes in the entertainment industry twisted the truth and spun a web of lies that the public sometimes would actually believe.

I got on really well with Ray Slijngaard, who was the rapper from the group. He did something similar to what I had done with L.A. Style, the difference being that the people he worked with in Belgium coordinated the project properly and executed it perfectly and they seemed like straight up players, unlike the clowns I was with.

I got to working on a track called 'No Feelings,' which went under a project name entitled FOXX. The project consisted of Sander, a rapper called Rowdy, and I. It was fascinating: a white man, a breed and a black man; we looked like the United Nations or something, but the track was phat.

Ray absolutely loved it, and imminently decided that he' wanted to shoot a video for it in New York.

"Ready for Harlem?" he asked.

"Definitely," I replied.

And off to Harlem, New York, we went. I was back in the United States and boy it was a fun time. We were in the ghetto, but the people there were gems. Some of the kids I'd meet were unbelievably talented and the rappers were phenomenal. It was definitely a lot better than the ridiculous video I was featured in while working for L.A. Style. Whilst shooting the video one of the guys off the street came up to me and said it was strange to see a white guy in his area. I explained that Sander was the original 'Wigger.' He laughed and before you knew it, he was joking around with Sander.

New York was a blast. We visited the Apollo theatre and ate at a 'Soul Food' restaurant in Haarlem. The food was delicious; I just couldn't get enough of it. Sander was in Heaven; all he saw were beautiful black girls everywhere.

The unfortunate side of it was that the record didn't really hit the charts, and so it didn't really hit the ground commercially. I had to give Wessel that, he knew about the business of the record industry, like kissing Mr. Lex Harding's ass or making people believe he was the white Quincy Jones. It didn't matter to me though, it was a great video and a superb track, and I had a great time with Ray and the others doing it.

While we were out there, shooting the video in Harlem, I was introduced to Shock G, who was actually working with Tupac Shakur at the time. Tupac wasn't a world-famous artist back then; he was another talented rapper.

"It's a real pleasure to meet you, dog. I'm Shock G," he said as he sat in his SUV.

"Nice meeting you, mate."

"Wanna hear a demo of the shit I'm doing?"

"Yeah sure," I said.

What I heard next was out of this world, and even though it was just a demo, I felt that it was better than anything I had done, or was doing. There was just something about the way he expressed himself, this Tupac guy; his lyrical flow, the way he played around with words. He had his own issues growing up, but had managed to articulate it immensely on a record.

Unlike that idiot MC Hammer, this rapper Tupac had real talent and the music was exactly the kind of music I had always wanted to make. Even though I was a pop star, and I played to more than sixty thousand screaming Japanese fans and all over Europe and the US, it was nothing like what I'd heard on that demo.

There I was, in my late twenties, with a reputation, with everything any other guy would dream to have. I was grateful and proud of what I had achieved, but also accepted that there was real talent out there who deserved it more than me.

The Fat Lady had sung and I knew it was over.

CHAPTER 33
Welcome to Manila

It was 1999, and I'd spent the last three years living off my earnings from touring and royalties. I didn't have any idea where I was headed to and what I would be doing, the obscurity of uncertainty weighing down upon me like an anchor.

My relationship with Nadia was my saving Grace: it was growing on a daily basis and I was now a father to three great boys. Nadia already had a son called Rishi from a previous relationship, but in my eyes he was my own too and together with my biological boys, I was trying my best to balance things out and be the best father I could. I freely admitted to getting many things wrong, but Nadia and those boys would always be my focus.

It was sourly difficult, especially as Carlton's mother just didn't make things easy for me, but at least I got to see him, maybe not regularly, but occasional was more than what I could ask for given the circumstances.

Ryan was a strong kid, but tended to display bursts of emotion because he missed me and was very close to me. It was particularly hard for Nadia, because while she'd push me to see my two boys, I think she was careful for Rishi to not get too close to me, for the simple reason that his biological father, like my own, had abandoned him and if things didn't work out with the two of us, she would be left to pick up the pieces yet again.

I hadn't and couldn't write anything anymore, I suppose they call that writer's block. I call it losing faith and inspiration.

During that time I'd gotten friendly with one: 'Glaze.' He was also a rapper and had worked on a very successful project called 'Flip Da Script,' but like with everything else in that shitty industry, he too had been completely ripped off.

Glaze was actually from London, but had lived in New York for quite some time, and I think he was half Jamaican and half English. Whatever the mix, he was a breed.

We got on well, but Glaze was only concerned about himself. He'd pass by quite often, sometimes with his son AJ, who was a sweet kid that hardly ate, which I found weird because how else was he going to grow? Glaze's girlfriend Anna Garcia was a charmer and a great girl, and in the end, she would leave him for Hollywood. Not surprisingly, she actually made it there.

Glaze sure was crazy. He'd always have escorts and I thought he was a bit of nympho, but all in all he came across alright. He was also friends with another rapper that called himself D-Rock, but his actual name was Rene. He was in a group called '2 Brothers on the 4th Floor.'

I didn't like 'D-Rock' much, especially not the way he'd stare at Nadia as though he was in love with her or something. One day he turned up at Nadia's house with flowers, not knowing that I was there. I listened at the door as he told her how much he loved her and wanted to be with her, and when he realized I was there, he panicked and ran away.

Glaze came to me and begged me not to beat him up for trying to go behind my back and get with Nadia. I agreed because it was Glaze, and D-Rock stayed away from me. Those two were tight and they went on to present a rap show on Dutch TV called 'The Pitch,' which I found hilarious, because I saw Rene acting all street and tough, like he knew what it was like, when out there, he was not all that.

I had completely lost interest in music by then. I had loved it, it was a thrill ride playing all over the world; meeting new people and also finding the next generation of stars, but the industry was so controlled and corrupt I just couldn't stomach it.

The year seemed to be going nowhere. I found myself spending most my free time in the Leidseplein, hanging with Bryan, hitting the clubs, trying to make connections in whatever there was available.

It was the kids I was concerned for. In those days Nadia worked at her father's restaurant and other times at the local coffee shop, so she was the real bread earner. We didn't live together, but she'd always cook for me or buy me things, which showed just how terrific she was. It was also a cause for embarrassment for me and that was my cue to get my shit together.

Once, Bryan and I were hanging out at the bars in the Leidseplein, when I got acquainted with Ian. To sum him up in a nutshell, I would use the word 'flashy'. He looked like he had a lot of money and he spoke with a broad London accent. He'd buy the drinks, which suited me well because I didn't have a penny to spare for alcohol at the time.

We were discussing boxing and the great boxers from the past, when he pulled an Ian out of the hat saying, "Frans, I don't give a fuck, life is for living and that's what I'm doing: living mate, when I die that's when I will sleep." Right there in the bar, in front of all those other drinkers, he'd do a line of coke to prove himself.

The one thing Ian had was the 'Gift of the Gab;' he could talk or buy his way out of anything. So I started hanging around with him and he introduced me to his friends.

There was Lucas the breed, who also looked as though he'd lost his marbles, or maybe borrowed some of Ian's. He also looked violent, like he'd shoot you for looking at him in the wrong way. And then there was Greco, who was an Italian bloke from Canada that acted like he was Scarface. Dave looked like the Terminator and spoke with a robotic North-Americanized voice. Their forces combined, they all had one thing in common: money. Lots and lots of money.

On one occasion Bryan and I were chatting with Ian talking about the usual shit: his ex-wife, boxing and who he was trying to fuck, and somewhere in that conversation, he said, "Guy like you should be in sales, mate. You can make good money, you got the gift of the gab, like me, bruv."

"I don't know, mate, not really thought about that," I said.

"Yeah, I'm telling you, mate, I know a salesman when I see one. You know what, mate; why don't you have a chat with Dave. He's looking for people, would be sweet for you and Bryan."

Bryan intervened, "Frans, let's do this, we ain't doing anything so let's have a look and see."

"Okay, we'll check it out," I said.

"Let me call Dave…" He made the call. "Right he said swing by his office tomorrow and he'll explain it all to you."

"Okay, mate. Thanks, Ian, appreciate you looking out for me."

"Yeah no problem, bruv."

The following day, Bryan and I went to Dave's office to see what he had to show. His office was in a fairly expensive area in the centre of Amsterdam, so I guess that the first impression exceeded expectations.

We walked in and were greeted by a small Asian lady called Connie. "Hello, sir, you must be Mr. Frans and Mr. Bryan. I'm Connie from the Philippines," she said proudly.

"Hi, Connie, we have an appointment with Dave," I said.

"Yes he will be right with you. Do you want a coffee or tea?"

"No thanks."

We waited for around ten minutes, when in walked Dave looking sharp in his expensive designer suit, but walking like a stiff robot.

"Hello, guys, glad you could make it, let me explain what we do here and what I'd like you to do."

He told us about how he was selling rare American coins, which had different grades and levels like MS65 or MS64. He also explained that he had a long list of existing clients, but we would not be speaking with them yet. He told us that we would be qualifying leads and finding new clients and explained that he had a call centre in the Philippines and they would pre-qualify potential clients and we would re-qualify these leads.

"Why the Philippines?" I asked.

"Cost of hiring there is drastically lower than in Europe," he said. He also explained that there was a set pitch, which we would read to the clients and if they were interested we would pass them on to the account openers or as he put it 'Openers.'

He asked if everything was clear, and once we nodded our approval, he set us up to work.

Bryan and I spent the day calling and speaking with people from Asia, and most of the time nobody understood us. And when we asked why we

240

couldn't speak with locals or British people or North Americans, Dave told us that he wasn't licensed to speak with them.

We didn't really get anywhere, but just plodded on as Dave had mentioned that we would get a 'Draw' at the end of the week, which was an advance on future commissions and costs for travelling to the office.

I'd noticed there was somebody else in another room that sat by himself in his own office and I wanted to know what he was doing.

"Connie, what's that guy doing in the office?" I asked.

"Oh he's the 'Loader.'"

"What's a loader, Connie?"

"Well once an account is opened by the opener, it's then passed on to the loader and he loads the account. It's the best job and he makes the most money, apart from the owners. If you do this for five years, let's say two years qualifying then three years opening then maybe you can be a loader."

Five years was a stretch for me, and I marched straight to Dave's office and explained that I too could be a loader.

"Steady on, Frans, you and Bryan have only just started, in time you can move on to being an opener then maybe a loader."

"Nah mate, we need to make money now, can't wait that long, let me show you what I can do, let me open a few accounts for you."

He must have appreciated my brutal honesty and confidence and said, "I tell you what, Frans, I will give you boys a go. You seem eager and hungry and I've got a good feeling about you."

I began opening and my first impression of the job was that it was boring: listening to people bitch about their wives or work while at the same time explaining to them the benefits of buying American coins. We were like B actors with our scripts saying the same thing over and over again until someone would bite. We just got on with it and sure enough we made the sales.

Dave was impressed. We got on well with him to the point where he would tell us about how his life was a mess because he'd found out his woman had been cheating on him with a Rasta guy. He'd sit there and say,

"I give that bitch everything, money, a car and the freedom to do whatever she wants."

It got so crazy that on a few occasions he'd break down and cry while saying he had a gun and should shoot her. I'd spend most of my time listening to all this while not being on the actual phone, but he valued my listening skills and said, "Don't worry about the sales I will sort you out with some money."

The boredom became unbearable and after only a few weeks I went back to Ian and asked if there were any other openings.

Ian asked, "Well, how was it at Dave's joint?"

"Fuckin boring, mate, not really for me," I said.

"Okay. Guy like you needs something where you make some real money. Tell you what, you ever been to the Philippines?"

"Nope," I said, which was true. L.A. Style had never visited such countries as Indonesia, Malaysia and the Philippines.

"Right, I've got an opportunity for you and your friend. See there's this investment firm; you'll be speaking with in-house clients there. It's a licensed brokerage and I'll tell you what, you'll make some good money there. Also, they pay your flight ticket, and provide you with nice accommodation until you're able to get a place of your own, which should be fairly easy after a few weeks working there. It's a chance in a lifetime and I know you need the money and sitting around here doing nothing ain't gonna help."

I didn't really understand what a brokerage was, but thought if there's money there and I have to do what I have already done then no problem. I knew all about seizing whatever opportunities came my way, and I accepted saying, "Okay, bruv, will give it a go." I thought that I might as well make something of it, and that it might just be the thing for me. As they say, 'No harm in trying.'

I left Amsterdam, and the flight could not have been any worse. I flew via London then Hong Kong and on to Manila and that took forever. The plane was packed out, as I sat in between two Asian ladies and had no room to move and I didn't sleep one bit.

I was so relieved to get off that damn flight. I had travelled alone as Bryan would be joining me later, saying he had to sort things out at home.

I landed in Manila and as soon as I stepped out of the plane the heat stifled me. Once I got through the customs, it was complete chaos waiting for my luggage, which seemed not to have made it. By some miracle, it actually arrived, and as I stepped outside, there were people coming up to me asking if I needed a taxi or wanted a hotel or a woman.

I finally got what seemed like a normal taxi and told the driver where I needed to go. We drove away from the airport and through what, to me, looked like a warzone. There were homeless people everywhere, the buildings were crumbling and looked as though they would collapse with a gale. There was garbage strewn all over the place, and even though my window was up, I caught the stink from outside.

I took a look at the sheet of paper with the hotel name on it. I wondered what kind of a place it was, and I asked the driver, "This place, that we are going, is it good?"

"You will see, sir, area is okay but this not a hotel, it's a kind of service apartment," the driver replied.

The driver explained that the area we were driving through was the business district called Makati, which looked rather slick, and not half as bad as what we'd already seen.

"It says the area is called P. Burgoss, is that also a business district, sir?" I asked.

The taxi driver laughed and said, "No, sir, that is not a business area, but we are there soon."

Sure enough, we arrived at the area known as P. Burgoss. It certainly wasn't the business district. It was a dump, infested with hooker joints, junkies and the whole place looked a real seedy place. Manila had its very own red light district, just like Amsterdam and I was going to be staying in the heart of it.

"Is this the place?" I asked.

"Yes, sir, this is your hotel apartment."

I thanked the driver, paid him and walked towards the entrance of what would be my new home. I explained to the receptionist who I was and she confirmed that they had a room ready for me. She gave me the keys and said, "You go to the fifth floor, room fifteen." I thanked her and went straight to my room, opened the door and at first I thought that I could deal with it, seeing as I had slept in a coal yard as a child.

It wasn't until I needed to use the toilet, and opened the bathroom door, that the place showed its true colours. It was occupied by a family of monstrous cockroaches, some lying on their backs, their legs squirming, others wriggling about, scuttling along and disappearing inside the cracks and holes everywhere.

I went back downstairs and explained to the lady who laughed and said, "You clean them up yourself this not five-star hotel. They don't bite, sir."

The woman then said she had forgotten to give me a number I had to call once I arrived and instructed me to get a chip for my phone saying I could get one across the street. I got the chip and made the call.

On the other end was a Filipino guy called Anthony. "Okay, sir, good you arrive, I come see you now okay?"

"Okay, mate, see you soon," I said.

A couple of hours later I met with Anthony and he explained what time I was expected at work on Monday morning and that for the first few days he would take me to the office until I got my bearings right. He pulled out an envelope and handed it to me saying, "This should be enough for the weekend, so you can get settled and everything."

I accepted the envelope, thanked him, and went up to my room. There was dust everywhere, the curtains were moth-ridden and the walls were mossy, not to mention the mite and roach infestation. I was exhausted from the flight, but didn't have the stomach to undress. I couldn't even go to sleep, and so I just lay there staring at the ceiling fully clothed.

I cursed Ian, and was certainly not looking forward to seeing what else he had set up for me. My only consoling thought was that at least if I made money fast enough, I'd be able to get away from there and find a better place to stay or make a break back home.

Monday arrived, and I was out of the apartment block at seven a.m. I wandered across the road to grab a coffee and wait for my pick up. As promised, Anthony arrived at eight sharp and we headed out to the office.

The traffic was horrendous: this wasn't Japan; it was dirty and disordered. The good thing was that the people were friendly and I respected them so much because it must have been hard living in a pollution-zone like that.

We arrived at the office. It was a tall skyscraper in the middle of the business district opposite a mall called Mega Mall and another big building called San Miguel, which later I found out to be the name of the local beer. I was greeted by guards at the entrance, and after going through a security check, I was directed to the top floor.

As I came through the office doors I was instructed by the bimbo receptionist to go and wait in a separate room. After about thirty minutes a tubular, white man walked in and identified himself as head of security. Without as much as a hello he said, "You need to piss in this, make sure you're not on drugs."

"What you mean mate? I don't do drugs, never have and never will," I retorted angrily.

"Yeah whatever, mate, I don't give a fuck, you need to piss in this, get on with it!"

I stood up and clenched my fists. I could feel my ears get red and I said through gritted teeth, "I'm not pissing in your pot!"

He squared up to me and said, "You deaf, mate, I'm not asking you to do it, I'm telling you to do it."

I measured him up. "Make me, fat boy, fuck this place and you, step away, you cunt."

All of a sudden it was clear to him that to make me do something that I had refused to do would mean serious pain. "Err sounds like you got a Yorkshire accent there, mate, where you from, who do you support, mate?"

"What?" I asked.

"Who do you support, mate?"

"I'm a Leeds fan, but what's that got to do with anything?"

"Mate, me too, name's Simon, err forget the piss thing, just we've had some right cunts here, but since you are Leeds then let's leave it, mate," he said nervously.

"Yeah alright."

"Listen, mate, I run the local Leeds supporters club here so if you ever want to catch a beer and hang out..."

"Yeah ...will let you know."

A few moments later, a member of staff came up to me and said, "Hello, Frans, Ian's talked highly of you, looking forward to seeing what you can do. Please walk this way, this booth is for you. On the wall are all the rebuttals and of course the pitch, if you have any questions just ask. Good luck."

I asked him where my stool was. He just smiled and said, "No stools or chairs, you have to stand and with the air-con down to freezing it will keep you warm and actually makes you harder."

There was no training. Someone just shoved a sheet under my nose, calling it the pitch, and I just had to get on the phone and get on with it. I was not happy about the chair situation.

"Listen up I'm getting a chair and if you wanna stop me then try," I said.

"But Mr. Frans our office manager Mr. Chris will not be pleased."

"Yeah well he can tell me himself, mate," I said.

As I sat on the stool, going through the list, the manager walked in. "What do you think you're doing? Nobody's allowed a stool, get rid of it now!" He was 'Sweaty' Chris. I named him that because he always had sweat on his upper lip and he'd wipe it off with his middle finger and it caught on.

"You'd best get out of my face before I throw you out the window," I said.

It was turning out to be a disaster for a first day. I was still jet lagged, I was stressed and missing Nadia and my kids and at the same time dealing with so-called tough guys in a wacky office.

"Calm down, mate, take it easy, I was just saying, just informing you about the company's policy," he said.

"Yeah well my policy is to work in a normal way." He scurried away, leaving me incensed.

Ninety nine percent of people I called just hung up or said, "No English solly."

Opposite me was a bloke who had what sounded like a German accent, and we got to talking. "Alright, mate, how you doing?" I asked.

"Ya good, my friend, my name is Jorg, I'm from Austria."

"Nice to meet you, Jorg, so how long you been here?"

"Oh for quite some time, I can't go back to Austria, I have some problems there but it is a long story."

Jorg also introduced me to the others in the office. They were actually pleased with my boisterous entrance to office life. It seemed like fatty boy Simon our security was a real bully, but I had put him in his place. There was one man who called himself Nigel, and he really was one of the funniest people I'd met. He was from Barnsley in South Yorkshire and knew Ian well. He laughed when I told him it was Ian who had arranged the job, but I was beginning to regret coming.

"Fuckin Ian, you know mate for every person he brings in they pay him and he also gets a cut on any commissions you are paid, that's why he pained the rosy picture, mate," he said laughing.

"So in other words it was all bullshit. When I see that cunt again I'm gonna sort him out," I said.

"Don't stress it, mate, apart from some of the idiots here, it's actually okay and they are a fully licensed brokerage, well under the Philippines they are, and some here actually make big money, I mean you could have ended up at some slop place."

"What's a slop place, mate?" I asked.

"Will tell you another time, anyways it's a numbers game here and you just have to keep calling."

I was angry to learn that Ian thought he could get away with setting me up like that, and it seemed as though Sweaty Chris sympathized with me. Maybe that's why out of the blue he came to me and asked nicely if I could drop off some papers upstairs and if I needed a coffee I could grab myself one since it was my first day.

"Okay, mate, will drop this off then grab a quick coffee," I said.

"Yeah, mate, don't stress it's your first day," he said still looking nervous.

I got into the lift and went upstairs. There, the office had desks and chairs and looked like how an office should look. It also wasn't freezing cold. I was told to hand the documents to somebody called Jack. I asked the secretary and she said, "Wait I will see if he is available, sir."

As I sat there out walked a tough-looking guy, but he asked me with a friendly tone, "Hey buddy, you the new kid here right?"

I had to laugh as I didn't consider myself a kid but replied, "Yeah, mate. Name's Frans, nice to meet you."

"Nice to meet you too, bud. Name's Jack, heard you were having a bit of an eventful day so far, don't stress it, Frans, this is Asia and it's fuckin nuts here. Tell you what after work lets grab a beer and will get you up to speed on everything here."

"Yeah okay, mate, anything's better than sitting in that shit hole where I'm staying, gotta tell you I haven't got any money for drink mate," I said.

"Don't worry about that bud, meet me downstairs at the entrance at five."

"Okay will do."

Jack and I got on great after that. He was originally a 'Hells Angel biker,' had tattoos everywhere and always wore long sleeved shirts to work to cover them. I used to laugh because he sounded like John Wayne when he spoke.

I was always grateful to Jack: because of him I ate well and the time passed off a little easier. He was a loader and that meant a main guy there, the one who made good money and I mean real good money, and the openers were jealous.

I got on with the four other loaders as well. Jack had told me that the owners were two guys, one was English called Greg, who was an ex-Army officer and the other was a raving transvestite called Ding. From what I understood, Ding was powerful and worth millions, and nobody dared cross his path because he was a loose cannon.

About Greg, Jack said, "If he likes you then things will be smooth sailing but if he doesn't then let's say you will be out of here on the next flight home. Greg's an alcoholic but I get on with him fine, most here kiss his ass but not me, bud. I just do my job and that's that."

After about a week there I was starting to get used to the place. Sometimes I'd hang out with Jorg who was always stoned. Other times I was with Jack who'd tell me all about his Harley and kids and the secret of selling, which wasn't much but I'd just listen out of respect.

The second week arrived and it was the week that Bryan would land. I felt good knowing someone that I knew would be here with me. I was in the office, when all of a sudden everybody stopped working and stood at attention. Jorg whispered "Hey, bud, the boss is coming." I had to laugh to myself, it was like royalty or a general was arriving.

I whispered back to Jorg, "Is it Hitler, mate? Let's do him in and bring him to Israel." Jorg was laughing while at the same time telling me to be quiet. As the door opened, a small man walked in. He reminded me of Sergeant Pluim because of the way he walked.

"Good morning, ladies and gentlemen," he said.

They all answered at the same time: "Good morning, Mr. Greg." At that moment Greg the boss walked towards me followed by his entourage of five bodyguards.

"Morning, lad, and who may you be?" he asked.

"Morning, mate, I'm Frans, how you doing?" I said.

Everybody looked at me as if to say, don't talk to the boss like that, but I stood my ground.

"Morning, Frans, yes I'm fine, how long have you been with us?" he said smiling.

"Been here a week, mate, living over in the shit hole of P. Burgoss, but I guess once I start making money I will be alright."

"Keep at it son you will get there, come and see me later for a quick drink, I will be at TGI Friday. Jack knows where that is, just ask him, okay?" he said.

"Okay, mate, will do."

I met Jack at the usual time and we had a laugh about me meeting the boss and he said I had done the right thing by just being myself and we went off to TGI Friday' to meet with Greg.

We entered the bar and it was quite busy. I'd noticed a few spare seats at the bar and headed straight for them, while Jack went to the toilet.

As I sat down one bloke came over to me and said in a very girly English voice: "You can't sit there, that's my brother's stool."

"I don't see him around so since he's not here I'm taking it," I said.

"Wait till my brother comes then you will have to move," he said.

"Yeah whatever, Sandra, I'm sat here, let me know when your brother arrives."

Jack was at the other side of the bar talking to other people, so I ordered a beer and just sat there, occasionally being approached by the local brass, which meant hookers, and explaining to them politely that I wasn't interested.

The bar was filling up and there were people from my office in there. I didn't really mingle with them and would just greet them out of respect. And then a black guy sat a few stools down, said to me laughing, "I say chap, you northerners know about rugby right, well you play the backward version, what's it called Rugby League?"

"Yeah we play Rugby League so what, it doesn't really interest me, but it's a lot better than Rugby Union."

"Listen chap I played Rugby Union and it was a tough old sport, but with due respect, not like that barbaric version you lot play."

"Firstly, mate, who the fuck are you and why are you asking me about rugby, seems like you got a problem with northern people."

"Oh forget it," he said and then turned to one of his friends. He laughed and said audibly, "I told you those northerners are just a bunch of Neanderthals, they are not really that bright."

I stood up and walked over to him. He was a big lad, but I wasn't going to let him insult me or where I came from.

I said angrily, "What's your problem, bounty boy?" A bounty boy is what we used to call black or Asian guys who acted white. It meant brown on the outside, white on the inside.

"What did you call me?" he said as he stood up.

"You are a fuckin bounty, think you are hard with your public school pussy friends."

At that moment Jack was standing next me and said, "Any of you boys got a problem with my mate you got a problem with me."

The black guy backed off and said, "No, Jack, just having a light-hearted discussion, you know how it is north against south."

"Yeah whatever fuck off," he said and I laughed.

Jack was not only respected in the office, he was also feared and not just because he could get anyone fired, but also because he was from the streets, like me, and didn't take shit.

I walked back to my seat just as Greg walked in.

"Hello, mate, bit late aren't you?" I said grinning.

The same bloke who warned me about his brother ran up to us and said, "Greg, that's the cunt who took your seat."

"Calm down, Ian, he's a guest of mine, now leave us," said Greg.

"Who's the puff mate?" I asked.

"That's my little brother, take no notice he's had too much to drink plus he just broke up with his boyfriend," he said laughing out loud.

"Sorry, mate, didn't mean to offend your brother," I said.

"Don't worry about it, but that is my stool my name is literally on it, anyway what you having?"

I looked and he was right, but I had taken the reservation.

I sat there the whole night as Greg explained he was originally from Norwich and had been in the army, but was then married to a Filipino and that he had given up his British nationality and taken a Philippines passport. He loved it there, and I couldn't see why. He was like a king there. I asked him about any loader's positions that might be open, and he said if a position became available he would consider me.

I woke up the next day, as did the rest of the vermin in my room. It was Saturday and I would be picking Bryan up from the airport. Jack called and asked, "What you doing today, bud?"

"I'm picking Bryan up from the airport, mate," I said.

"Okay, will give you boys a lift, what time is he coming in?"

"Around nine tonight."

"Okay, will pick you up at seven."

"Thanks, mate."

I appreciated the gesture and thought Bryan at least deserved a better welcome than I had.

I spotted him wheeling a trolley, looking dumbstruck as he took in his surroundings. I smiled and shook my head as he spotted me. "Ey, bruv, welcome to Manila. This is Jack. Jack, my mate, Bryan."

"Nice to meet you, buddy," Jack said.

"Yeah, likewise. So this is…" Bryan said.

"Yep this is crazy Manila, let's go eat guys, I know a great little Belgian restaurant in the better area."

Jack drove us back to Makati Manila, to the Belgian restaurant. He explained that a couple of people from the office would be there. He mentioned Nigel, the English guy who made me laugh as he smoked cigars and looked like something from the Godfather, and Melanie, the English lady.

We arrived and we noticed there weren't many people in there, but the place looked fancy. As we sat there, I saw in the corner that there were three fat lads who were quite loud. Two of them sounded South African and the other was definitely an Aussie. They had a hoard of hookers with them and as usual they were just disrespecting them. At that moment one them noticed me looking over and said to his mate, "See over there, couple of fuckin kaffir, one's been looking at us."

I nudged Bryan and jerked my head in their direction. One of the South Africans walked over to our table and addressed us, "What are you blecks doing here and what you looking at?"

That kicked everything off and I charged the fat Aussie, got him in a headlock and slapped his bald head with some neat forehands that Roger Federer would be proud of, leaving a handprint.

I think Jack would have been pleased because it was like something out of a John Wayne movie as plates, glasses, tables and chairs were smashed all about us. The best move was seeing Bryan doing a spinning back kick on the other South African, knocking him cold out.

In all the commotion Jack never once got up to help, because he knew we didn't need it. After some time, however, he eventually stood up and said, "Guys we best get out of here before the cops come." As we headed outside the original guy that I had decked came charging to confront me again.

"Put up your dukes," he said.

I rushed at him, grabbed his head while at the same time pulling it towards mine and gave him the hardest head-butt imaginable, and then for good measure decked him properly with a double overhand right.

Jack shouted, "Get in the car, bud, they've called the cops!"

As we were about to get into the car, a Filipino came running towards me from across the street. I froze, with my hand on the car door handle, as I saw he had an Uzi in his hands. I thought he was going to pull the trigger at any moment and end it, but he came up to me and said, "What a great punch that was, sir, you a boxer."

I was relieved and said smiling, "I used to be, mate."

He walked away shaking his head saying, "Good punch."

We got in the car just as the police arrived. "Let me deal with this," Jack said. They were flashing their lights into a van, and Jack approached them. We could see he was in discussion with them, dealing with the situation, and after that familiar exchange of money, Jack got back to the car. "Apparently those guys you both bust up were pimps and are well connected. Let's get out of here."

Welcome to Manila.

CHAPTER 34
Thriller in Manila

We returned to the office the following day. The previous day's events were a secret, so naturally the whole place was buzzing about it. As they gossiped, the story reached Greg's ears, and Bryan and I were called into his office. We were accompanied by a couple of bodyguards, and didn't know what to think or expect.

"Take a seat, chaps, take a seat." He indicated two sofas on the other side of his desk. I really didn't mind getting fired because it had all been a complete waste of time anyway and I then had an excuse to go back home. Greg resumed, "I heard something about an altercation yesterday?" Bryan and I did not respond. "You got into a fight with some racists and an Aussie. Let me make this clear, lads." He put his hands together, and I braced myself for it. "I fuckin' hate racists, I got mixed kids myself. From what my guys have said you beat the living daylights out of these racist scum, Frans."

Bryan and I exchanged surprised glances and I said, "Yeah we kicked the shit out of them, Greg, they deserved it. Sorry for all the bother, mate."

"Absolutely no problem, lads, good on you! And for that, I'm giving you both a bonus at the end of the week. Great job, boys! Alright, boys, carry on as you were," Greg said.

I thought fast and replied, "What about the loader's job?"

Greg sighed and shook his head saying, "Difficult, mate. The loaders are making lots of money, so there's no positions available."

I decided not to insist, and said, "Thanks anyway, mate."

"Have a great day, boys, and congratulations once again on thrashing those beastly people."

Bryan and I left the office, this time without the usual bodyguards, and as we returned to the office floor, I got to scheming about how I could hustle and make money anyway, loader or not.

The days dragged on, and Bryan and I went to work every day. I had to count my blessings, because Greg made the arrangements to transfer us to another hotel called, "the Legend Hotel." There was nothing legendary about it, but it was a definite upgrade from the roach-infested shoddy apartment.

The problem might not have been roaches, but I nudged Bryan as I saw some creatures scuttling around outside and asked him, "Bruv, see those dogs running around?"

Bryan shook his head and said, "Nah mate, those not dogs bruv, they fuckin rats!" Sure enough he was right. I had mistaken mutated, humongous rats for dogs.

Bryan and I decided to shave our heads clean, and walk about Manila in that blazing heat. We did it because there weren't any decent barbers around. It was only a matter of time before I got sun stroke, and was down and out for some time, while I tried to recuperate.

At least my recovery was imminent, unlike never being able to. One day, as Bryan and I headed to work, I heard shouts from a building, which was undergoing construction. They used to have bamboo scaffolds, which I always thought was stupid and dangerous, and sure enough, right in front of us, two kids fell off and came to a messy, bloody end. You'd have thought that would draw a crowd or something, a couple of women would pull out their tissues and sob, or a few men would stand around with their mouths open in shock.

Nothing of the sort happened. People just went about like nothing happened and those kids lay there dead. Bryan and I exchanged shocked glances, reflecting looks of sheer disbelief and horror.

We eventually moved along and made it to work on time for another sloppy day. During our breaks, we never really hung out with anyone there. Instead, we frequented Mega Mall and I noticed that there were lots of people around.

I had heard talk about how malls were packed out with shoppers because in Asia everybody had so much money to spend. Once again, that famous veil of ignorance was lifted off me, and I saw the truth. I would guess that of all the people at the mall, only around ten percent were actually shoppers. The rest of them were poor people, who were only there because of the air conditioning.

One of our neighbours, Capola from New York, had been living in the hotel for quite some time and had been working at our place for an even longer time. I used to see him now and again with his Filipino girlfriend and just chit chat with him about New York and how I thought it was a great city when I visited back in the day.

Once I went up to his room and he told me how he was with his girlfriend for over seven years and that he reckoned another three years at Greg's office and then he could start his own business. He had plans, but like most in that office he loved his cocaine.

He asked if I wanted to come up to have a coffee, and I said, "Sure." We went to his room and his girlfriend was there. He got round to telling me that he wanted to buy his own bar and that he was saving his money for it. He walked over to this cupboard and opened it and sure enough there was a huge pile of cash.

I said to him, "Wouldn't keep your money here, mate."

He laughed and said, "Nah it's all good, bud, my girl and I are here and I lock it in my safe. I'm not putting it in the bank so Uncle Sam in the States knows I'm making money, you get me," he said, winking.

I shrugged and said, "Yeah your money, bud."

One week later there were police all over the place. It seemed Capola's girlfriend of seven years decided she wanted to get paid and arranged with her brothers to kill the man. They stabbed the poor guy forty-four times and took all his money.

Since he was from the States, it was all over the news. They caught the girlfriend and she confessed and the police actually killed one of her brothers in a shootout. I sure felt for Capola; all that shit for nothing.

Unlike Capola, Bryan and I actually got on pretty well with the locals, with whom we were generous. It started off while we were on our way to work one day, and these poor kids came running up to us asking for money.

I just could not deny those innocent younglings, particularly not when they used those pitiful eyes so effectively, such that I had no choice but to give them a little something from my pocket. Little had I known, before, that just around the corner was an agent from a crime network that collected the money from these kids, and set them off to beg for more.

As for the other locals, we had gained their trust and respect because unlike other Westerners, we respected them. We did not do drugs and weren't drunk and hanging out with hookers. They despised foreigners, and I had to admit, most people who came to Manila made a terrible job of upholding a good reputation, especially when all they did was abuse the women and children.

It was great for us, because we would walk around at night time without a problem, while any other foreigner would get shot or robbed on the spot. I really did admire the people there, and loved to spend time with them, whether it was grabbing a beer together and sharing light-hearted stories or just bumping fists while walking down the streets.

On our way to work, Bryan and I had to cross a street. There was always a gentleman there. He put a smile on my face, because he looked like the Asian version of Bryan's cousin whose name was Willgo, so we started calling him Willy, with big buck teeth.

We'd slip him twenty cents every day, which was a small price to pay for the way he'd stop the traffic for us. Like some sort of superhero, he'd just walk right onto the busy road and put up his hands for them to stop. How he didn't get run over amazes me to this day, but because of that we could get across safely.

And after work, we'd sometimes hang out at the Filling Station, which was a sort of pool hall. The locals knew us there so it alright for us to be there, and even though sometimes it got heated at the Filling Station, and somebody pulled out a gun and pointed it around, we just became immune to it.

I wanted to keep my slate clean with the locals, and that was why I didn't want to hang out with any of the others at work. One of them was a black guy called Owen, from London. He had married himself a Filipino girl and had about seven kids with her. He told me he never wanted to go back to 'Blighty,' which was slang for England.

He was running his own sales room and from the money he made he opened his own "Titty bar." It was full of half-naked women dancing and serving drinks. Naturally, the foreigners loved that place. Whenever he asked Bryan and I to go with him, we respectfully declined.

I realized that all those stereotypes about how people employed by firms like mine were mega rich, and rolling around in money, was total bullshit. Only some of the loaders, like my mate Jack and the owners were making lots of money, but it wasn't the case for everybody else.

While Jack was riding his bike to work one morning, he flew off and got himself shredded in barbed wire. It was horrific and took half the skin off his body. He was taken to the hospital, where he lay, which was a sore sight because he was tough.

I truly felt sorry that he had to spend time in the hospital there, because there was one place other than the 'Titty Bar' I would never want to be and that was a hospital in Manila. Luckily, he was making great money so he could afford a decent hospital and doctors, but if he had nothing, like the locals and Bryan and I, he would have been in real trouble.

I was sick and tired of calling up the leads and nine out of ten times, the person on the other end would be a Chinese lady saying, "Weh?" It was the most annoying thing in the world, and I didn't care what the script said about how to respond to "Weh?" I wasn't going to follow through with that.

Bryan said, "Bruv, we got to do something."

"Yeah we gotta get home, but we gotta make some coin before we go back. I got an idea," I said.

"What idea?" Bryan asked

"I'm gonna start a rumour and so are you, saying we have the hottest leads. I reckon once that's circulated we can sell them, get our tickets and get the fuck out of here."

"You think that would work?" asked Bryan.

"Yeah it will work, you know how these cunts are, we just need to pick the right ones, and you know the gossip type."

I sent Bryan off to spread the rumour. He bragged about how I had the best leads in the company and that they were worth millions. After a little over a week the actual rumour was told to me that somebody in the company had the best leads.

I waited and watched, then as I suspected Greg called Bryan and I into his office. We sat opposite him and he said, "Yes, old chaps, I've heard that you might have something interesting for me?"

I had been waiting for it and Bryan knew the script. He was not to speak and was to let me do the talking. I said, "Well, dunno mate, this is the best of the best mate, I reckon you could make millions from these leads."

"Well I'm sure we can come up with an agreement for this, mate? You're a reasonable man, right?" Greg said.

"Well, Greg, if I am gonna sell these leads it's got to be worthwhile as I wanna go home to my family, you know I miss my missus and kids, you understand that right, mate?" I said.

"Well, I'm sure we can come up with something, some sort of an agreement, what do you say, old chap? How much are you looking for here?"

I was not expecting more than a couple of grand, but I didn't say so. "Make me an offer mate."

He pulled open a drawer, shuffled around, and then pulled out a serious bundle of money and pushed it over to me. I felt Bryan get excited beside me. Greg said, "Thirty grand, I think that will suffice."

Bryan and I froze. We were lost for words, and before we could find them, Greg turned around and said, "Your silence is telling, I guess I will have to up this, but this is my final offer, fifty grand, Frans, and that's it, chaps."

We were completely flabbergasted, but I played it cool again and said, "Well, since it's you, Greg, I think we can agree on this."

I pulled the two discs out of my pocket, which contained the 'Yellow pages' lists and handed it to him and this time he was the one that looked as though he wanted to dance around his office. "Excellent! Great stuff, lads, what do you boys say to a drink?"

"No thanks, mate, I just want to get some clothes and stuff from the mall and then I best get ready to leave."

"Well, chaps, I'll see you both soon then, have a great day, and I'll have one or two for you!"

"Thanks, mate, see you soon."

I put the envelope in my pocket and Bryan and I left the office. I had a score to settle with someone and I marched straight up to Sweaty Chris, and said, "Chris, you sweaty fuck, you know what you can take your job and shove it up your ass." He stood there and had no idea how to respond to me, but I didn't wait for it and I walked straight out of his office.

As I made to exit, I said to Simon the security guard, "Fat boy, I'm going."

He replied, "Yeah, mate, stay in contact, alright?"

I didn't respond as Bryan and I walked past the armed security guards on our way to the elevator. One look from me, and they understood what had happened and they laughed as we pushed the down button and waited. The lift finally arrived, and it was the most pressing few seconds as we waited for the doors to shut.

We could barely contain our excitement, and finally when the top floor was blocked from view by the metallic doors, we began jumping up and down, holding on to one another, smiling widely. "Maybe there's a camera in the lift, keep cool," I said, and we paused looking stern for a minute, and then shrugged, laughed and resumed the dance of joy.

We went straight to the mall and went on a spree. We bought all kinds of things, like gadgets, a few clothes and sneakers.

I called Jack and he wished me luck and I wished him well.

"Hope to see you again, bud," Jack said.

"Yeah mate, take care of yourself and thanks for everything, I won't forget what you did for me."

And then we were out of the thriller in Manila.

CHAPTER 35
French Connection

A few days later I returned to Amsterdam and met up with Ian. I wanted to wring his neck for setting me up at a place that had the worst conditions.

That old sod still had his gift of the gab, and in the end I just said, "Well, it didn't work out, but it wasn't all that bad, I met some great people and everything turned out fine in the end." I thought, well I got back safe with some money, so might as well leave it at that.

It was true, it could have been much, much worse out there in the Philippines. It was the Wild West of the Far East; without any rules. There was anarchy, and violence, but I was kept safe by the locals taking a liking to me.

The year was 2000 and word had gotten out about my salesmanship. It was only a matter of time that the phone rang, and on the other end was a Canadian fellow called Ormy. I would say he was probably a little bit better than Ian, who just looked to make a quick buck by exploiting people. At least with Ormy, I knew I was dealing with a professional recruiter, because what he did was place people in jobs all over the planet.

"Frans? How are you?" he asked.

"All good," I said.

"My name's Ormy, Frans, sure you've heard about me from other guys and I've heard a lot good stuff about you. Now, are you still looking for work, because there's a job going down in Spain if you are interested, with a company called World Health?"

"What sort of position is it?" I asked.

"It's an Opener's position and it's a new up and coming company. Their leads are generated through financial magazines and their patron is

Prince Michael of Kent. If you've got someone else looking for work then let me know."

"Great, count me in and I think my mate Bryan will want a job," I said.

"Excellent, Frans, I'll email you details of where you need to go to be briefed and then how you can get to the office in Spain."

I hung up the phone with little to no expectations about the job. As it turned out, Bryan also wanted in, and so off we both went to Spain.

Malaga, to me, was not so different from Bradford, only the weather and food were better and the people spoke Spanish instead of English.

I arrived at the offices there, and met the office manager. He was another Greg and he was from the United States, or as he said, "From New York, man." He was an Italian New Yorker, and the accent could not have made that clearer. "Well, this is the job guys, there's a list of existing clients that are interested in buying pieces of the company. They've already applied for a stake in the company so it's really easy guys, anyway you know what to do."

It was a reputable company, and I really did see that Prince Michael of Kent was the patron. The job wasn't all that bad either. We were making decent money, and taking it one day at a time.

I actually ended up loving Spain. In the morning I'd get my coffee and sit on my balcony, with a wonderful view of the cute cobbled street below, and since it was close by Amsterdam I could head back home anytime I wanted to see Nadia and the kids.

After a couple of months, Bryan told me that he had to get back to Amsterdam for good as his dad was ill and he wanted to be there for his mother. "Alright, bruv, I'm going to stay a while longer," I said. He went back and I kept it up at work.

Around two weeks later, Bryan called me and told me about his new job. It was another opener's job with a Spanish telecommunications company called Spantel. They had an Investor Relations office in Amsterdam, with what he explained to me was an IPO, which stood for Initial Public Offering, and that was when a private company sold shares to the public for the first time. It was great for both he and I, because he bigged me up there, and so I was in for a chance to go back home and work.

During my time in Spain, I became great friends with a guy called Christian from Canada. We hit it off, and started hanging out together. He was extremely intelligent and also had a rough upbringing; his mother was Canadian and his abusive father was a Native Canadian.

He told me how the abuse got to her, and she eventually divorced him and got remarried to somebody better. Luckily for Chris, his step-father was a top guy and not a freak like Beacher.

We would also go to the gym together, and talk about sports. He loved his ice hockey and I, my boxing, and it was great recounting the tales of my favourite uppercut. Next to Bryan and Roger, he became one of my most trusted friends.

"Chris, Bryan has started a new job as an opener in Amsterdam for some Spanish telecommunication's company and he might have sorted me with the loaders job, if that's the case I'm heading back to the Dam, which is great because I'll be near my kids and Nadia, and on top of that he said there's great bonuses and commissions," I said to him, as we worked out in the gym one afternoon after work.

"Sounds like a sweet deal, man," Chris replied.

"Yeah, but I will push to get a place for you too, bubba." I started calling Chris bubba, or Bub. It seemed to suit him as he was like a little brother to me.

"No problem, Frans, I'm gonna hang here a bit longer with Tim, but let's keep in touch, I'm sure in the future you and I will do something together."

Tim was another Canadian who worked there, but he was totally different to Chris. He had a great up bringing with supportive parents, silver platter stuff. I had an amusing tagline for good old Tim: 'Tim: nice, but dim,' which I got from a comedy sketch on TV in England. Tim's ideal life was to watch that nauseating American TV series called 'Friends.' He wasn't a bad guy at all, just very sheltered and someone that didn't really understand what it was like coming from the streets, and I loved to pick on him.

He'd always hang out with the office manager and they'd go to play golf together. They even took me along to the golf course once, which wasn't the best of times for me because I just didn't have the patience for the game.

I loved it, but couldn't play all that well. And it wasn't just me that went to play golf with the boss and Tim. Somewhere in between, I'd managed to get an old friend from the Philippines a job with my firm, that friend being Nigel and as always, he was a real show grabber.

Chris couldn't be bothered to come along for the round, but I decided that it would be worth it for the laugh. It was therefore the four of us on the course: Nigel, Greg, Tim and I.

"Take a shot, Frans," Greg said, as we lined ourselves up at what they called the tee.

"Okay, here goes," I said.

I took a deep breath, tried to keep my eyes on the ball and swung the club. I hit that shot with tremendous force, and Greg was impressed.

"You say you've never played before, bud?" he asked.

"Nope never," I said.

"Well that was a fuckin fantastic shot, it's an easy three hundred yards."

I shrugged my shoulders and said, "Your turn, Nigel."

Nigel was completely drunk at the time and couldn't hit the ball. He started to get so frustrated that he literally started hacking away at the neat turf, grinding his teeth and muttering in a slur.

He then jumped into the golf buggy and shouted to me, "Bruv, come and drive this fucker, had enough of this crappy golf." The look on his face said he was serious, and I spared a thought for the neatly pruned grass as I jumped in the driver's seat and we sped off.

It wasn't long before Nigel fell off the buggy and passed out on the grass. Greg was furious, telling us we would get him banned and sure enough before we knew it, Nigel and I were banned from the golf club.

There were other strange characters working at the firm. One person I would never forget was a Dutchman called Frank Top. He was actually from Amsterdam and he'd sit by the phone speaking with his clients. Once he'd put the phone down, he'd start crying and saying that his life was shit and then he'd swallow so many pills, which he claimed were painkillers, that by the end of the day he'd truly be out of his mind. Pills aside, I recognized that he was probably one of the best sales guys I had ever seen and heard.

Through all the craziness and golf, I suddenly felt the need to head back to Amsterdam. Nadia and my kids were there so that's where my heart lay.

I gave my notice in at work and headed back to Amsterdam. I had a rendezvous with Bryan and he told me that the job was still mine if I wanted it. I accepted it, seeing that I still needed to keep my accounts in check.

There to greet me at Spantel's office was a little Sri Lankan guy, who introduced himself as: "Jerome Andre, from London, but call me Jerome, Frans."

Jerome continued with the introduction. "Well, this is us; we are a fully licensed investor relations office and have our license with the AFM regulatory authority here in The Netherlands. We've heard a lot of good things about you from Bryan and a few other people, and we are looking for a top-notch account loader and head of sales with their own team. We think you're the guy for the job." I asked Jerome what the benefits were and length of contract, and he explained that I "would receive a salary, commissions and commissions on the room."

"What room?" I asked.

"The sales room here in Amsterdam. As the loader you will be the number one guy and the rest of the sales guys will be under you. You will need to appoint an office manager, but there's no rush mate."

"Okay sounds great, I'm ready to start," I said.

"We love people who are hungry to make money. Our company is owned and run by three important people. One is Mr. Mohammed Kashoggi, and then there's Mr. Frank Pulumbo and Mr. Robert Carling. These people are the directors and owners and should you wish to speak with them you would have to do that through me."

He continued to explain that he was the most trusted person in the company. He was full of himself, but I swallowed the pill because the job sounded fantastic. He also explained that he was running the other investor relations office in Spain called 'Goodman Hart & Associates,' and that all transactions, whether they'd be in Spain or Amsterdam would go through another company called 'Clearing Services,' which was exactly what the name stated: it was their legal clearing company for clients buying shares and also the company that would officially distribute the share certificates.

I asked him why the transactions would go through another company and he explained that ninety-nine percent of the clients didn't want to do onshore business therefore 'Clearing Services,' would do it offshore and it was run by the third director Mr. Robert Carling.

It was also the company that was legally recognized by the regulatory authorities. It was all a bit technical to me, but I was happy because I had a contract, great salary and great commissions, which I had gotten out of doing nothing.

"If you pick the right team, mate, you can make a lot of money because whatever the other sales guys in the room get, you'll get override commission off that as well."

"What about taxes?" I asked.

"All taxes are paid, Frans, otherwise we wouldn't be able to operate here in Holland. Everything's done through our accountants. Frans, here things are done the right way, we're fully licensed, transparent, you'd have to sign a contract and everything, and it's all very official."

"Sounds fantastic and I can't wait to start, Jerome," I said.

"Excellent."

"If I may ask Jerome, why Amsterdam?" I asked.

"Well, Amsterdam is a world city, and we wanted a second office plus did you know, Frans, that this city was the original place where stocks and shares were traded so it's all very traditional, and so with that said, we set up here."

I got started at Spantel's office in Amsterdam, and we were selling the Spantel IPO, which was fairly straightforward as the account openers would call up the clients, and after they had returned an application about subscribing to the Spantel IPO, they'd offer the clients shares in the company.

Within no time, the money started rolling in. It was the beginning of the two thousands and European regulations were being relaxed, so for the telecom sector, many new dynamic companies were springing up and Spantel was one of them and a major one at that.

I was also asked to assemble my own team. In the end, I called on Ian with his gibbering talents and I also asked two blokes called Paul and Alan to come on board. The final addition to my squad was none other than my mate Bryan.

There was already somebody called Jerry there when I arrived. I had to straighten him out after initial tensions in the beginning, because he had been rejected after applying to be a loader, and so he remained an opener.

"Company's made a decision that I'm the account loader here, you got a problem with that?" I told him, after he turned up to our first meeting in a foul mood. I think I got to him in the end, and he complied.

With Spantel, the work was different. They had placed advertisements in respectable financial magazines and that meant clients would apply for shares themselves. There was no cold calling, so it was really just order-taking like a waiter would do at a restaurant.

I started to enjoy my position as a leader, and unlike that sweaty Chris in Manila, I did not abuse my position of authority and act the dictator. Ian would come into work and do his lines of cocaine while talking to clients, dressed in beach shorts. Once, he was speaking to the Chairman of the Royal Bank of Scotland, and I had a real laugh watching him in action.

He spoke with this posh accent while sipping on whisky and snorting the white powder, and after he hung up, he started laughing and shouting in his cockney accent. It was most unusual, but entertaining all the same.

The company was growing in stature. I had gotten to know that one of the directors, Mr. Mohammed Kashoggi was the nephew of the famous arms dealer Adnan Kashoggi and together with Frank Pulumbo and Robert Carling, they were doing their best to expand Spantel's scope.

I was well compensated with a bucket load of money. Not only that, it was an entirely legitimate operation, and the best part was I only had to talk to existing clients, which was not every day.

When talking to the clients, I didn't have a sales speech or anything. I just went with the flow and when I got hold of the client, I gave him or her the latest news that I received directly from Spain, and they kept asking to buy more shares. From my point of view, I really did nothing while my pockets filled up.

There was one particular client who really loved Spantel, and he bought heavily. The competition's ears began to perk up and that just happened to be Jerome, who was the loader and sub-director at Spantel's Malaga office. My office was performing better, and I wasn't doing much to make that happen, and it completely made sense that he started to hate me.

And I didn't mean to pile on his hate, but there was another client that had invested quite a few million and who had requested the possibility to meet with the board of directors. I knew that Jerome was close to the bosses and could set it up without a problem.

I got in touch with him and said, "Got this massive client that wants to do a meet and greet with the directors, can that be done, mate?"

There was a pause on the other end, and I knew he probably wanted to strangle me, but then he said, "I'll let the bosses know and get back with you."

A couple of hours later, Jerome called back. "Frans, they've agreed to a meeting, but said that they want you to be in Madrid as well."

Before I could answer, he cut the phone. I felt the corners of my mouth curl up in an evil grin.

The company secretary Miss Justine who after Jerome was the most trusted person at the company made the appointment and arrangements. I headed out to Madrid to meet with Misters Pulumbo and Kashoggi. I arrived to the Madrid-based office, and it was an old-school style boardroom fashioned like an old man's gentlemen's club with its Chesterfield couches, leather seating and mahogany touches.

I went up to the boardroom and as I walked in, I found the two power horses already present. They were extremely affluent, in their fancy suits and with that million dollar eau de cologne. It was like being in that 'Scarface' movie and seeing these riches guys sat around the table, waiting to talk business.

The client walked in and took a seat at the table. As he spoke with the directors, I just sat there and smiled and nodded. After a while the client stood up, shook the directors' hands and thanked them and even me and he ended up writing out another check for a few million dollars, which concluded negotiations.

After the client left, Mr. Frank Pulumbo addressed me and said, "You done a great job, Frans. Come to Marbella, we can celebrate there, also we can show you around Spantel's office there and show you first-hand how the company is progressing!"

I was being treated like the main guy, something Jerome wasn't please with as I said excitedly, "Okay, sounds awesome."

Out of nothing I was one of the best salesmen on the planet. Around that time, while everything was happening with Spantel, my good friend Chris was busy trying to set his own company up with other interested parties. The word had gone round that my team and I were doing a superb job and making serious money. Chris wasn't performing too badly himself, but it was no secret that I was doing far better than him.

Marbella was famous for its beaches, and I definitely enjoyed the vibes as the bosses took me out with them. They were on a whole new level of financial wealth. They had what seemed like their own club. They drove Ferraris and other fancy cars, and drank the most expensive champagne like it was water, ate whatever they wanted, whenever they wanted, without a single worry in the world.

I don't know if money gives happiness, or insane happiness, or no happiness, whatever happiness was anyway, but they sure seemed happy.

After joining them in a few glasses of champagne, I visited their offices in Malaga. They had high quality Spantel banners, which was very impressive. They had a huge team of people manning the phones and Jerome explained that they had just started a new company called Ad-Rent-a Car where a person would hire a car and the costs would be paid for by the ads, which were splashed all over the vehicle. It sounded like they were onto another winner.

I was amazed at just how much money they were making from the simplest ideas. I networked with various people involved, and I was sold on how great they and their companies were.

While I was in Madrid I'd noticed that the bosses were marginalizing Jerome. This was put further into evidence when I was sat there in that boardroom. He was instructed to wait outside, which didn't go down too well with him. So with each passing day, Jerome grew more and more jealous. I was sure he had nothing better to do than to find ways to screw me over, and sure enough he called me up one day, saying,

"Frans, we're setting up a new office in the Philippines. Big investor relations office for Asia, there's huge, big, big money involved and together with Amsterdam we'd like you to run it, so you'd commute between the two offices. This would be perfect for you, a great addition to the Amsterdam office, you interested?"

At the time I thought that I was performing brilliantly without doing much, and could do with a challenge. I said to him, "Okay."

"Great, I think you're going to be a hit there, mate, you're the guy for this."

"Okay," I said again, and put the receiver down.

In between all the sealing of deals and the business, I had driven to and from Bradford. I had become some sort of Robin Hood for my comrades back home. I gave Roger everything, from clothes to accessories. In hindsight, I felt as though I owed him one after all the times his mother took care of me when I had nothing.

They say charity begins at home and Lateef was keen on that, playing the cool brother. All of a sudden, he wanted to hang out, and "catch up" and whatever else, and sure enough, after the smiles and laughs, he got straight with me.

"Zahid, I don't know how long I can keep working in the factory with my arthritis, my hands are getting really bad and the polyps I have in my intestine are bad and the doc says I need a major operation," he said.

"Okay, Lateef, I will lend you the money and you can pay me back over time or if you ever sell the house then you can give it back to me then."

"If I sell I will pay you interest, what's yours is mine and what's mine is yours brother," Lateef said. I took pride in the fact that I could do something for a member of my family.

"No need to pay me interest, I'm your brother not a fuckin bank, Lateef."

"Thanks, brother, I will never forget this, you just like dad, you always make money and you've succeeded in whatever you have done."

"Yeah no problem," I said.

Robin Hood or not, I pulled out eighty grand for him in one go, so that he could pay it off. I even went the extra mile and bought his son a car and gave his kids lasting pocket money. .

And it wasn't just Lateef coming up to me with requests. I had Zak poking his head round the corner every now and again, having a sniff. He had gotten himself a job as a social worker, and because he had no qualifications or anything, he was at the bottom of the food chain trying to make his way up.

He did not have much money to start off with and so he, too, benefited from my funds, while I bought his kids all the newest gadgets and toys.

And even though I was driving around in a Porsche, spending big money everywhere, I kept my head out of the clouds. I still attended those Blues parties, met up with old friends, ate at the local fish and chip shop or the greasy cafe, made sure Roger was alright and brushed off those points and comments about me being some kind of superstar.

Jerome sure lured me in with the offer to go to the Philippines, and it seemed as though he was going to follow through after the company presented me with a first-class ticket on Emirates Airlines.

I got to London, and over there, at the check-in counter; an Asian ground stewardess said to me, "Sorry, sir, economy class is further on."

I laughed out loud so people would hear and I ground my teeth, as my fists curled up into balls. I brandished the ticket like a sword and shoved it under her nose, saying, "Check out my first-class ticket."

The look on her face was priceless as she replied, "Oh, err, sorry sir! Would you like some champagne?"

I thought, fuck your champagne, and made my way into the lounge to rest before the flight.

First class ticket, and an enjoyable flight, it was a recipe for a dream, but I started to have a funny feeling about it all. And sure enough, I had landed right in the middle of a military coup against President Estrada. If it was a warzone before, it was nothing compared to what it was like then, with tanks and armed military personnel marching the streets.

I got to the office in one piece, and approached the person who was setting it up there. He was a white guy from Manchester, called Brian. He told me that he had come under the impression that there was an office with people working and it was a complete set up.

The reality was there was a small office, no direction, no leads or proper promotion and he was still waiting for clearance from the regulatory authorities to run the office. He too had been lied to by Jerome and explained that he had worked at his office 'Goodman Hart' in Spain and that Jerome had spun him the same story as what he had spun me.

I had to put my rage towards Jerome aside, as I thought about getting back to Amsterdam. After less than a week of trying to get things started I admitted defeat, handed my notice to Brian, while promising to stay in contact, and got out of there.

I was being driven all the way back through Edsa, watching the tanks and soldiers patrolling through my rolled-up window. There was a manic rush at the airport as people were trying to flee, but because I had a first-class ticket, I was given priority access and got to the front of the line without a problem.

I arrived back in Amsterdam, and got the message out to Pulumbo and Kashoggi what they needed to do before that place could become operational. I will give Mr. Pulumbo this; once I was back in Amsterdam he called me and apologized and said I should focus on the Amsterdam office.

Back at work, I got another telling phone call. "Frans, Bob Carling here, we're looking for somebody to go to Paris. We have a client there, Madam Lacroix, and she would like to receive share certificates in person and since you did a great job in Madrid we thought it would be a great experience for you. Also it will be an all-expenses paid weekend trip. I think Mr. Pulumbo and Mr. Kashoggi wanted to do something nice for you after the shambles of the Philippines."

It was not every day a regular breed would get to go to Paris without pulling a penny out his pocket. "Yeah, sounds good," I said.

"Excellent, take your office manager with you as your assistant."

I would have asked Bryan to go with me, but he was making a lot of money and had bought himself a jeep. He spent most of his time at the beach getting stoned and getting busy with a variety of girls, and so I ruled him out for this trip. "Yeah, okay," I said again.

I had made Alan the office manager. He was from Manchester, a family man and wasn't wild like Ian or my mate Bryan. He was loyal and like me enjoyed working and earning his money.

I called Alan in and briefed him. "What do you think about going to Paris for the weekend, mate?" I asked.

"Why what's happening?"

"There's a client there and the bosses have asked for me and you to present her share certificates on behalf of the company."

"Okay, mate, understood, when do we leave?" Alan said smiling.

I wanted to make it an enjoyable trip, and so I dialled Chris up next. At the time, he was also in Amsterdam, busy with his own line of work, but I was certain that he would not refuse the trip with me. "Bruv, you me, Alan my manager, Paris, this weekend. What do you think? All expenses paid."

"Wow Frans, that really sounds grand, yeah I'd love to go."

"Okay, cool, I'll see you later on to discuss, but we leave this Friday."

Friday arrived and we got on the plane, destination Charles De Gaulle airport in Paris. The meeting was to be held at the Ritz Hotel, the very same hotel that Princess Diana exited the night she died. It was Mr. Khoshoggi's cousin's place. He too was famous and went by the name of Mohammed Al Fayed.

We arrived in Paris and it was altogether different from the last time when I didn't have a dime on me and was trying to sign up for the Foreign legion. One thing that hadn't changed was how stylish and chic the city was. We all jumped into a taxi and told the driver to take us to the Ritz Hotel.

We entered the hotel and it was a sight to behold. If anything spelt mega-star luxury, it was that. The lobby was over-the-top lavish with a rich décor, complete with crystal chandeliers that just oozed with confidence and glamour.

"Damn Chris, some people live large," I said to Chris, while he and Alan ogled at the surroundings.

"Fuckin 'ell," Alan said in his broad northern accent.

"Yep this is phat," Chris added.

"Yeah, hang on I'm going for a piss," I said.

"Wait, I'll go with you, need it too," Chris said.

The concierge directed us to the men's room, down the hallway. If what we had already seen was over-the-top, the taps definitely completed the whole enchilada. They were gold plated or solid gold, either way they were expensive looking. "Chris, reckon we could chip these off and take them back with us to sell?" I laughed with Chris.

"Imagine that, here's your twenty-four carat gold...tap!" we laughed some more.

"Alright, alright, let's be cool now, I need to go and give this lady her share certificates with Alan and then we can go sightseeing and have a laugh."

We wandered into the restaurant, where Alan had already gotten a table at the far end. Something felt weird as we walked into the place. The atmosphere was somewhat artificial, like I was a part of a stage play or something, but I couldn't quite put my finger on what really was wrong. All I knew was that it made the hair on the back of my neck stand up.

I shrugged it off and ordered the salad. It the most expensive salad I had ever had.

Alan was placing his order saying, "Fuckin 'ell, mate, bit expensive here."

"Yeah I know just get the salad," I joked, and Alan laughed.

"That must be her, damn," Chris said, nodding his head in the direction of the entrance.

She was like something out of a sixties film, with big shades on and a classic look. She was with a weedy looking guy, who was also appropriately groomed for the occasion. "Monsieur Merkx?" she said, approaching our table. "Madame Lacroix."

"Nice to meet you, this is our colleague Alan Ingham, and this is a friend of ours, Christian," I said.

"Enchante," Madam Lacroix said in her snotty voice with a French accent.

"So we've got here your share certificates that you wanted in person, and on behalf of Spantel we are very pleased and honoured to have you as a shareholder. Alan has your share and should you have any questions then please feel free to contact Mr. Jerome Andre or myself. Please accept my business card," I said.

Alan passed over the shares to the gentleman and I waited expectantly, secretly hoping to get out of there as I wanted to check out the rest of the city.

The gentleman cleared his throat, glanced over his shoulder and then leaned in to talk to me in a low voice, "Monsieur Merkx, I have here with me, in this briefcase, five hundred thousand dollars. My mother would like to buy more today."

I was taken aback. "Excuse me, no I cannot accept that, you have to go through the normal channels."

"Well, we would like to buy more shares from the company today, so, I'm sure you understand?"

He had discretely pushed the suitcase closer to me, but I pushed it straight back at him. "I am not allowed to take money, as I said, sir, it has to go through the company."

The gentleman was adamant, "But we want to buy shares."

"I understand, but you will have to go through the normal channels. What I can do is inform the company that you wish to buy more. But I can't accept money from you and your mother. I'm director of sales not a board director, so I can't sanction or accept this."

Madam Lacroix interjected, "Mais, Monsieur Merkx, we really would like to buy more, we've been thinking about it for a while now."

"Well, that's great and everything, but I'm going to ask you to do it officially."

Madam Lacroix sat there with those big shades and no expression on her face. After some time, she finally said, "Merci" and she left, taking the envelope with the share certificates.

"What was that all about?" Chris asked.

"I don't know but she can sort it out with Jerome," I said. "Anyway, want to check out Paris?"

"Yeah let's get out of here," said Chris.

We proceeded to the exit. I was still admiring the hotel and walked outside when I felt my insides twist. I was pushed up against the outside wall and felt something very hard pressed in the back of my head. "You are under arrest."

"Hey! What the f-" I couldn't even finish my sentence.

"Shut up, hands behind your back!" I couldn't see anything, but I knew the smell of a rotten copper in the morning. Out of the corner of my eye, I spotted Chris sprawled on the floor, also cuffed with a gun to his face.

Before I knew it I was thrown into the back of a car, hands cuffed behind my back.

"What the hell is going on?" I yelled.

One of the coppers responded, "Shut up, you know what's going on. Swindle!"

"What the fuck are you talking about?" I asked.

"Shut up! You know, you know that this is swindle!"

We sped through Paris, past red lights and then all of a sudden we were going underground, round and round deeper into who knew where.

CHAPTER 36
Le Santé

The beautiful streets that I had always admired had now become the Devil's playground. And the Devil himself was staring daggers at me, his eyes narrowed, and his first-class Gendarmes attitude intact.

"What the fuck is going on?" I demanded.

"You know what's going on, this is swindle!" the copper said in a thick Parisian accent.

"Swindle of what, what you talking about?" I asked again.

"Shut up, you know, you know, this is swindle!"

There was no use arguing, so I peered out the window and saw that we were driving underground, going deeper and deeper, round and round. It seemed as though we were entering an ever-lasting labyrinth like in Alice in Wonderland, snaking its way to the bottom of a bottomless pit. There was no light, no life, save a few scurrying rats that we would hardly see as we drove on and on into the unknown.

I thought it would never end, but the car finally slowed down and then stopped. We had arrived to a base located underground. I was certain that most Parisians had never heard of this place, as they naively munched their croissants and troubles away. Maybe it was the old place where the resistance hung out back in World war two.

I was marched into the building, and it seemed like I was being brought through the back door as I didn't see many police about. I was escorted to the day cells further down, and the copper threw me into one. Chris was brought in too and thrown into the cell next to me. There was no wall separating us only the bars so we could at least talk. And then Alan arrived and he was tossed into the cell next to Chris.

As soon as the copper left, Alan turned in my direction, whimpering, his face chalk white, and said, "What the fuck is going on, Frans?"

"Dunno mate, have no idea," I said. I tried to think about what it was all about. There we were, at a restaurant in the fancy Ritz hotel, having taken a piss in a golden urinal, when suddenly there were two shady characters, Madam Lacroix and her son. We gave them their share certificates, the son offered us money and we refused the briefcase. Why then, why were we here? Were we being followed? Watched?

Chris shouted over to me, "This is bullshit, they can't just hold us like this."

At that moment a police man came in and asked, "You want to eat?"

"When will we see our lawyer?" I asked.

He ignored me and asked again, "You want to eat yes or no?"

"When are we going to see a lawyer?" I asked again, adamant to get an answer from him.

"I ask you, are you hungry? Or you will not eat?"

"Yes I want to eat," I said.

"We get McDonalds for you, okay?" The copper said.

There were a few moments of silence as we all expected slop or maybe 'Duff and custard,' but not McDonalds.

"Yes, McDonalds will be fine," I said.

The overpriced salad in the Ritz had done nothing to brighten my day, and my belly was aching with hunger.

A burger, fries and cola later, a bald copper approached our cell. He unlocked the door, pointed at me, and gestured for me to follow him. We wound up in an investigation room, and he closed the door behind him. "Your name?" he asked.

"Frans Merkx," I said.

"You know why you are here?" he asked.

"No idea, sir," I said.

"You are here because you tried to swindle Madam Lacroix with shares from your company."

"I didn't do that, where are you getting this information from?"

"Frans, listen. The client says you tried to swindle her. Let me tell you something, that restaurant you were meeting her was full of undercover police."

"Well then, they all would see that I didn't do anything!" I said.

"She said she felt like she was being swindled by your company."

"Well, I'm not the company, I don't decide anything, that's the company, and I have nothing to do with anything that goes on when it comes to decision making."

"Well on your business card it says 'Director of Sales.'"

"So what, I am the Director of Sales but I'm not the director of the fuckin company mate."

"Watch your language, Monsieur Merkx."

"But I just work at the company, I am from Amsterdam and that's where our offices are."

"Okay but why did you come to Paris, you cannot hand over securities like share certificates to people, this is against the law here in France."

"Sir, I didn't know that, we were just told by the company directors to hand over the certificates to Madame Lacroix as she had insisted that she receive them personally from the company. And I agreed, because firstly it's my boss telling me this and secondly it was an all-expenses paid trip to Paris, so I thought why not: a free holiday and then we can hang out for a couple of days and have a laugh here."

"I see."

"I'm just a worker doing his job, nothing more, did you see her son trying to pass me money? I told him I wasn't allowed to take anything, if I was the swindler that you and your colleagues keep screaming at me then I would have taken the money, don't you think so?" I said desperately to the copper.

"Yes, yes I understand. Calm down."

"When can we get out of here we've done nothing wrong?"

I loathed ninety nine point nine percent of coppers, but right there, in that room, I looked into this coppers eyes and saw, incredibly, that he was starting to believe me. He even nodded his approval, and gave me a small smile.

"Why don't you check who I am, my background, I got nothing to hide," I said.

"It is Friday, I won't be able to check anything today, but I will let you know. I am going to get your friend in now." He left the room, closing the door behind him and leaving me wondering what that was all about.

A moment later, the copper returned, accompanied by a teary Alan. "You are?"

"Alan," he stammered, his lips quivering and his eyes swollen and red.

"You know why you are here?"

"No, sir!" Alan said looking confused.

"You tried to swindle Madam Lacroix, did you not?"

"No, no of course not, we were just doing our job, which was to drop off the certificates!"

"Madam Lacroix issued a statement to the police that your company tried to swindle her."

"Sir, no I'm...I just work for the company I, I don't know about anything else!"

The cop exchanged half a glance with me. I guess in a way we both felt bad for Alan, who looked as though he was going to shit himself. "What about the other guy?"

"He's just my friend," I said, "he just came along to have a laugh in Paris, he doesn't work for Spantel."

The copper nodded his head as he took a moment to think. "I see. Well in that case, we will let your friend go, but not the both of you."

"Why not?" I demanded.

"We have to investigate this further and see if what you are saying is right. Also the commandant will not allow it until we check things properly."

The copper stood up and took Alan back to the cell, turning to tell me that he would be back. There I was, in my Hugo Boss designer suit, on the receiving end of a false accusation, somewhere underground in the middle of God knows where, without the faintest idea what was going to happen to me. At least at Armley and the Borstal it was clear, but out here, everything was up in the air.

Finally, the copper came back to break the tension, which was starting to eat me up. "Well, your friend Mr. Christian is going to take the train back home."

"Okay, so what now?" I asked.

"Listen to me, Frans. My boss the commandant believes you and your company did swindle Madame Lacroix, I do not believe that plus if it did happen then I believe we must speak with your boss and not you. I would like to see you go home because I believe we are wasting our time but that is not going to happen. So what we must do is make a statement to clear this up and then I will speak with our Commissioner."

The warning bells began to ring, and there was one thought on my mind: never, ever, trust a copper. And yet, I had a feeling in my gut, a strange, crazy, insane, feeling that this bald eagle, could be trusted. To be honest I was so confused that even if 'Inspector Clouseau' had asked me to sign my own death warrant I would have agreed.

We went through everything and he wrote the statement in French. When I asked him how I could sign something that I could not understand, he assured me that the way he was writing it would mean we'd have a better chance of getting out.

It was risky what I did and in hindsight really stupid, but sometimes the brain doesn't connect and you go with the feeling.

"Sign here," the copper indicated.

"What's going to happen now?" I asked, scribbling my signature at the end of the agreement.

"Now I will make a similar statement and your colleague Alan must also sign, then I will present to the Commissioner and hopefully you can go home."

Alan was brought in and sat down next to me and I explained what would happen and what he had to do.

"Mate, just sign and do what he says."

"Can you trust this copper, Frans?" Alan asked nervously.

"What choice do we have, mate? I mean we've done fuck all wrong, we just work for those cunts and if there is something wrong then it is the company that has to answer not us."

"Okay, mate if you think we should do it I'm with you," Alan said.

The copper proceeded to explain the statement and instructed Alan where to sign and what to say.

Once we were done the cop explained that the Commissioner would be passing by to speak with us and she would decide whether we stayed in jail or went home. We were escorted back to the cell to await our fate. After an hour or so I was brought back to the interview room and there I was interrogated by the Commissioner.

She was a nasty looking woman with the ugliest and meanest face. "Why were you handing over securities, you know it was swindle, admit it!" she screamed.

"No, we were just doing our job, we were not trying to swindle anyone, we've done nothing wrong!" I shouted back.

"I do not believe you and you look like a liar to me!"

"I swear we just work for the company; we've done nothing wrong!"

"You are a liar, Monsieur Merkx, you will not be going home, I want to make sure that your story is true," the Commissioner said.

She stormed out of the room leaving me sat there with the bald copper.

"So we have to stay here the whole weekend?" I asked.

"No, no you cannot stay here, you will have to go to prison and stay there," said the cop.

"Why do we have to go to prison? We've done nothing wrong, this is fucked up. I've told you everything and done everything you've asked, I didn't even ask for a lawyer, you know we are innocent!"

"I understand, Frans, but the Commissioner is my boss so I cannot do anything, if what you say checks out then you will go home soon."

"What is soon, a few days, a few weeks, what!"

"I don't know, we shall see, that would be for my boss or an investigating Judge to decide."

He went on to tell me that the prison I was going to was the worst prison in France and one of the worst in the world. It was an unholy sanctum for the ghouls and degenerates of the society and was apparently very dangerous. The name she was given was Le Santé. I could actually see in his face that he was concerned for us, but he couldn't do anything.

"Listen, Frans, while you are there keep yourself to yourself and tell your friend Alan to do the same. I think you will be okay as most of the prisoners are either African, Arab or Asian but not many white people in there," said the cop.

Now I was getting worried, but I stayed calm and just thought I gotta use all my street shit to survive this nightmare.

"Frans, do you drink?" the copper asked.

"Sometimes."

"Here take a drink of this, you will need it," he said as he offered what looked like a bottle of cola, but once I took a swig it tasted like there was a good measure of rum in it.

Alan came in was told about Le Santé as well. With fear all over his face, he said nothing.

He took the bottle too, had a sip, and then drank a decent measure of the mix. I couldn't imagine how bad it was for him, when I myself was trying not to think about what was to come. It could be years until I got out. For all I knew, this was a set up.

The copper tried his best to keep us calm. He spoke about his football team Lyon and I spoke about Leeds United, but nothing could smooth over the fact that we were going to be thrown in a hellhole.

Like in the deep south of the United States, we were chained up, legs and arms, and marched off to a van, destination Le Santé prison.

We arrived at the place and were frog marched to the waiting area, which was full. It finally struck me why the copper was worried for Alan. There was not a single other white person there.

We found ourselves seats at the far left of the waiting area, and the clock ticked down the seconds to our impending fate. Each minute that past was as painful as the last. I just wanted to know what was going to happen, I didn't care about being in prison. In the end, Alan was called. I shouted at him to keep his chin up, he looked back and just nodded. I sat there and waited and waited while they called the other prisoners.

It was now just a round-bellied man and I left. He asked me, "Salam brother, where are you from?"

I said, "From England, mate."

"No brother where is your father from?" he asked

"Oh, my dad's from Pakistan, brother."

"That's good brother, I'm from Pakistan, good thing you are Muslim brother otherwise problems here, your friend is fucked they hate white people here." He proceeded to ask, "What you here for?"

"They arrested me for swindle mate."

"Wow that's big. I hope you get out, this place is hell on Earth." They called him and he shook my hand and left.

It must have been the early hours of the morning when they finally called me and I was brought to my cell.

I saw that there was a bunk bed for two and a separate bed, which was occupied by what looked like a lunatic, as he gave me an unblinking stare with his mad eyes popping slightly.

The bottom bunk was also taken, and that meant I was getting top bunk, which would be horrendous because they kept the lights on the whole night and that meant I would not catch an ounce of sleep. The cell was hot and stank of my cellmates' sweat and piss, the plumbing gurgled somewhere in the walls, the remains of a dead animal lay in a corner along with a few large dead cockroaches.

I made to climb up, when the lad in the bottom bunk did something that I did not expect. He stood up and gestured for me to take his bunk, saying in broken English, "Salam brother, you sleep here, better for you."

The man on the single bed looked delirious; his head was lolling about and he clutched his stomach moaning, "Mangé! Mangé!" over and over.

Not long after, a Parisian screw was doing the rounds. He stopped at our cell, and addressed me, "Your food?" It was a white plastic plate with a piece of moulded cheese and stale bread, and an apple.

"Mangé! Mangé!" he was getting louder and more insistent, and it struck me that he must be hungry.

I looked down at my plate and then up at him, and said, "Mangé?"

"Oui Mangé!" he nodded.

"Fuck off, this is my food," I said.

He scowled at me, but I knew the way inside. Once you show weakness they run over you, so I stood up and made clear if he wanted trouble he'd get it. He backed off still mumbling, 'Mangé, mangé.'

I sank into the mattress of my bunk, the springs groaning noisily, and just lay there. I had three cigarettes in my top pocket, and I pulled one out, but realized I didn't have a light.

The lad in the top bunk looked Arab, and I thought he must have one. I stood back up and hissed up at him. "Bruv, you got a light?"

"What?" the Arab brother sat up and looked down at me.

"Light?" I showed him the cigarette and he climbed down from the bunk. "Thanks, bruv…" All of a sudden the starved lunatic from the single bed moved forwards and tried to grab my cigarette. I shoved him right against the wall. He put his hands up in surrender, and I didn't pursue with a pummelling.

The Arab lad told me about how he and his mates had been running a credit card fraud operation and that they had all been caught. He looked upset and said that he was going to be stuck in prison for a while.

As though to pile on the misery, and rub salt in the wounds, he emphasized that this prison was the worst and that he was not from Paris, but from a place called Marseille.

He asked me what I was in for and I explained what had happened. He said to me, "You better pray, brother, that you go home. You, like me are not white, so here we are shit to these guards."

I did not sleep one bit the entire night. The anxiety kept me up like a drug, and I sat leaning up against the wall, waiting in earnest for what they were going to do to me the following day.

Dawn arrived, and the inmates were roused from their sleep by the screws. I was taken to a day cell, where they would process me. Alan was there already, and he looked absolutely distraught, like they'd stolen his soul and left with him nothing but bare skin and bones. "Frans, Frans..."

"How you holding up, Alan?" I asked.

One of the African men around approached me and asked "Is the white guy with you, brother?"

"Yes, bro, he's with me so leave him alone," I told him.

"Okay, brother, if he's with you then okay."

After a while we were sent back to the cells, and there I sat once again, my heart racing. I closed my eyes, but did not dare to rest.

It went on for the whole weekend. It was so excruciatingly hot in there; just as bad if not worse as the Philippines. There was no shower or anything else. I'd been sweating so much my shirt reeked.

Finally, after the weekend, they brought me back to the day cell. Alan was there, and after three days in prison, he was a total wreck. He hardly even recognized me as I stalked in.

A screw entered, and started yelling, "Merkx! Merkx!" I stood up, and so did Alan, but the screw yelled again, "You! You stay there, you!" They manhandled me and got me back in chains.

They were massive, at least a foot taller than me, two flanking my sides as I shuffled along. We emerged above ground to what seemed like the court house. "Wait here!" The prison guards said, and I sat outside the prosecutor's office.

After some time, they brought Alan upstairs, and he took a seat beside me. I whispered to him, "Whatever happens let me do the talking, keep your mouth shut, mate."

"Okay, Frans," he said nervously.

The door opened, and the prosecutor, and to my surprise a black brother, called us into the office.

We were instructed to sit as the guards stood behind us. The prosecutor looked at us with suspicion and said, "You have been suspected of swindle. French law is very clear, let me tell you how French law is. French law is concrete. You are guilty until you are proven innocent," he said while slamming his hands down on the desk.

"We are innocent," I said.

"What do you have to say about what happened?"

Alan looked on the verge of replying, but I gave him a stern look and he gulped.

"We have nothing to say because we've done nothing, sir, we just work for the company, that's it," I said.

"Under French law we can keep you here for up to fifteen months, but if you have nothing to say then you can tell that to the investigating Judge," the prosecutor said angrily.

Alan looked like he was ready to cry, but I held firm and just looked at the prosecutor in a way that he knew I wouldn't speak. We were taken out again and made to wait outside.

As we waited, another gentleman with a funny hat came up to us and said, "I am your translator for when you see the judge. Now," he gestured at the many doors on either side of the corridor. "There are many judges; the one you don't want is Judge Schoonwater, because she is very strict and can keep you here for a long time. But let us see." Eventually, we were called forward and instructed that Judge Schoonwater would be seeing us.

I was escorted to the office and as the door opened I walked in with the prison guards and was told to stand and wait. There in front of me was Judge Schoonwater. She looked like a twisted gargoyle, with not an ounce of emotion on her face.

Even I felt a shiver run up my spine as she glowered at me, her reading glasses perched at the end of her nose. She stared down at papers on her desk. "Sit down, Monsieur Merkx, I am reading your statement." I wanted to object, to be defiant, but before I could say anything, she said, "Silence. You will answer oui, when I say something, or non, correct?"

"Yes your honour, correct," I said. There were two guards either side of me, looking straight ahead.

The judge pointed at me and said, "It says here that you are a witness?"

I did not hesitate and said, "Oui."

"And you agree that should the investigation be necessary, you will come back to testify?" she asked

"Oui, but what-"

"Only oui, or non!"

"Oui."

The judge shuffled the papers without looking at me. I could not tell if she had anything else to add, if she was going to clear me or sentence me to years and years. And then she said, "You are free to go."

I was actually taken aback and asked, "Excuse me?"

"I said, for the last time, unless you want to stay, you are free to go. Now go." I turned to the guard who flashed me a little grin.

"Merci, your honour!" I said.

"Okay, go, go but do not tell your friend," she replied. I got out of the chair, and exited the chamber.

Alan was sitting waiting, "What happened mate?"

I looked at my feet, which were free from the chains and hoped he'd understand.

"Come with us!" two guards grabbed him up and shoved him into the chamber I had just left. Another set of guards led me to the reception area to collect my belongings, which included forty-four different credit cards. We then headed out of the prison, and I stood outside in the pouring rain, but I did not care. Nothing, absolutely nothing, could dampen my spirits at that moment.

I waited, allowing myself to get soaked, the rain washing me with relief. I closed my eyes and felt the cool water soothing my lids. It was a sensation that I would never, ever forget. After an eternity, the door opened again, and out walked Alan. Some of the colour had returned to his face, which reflected immense relief as well.

We immediately got into a taxi, and headed straight for Charles De Gaulle Airport. Our previous tickets were no good anymore, and we went up to the ticketing desk. "Need two tickets for the next flight to Amsterdam," I said.

"I'm afraid there are no more seats available in the economy class, sir, but we do have two in business?" the lady said.

"Give me two one way business class tickets," I said. And we were on our way back home to Amsterdam.

CHAPTER 37
Rollercoaster from down to up

As we headed back to Amsterdam, I came to the realization that everything was wrong with Spantel. I had always had my suspicions about Jerome, but now I saw that it wasn't just him. It was also the board of Directors, the legitimacy, the execution, all of it. I had simply done what I was told, and I was arrested and incarcerated.

What truly shocked me was the manner in which I was arrested and taken down to an unknown labyrinth, deep underground. I had gotten lucky and I owed that bald copper for being so honest and straight. He truly was one in seven billion.

I wanted answers from Spantel. After taking a couple of days to recuperate, I called Jerome and told him what had happened in Paris. The fidgety ferret stammered as he solemnly swore that the company had done nothing wrong and it was beyond him why Alan, Chris and I would be cuffed at gun point outside the Ritz hotel, while following his orders.

He did mention that he would speak with the boss Mr. Frank Pulumbo and get back to me, which wasn't necessary because for me it was over at Spantel. It wasn't just because of the arrest or the questionable legitimacy, but the mere fact that the company was not there for Alan nor I, and I had long since made up my mind to start looking elsewhere, only now I was given a harder push towards doing that.

I was devastated, and not only because I was doing a magnificent job for the company, but I'd also put together a truly world class Sales team. They were loyal, committed to the cause and determined to go the distance. It was a combination of these super powers that raked in millions for Spantel, allowing the company to grow exponentially.

A lot of people gave me the plaudits for the company's rise, labelling me a fantastic salesman, but I didn't see it that way. The truth of the matter was that we had clients calling in themselves and asking my team for shares in the company. All I did was take the orders like a glorified waiter, but what I had gathered from the acclamations was that reputation precedes all and I did not have a problem attracting a new job.

Upon hearing news of my return, Chris got straight in touch with me. We actually had a good laugh about what had happened in Paris, and he told me that he was working on something big. Apparently, he had been approached by Canadian investment bankers called Jupiter Capital in Vancouver.

It really is a small world after all, and I laughed out loud because the person that had arranged it all was none other than Tim 'nice but dim' Mason, my former colleague in Spain. Chris explained that he had done some work for them and that they had heard of Spantel's success and were eager to work with the two of us.

According to Chris, they wanted to open up their own investor relations company doing IPOs and Private Placements. At first I told Chris that Canada was too far away, and he in turn said that they wanted the office in Amsterdam.

Chis said, "We have to get a team together, but first they want to meet and discuss and iron out the details face to face." He went onto explain that he had already met them on numerous occasions and told them all about me, and they thought that it would be good to have someone with a Dutch passport on the team.

"Sounds phat, Bub, I've had enough of Spantel so fuck them let's get this done," I said.

We arranged a telephone conference call. I spoke with Bill McKay and his partner Randy Larson, and I had to say for big business guys they sure sounded like little kids.

"We can't wait to meet you, Frans, this is going to be fantastic," Bill said giggling.

"Well, Bill, as soon as you are ready I'm here in Amsterdam ready to start. I'd like to get the conditions sorted with you regarding my work contract," I said.

"No problem, Frans. We are coming in next week Monday and we will meet for a chat with you and Chris. Hopefully we can agree everything."

Monday arrived with the subtle scent of a mélange of hope and opportunity. Chris telephoned me, and said, "Yo Frans, meet you for coffee and then we'll drive up to the Hilton to meet these guys."

"Okay. See you in twenty minutes, Bub," I said.

I picked him up and we discussed what we would want in terms of the contract, salary, commissions and bonuses. Once we felt somewhat ready, we made our way to the Hilton hotel to meet with Bill and Randy. I hadn't told Spantel or Jerome what my plans were. I wanted to test the waters first, see if it would be something special, and then I would quit.

We made our way to the Hilton hotel's restaurant. I felt slightly on edge, and peeked over my shoulder more often than usual, however unlike Paris, the place was empty, which was a relief for me. Chris called Bill, who was in his room, to inform him we had arrived.

After about twenty minutes, in walked Bill and Randy. The former looked like an authentic redneck, with his fancy suit and ruddy face. Randy, on the other hand, reminded me a lot of Carel from back in the days of Infobeat, with that frail timidity that would belie the intelligence with which he was empowered to run such a company.

I was on the receiving end of some truly melodramatic praise, "...heard a lot of good things about you, Frans, we know the kind of money you raised for that company Spantel and we believe you can do even better with us. We'd like to offer you a position as Director of Sales. We can offer you a steady salary with excellent bonuses and commissions. On top of that, we are aware that to get your calibre of sales, we would need to offer you and Chris something special. Therefore, Randy and I are prepared to offer you a signing on bonus as well."

"If I may ask, Bill, how much would the signing on bonus be and are there any conditions attached? I asked.

"Well, Frans, we are in this for the long run and we'd expect the same from you guys, however we also know to keep guys like you we'd have to offer something special."

"Okay I'm listening."

"Yes so as I was saying we'd like to offer you and Chris tax free, three hundred and seventy five thousand dollars. You would need to sign up and commit to five years, but we think that would be a reasonable offer to you guys."

I looked at Chris and could see he too was stunned and excited like me, but before I could answer Bill continued. "We will pay you a monthly salary of eight thousand guilders and you will be entitled to commissions on the deals you make personally and you will both receive an override commission on the sales office."

It was an offer that I simply could not refuse, and I was blown away. I had been offered the dream job; security, in Amsterdam, and I would be my own boss. I could not muster the words to express what I was feeling, which was a blessing in disguise because the expression on my face seemed to probe Bill to saying, "Frans, I guess you have many offers, so I tell you what my last offer is. Five hundred thousand dollars tax free as a signing on bonus with all the other things I said. I can't do any better than that, what do you say?" he said while extending his hand.

I composed myself, even though inside, I was jittery with enthrallment. I maintained a firm voice and said, "I'd say Bill we have ourselves a deal." I reached out and shook his and afterwards Randy's hand with Chris following suit.

"That is absolutely splendid, Frans, I believe our clients and all of us are going to make a shit load of money, I think we could be like Warren Buffet," Bill said.

Bill explained that they had hired a world-class law and accountancy firm called Baker and McKenzie and had informed the Canadian Embassy about their plans to open an office in Amsterdam. It looked as though they were the real deal. Bill explained like with Spantel we would need a team and that the law firm would arrange Chris's work permit and the license for the investment office.

He then proceeded to ask me where he thought we should have the office. I explained the best place is in the Keizersgracht, which is in the centre and part of what they call the 'Golden Triangle.' To have an office there is the epitome of prestige. Bill agreed and said he would have everything arranged and in the meantime we could recruit the salesmen.

The company would be called Bentley Financial Services BV and Bill said that he loved the elegance of a Bentley car and felt that would be a fantastic name for the company.

"Why not Jupiter Capitol Amsterdam Bill?" I asked.

Bill replied, "Well for Canadian tax reasons we'd like to start a separate entity and then have a joint venture with Bentley and Jupiter."

"Okay, you the boss, Bill, but sounds all good to me."

"If you have any issues then please speak with our lawyers," Bill said confidently.

"Okay." Negotiations were concluded, and I left with a spring in my step.

After a few weeks Bill informed me where the offices would be and asked if Chris and I could go and get some office equipment, like desks, chairs and stationary. I checked the offices out, and I was left impressed and thrilled to be starting my new venture there.

Chris and I then decided to pay the lawyers at Baker and Mackenzie a visit, and they told us that they were busy with the licensing and Chris's work permit and would answer enquiries in due time.

The next thing that needed to be done was to assemble a dynamic sales team. I first approached Bryan, and he agreed immediately. I then reached out to Alan. I thought after all we had gone through in Paris, the least I could do was offer him a job, and he did not resent accepting.

I didn't want Ian as he was too wild. I thought back to Frank Top in Spain, but he'd made clear he didn't want to leave the country, so I had to think of someone else.

I had been in contact with my good friend from my time in the studios, Sander. I was telling him about how we were starting a new investor relations office and he asked me, "Any chance there's a job for me, Frans? I'm working part-time as a dentist, but I'm not making much and it would be nice to make some extra money."

"Sure, Sander, would love to have you on board, learn from Bryan and you will be fine," I said.

"Thanks, Frans."

I also had another friend that I knew was desperately looking for a job. His name was Joost, and I felt as though I could trust him. I called him up, "Hey, bro, how's things?"

"Yeah I'm okay, but need a job, getting loads of shit from my girlfriend," Joost said.

"Well looks like I've called you at the right time, bro. Fancy working for a new company?"

"Doing what mate?"

"Sales bro, if you are interested I can put your name forward."

"Is there a salary mate?"

"Sure is and commission."

"Wow, yes I'm in. Thanks, Frans, I owe you."

Joost was the last piece in the puzzle and I submitted the list to Bill. He agreed at once, and informed me that he would have his best friend Graham Douglas as the Managing Director. He also assigned the head of the finance department to Graham's daughter, Jenna Douglas. Finally, he said that he would send Tim 'nice, but dim,' Mason as the lead generator to coordinate Jupiter's clients and the new leads.

From the ashes, Bentley had risen.

CHAPTER 38
Falling

I fancied myself a Porsche, but I had to admit, Bentley met my fancy just as well. Like the vehicle, working at her namesake was smooth and easy. My job was to speak with clients that were brought in by our sales team. Sometimes I'd simply walk into the office, see if there was anyone I needed to speak with, and then leave again.

The difference between company and car, was that the former was decked with problems aplenty that restricted the cruise control and limited our scope. This was mostly down to the fact that the leads that Jupiter was producing were nonsensical.

I warned Bill and Randy about the shortcomings, but they repeatedly reassured us that things would pick up and that we were merely experiencing a blip.

I had finally gotten to know the Managing Director, Graham Douglas and his daughter Janna. I had no problems getting along with them, and I got close enough to Graham to explain to him that our team would need proper, qualified leads to get the deals in.

Just like Bill had done, Graham assured me that things would pick up, but unlike the boss in Canada, he acknowledged that both Bill and Randy were a little naïve when it came to running the business, and he affirmed that he would work on it.

As far as I was concerned, everything seemed to be moving in the right direction, and I promptly decided that it was time to do something to secure my family's future by giving them a proper home.

"Bub, I think I'm gonna buy a house, would be great for me and Nadia and the kids, you know a bit of security," I said to Chris.

"Yeah good idea, got anything in mind?"

"Seen something in a place called the Arke, it's right next to Osdorp in the west of Amsterdam. The house I want needs a lot of work but has great potential."

"Go for it, Frans!"

"Yeah, but I would need a mortgage, you think Bill would sign as a guarantor or something or change the contract so that's it's an open contract instead of five years?" I asked.

"Yeah I don't see a problem. Ask him, Frans. I mean once the deals are rolling in he might even lend you the full amount for the house," Chris said laughing.

"Okay, I'm gonna ask him and see what he says."

I rang Bill up and told him about what I was planning on doing, and I requested him to change the contract to an open one. I assured him that I wanted to stay long term with his company, and commit fully to the cause. Not only was he fine with it, but also thrilled that I was considering securing my future with his company. I soon had everything I needed to arrange a mortgage.

I proceeded with the bank, and they agreed to finance the mortgage for me. I visited the house and met with the owner, who informed me that he wanted four hundred thousand euros. I wheeled and dealt and got the price remarkably down. He simply could not refuse, and voila: I had my own mansion. I invested over two hundred thousand of my own Euros into the house: it was a palace and was worth close to a million Euros.

I was tremendously proud of myself, and as I cruised along the highway in my luxury car, the light breeze tickling my face and heads turning everywhere, I felt liberated from my inhibitions and exonerated from the bonds of conventions. I felt larger than life, and I knew I was a class act, cut from a different deck. I was able to look after my own family and I even made my closest friends a part of my success.

I travelled back to Bradford on a regular basis and my friends back home were impressed and proud of me. I think the biggest compliment was seeing the Rudeboys and them saying to me, "Zid, you haven't changed one bit, respect bruv, even with all your success." That felt so damn good.

I continued to serve as Roger's lead sponsor. Word about my charity spread, and Zak, too, was a beneficiary. I gave him whatever I could so he could have the finer things in life. I saw that he was eager to follow in my footsteps, but a businessman he was not, just an estranged Casanova. He was my brother and I felt the need to help him.

One day he came to me and asked, "Zid, I'd like to do the work you are doing, can you arrange a job for me? I've got four weeks' holiday from my work and I'd like to use that time and see if I can do this sales work."

"You sure because it ain't easy and I'm not the easiest person to learn from, Zak," I replied.

"Yeah I'm sure, give me a chance. I'll try my hardest."

"Okay, you can start Monday."

A week after starting, Zak gave up. He didn't have the patience or that pizzazz for sales and admitted defeat. I suppose that's what separated me from my brothers and sisters; I never gave up and always believed I was destined for greater things.

And even my own mother, who hadn't been the best mother in the world, needed money. She sent me a copy of her bank statement showing she was in the red zone. I duly delivered, but with an ulterior motive. Apart from the fact that she was my mother, I also wanted to show her what I'd made of myself, and the two combined were enough reason for me to provide her with financial assistance aplenty.

At that time Chris had said he wanted to bring in more sales people to complete the sales team and especially a proper office manager. He knew someone in Canada called Mike Swift who was experienced and had run numerous successful sales offices.

"I think we should get Bill to hire this guy, he's got a good rep, Frans."

"Okay, Chris, but is he working now or is he looking for a job?" I asked.

"Ormy says he's looking for a job. We also probably need a few more guys then this team will be complete, Frans."

"Okay, you sort out some new guys, Bub," I told Chris.

During that week Bryan approached me and informed there was someone looking for work and his name was Robert van der Braak.

"Who is he Bryan?" I asked.

"He's the brother in law to that guy we know in Spain, Frank Top," said Bryan.

"Oh Frank Top, fantastic account opener, but hooked on medication, yeah I remember him. Okay, tell him to come down so we can have a chat with him."

I met with Robert and he explained that he wasn't an opener or any kind of sales person, but he had worked at various companies as security. He would always make sure that the company information stayed confidential and data would not be taken from them. He would also make sure the office would run smoothly.

Chris and I had let our guard down and were enjoying our lucrative salaries. I was either on holiday in Miami with Nadia, or taking my kids everywhere and buying them everything or hanging out in Bradford. I took Nadia on a private cruise around the Caribbean and we had our very own butler. We ate at the best restaurants, I bought her everything and I guess we both took the good life for granted. I was getting lost in the success.

To have Robert in the office was another excuse for Chris and I to be even lazier and even more of a reason not to be there. I informed Bill and he actually thought it a good idea. Then again, anything I came up with was a good idea to him.

Robert became a kind of deputy office manager slash security man and Chris informed me that Mike Swift had accepted the offer to come to Amsterdam to take up the position as Office Manager.

I remember the day he arrived. He flew in from Canada with his Thai girlfriend and it was clear why he was out of work. He was a full on alcoholic and his wife was the kind of person who wanted the best in life and demanded it. Both Chris and I realized it was a mistake asking him to come, but because we had become so nonchalant in our attitude we didn't do anything about it.

I'd noticed that Bryan had gotten close to Robert. There was something odd about that Robert, but I couldn't put my finger on it. Perhaps I was just too lazy to bother.

Bryan and Robert didn't like Mike Swift and made that clear by always telling me that he was a waste of space.

"Look, Frans, the guy has been in the office twice since he arrived. I hope he comes today because I got a surprise for him," Bryan said.

"What you gonna do, B?" I asked.

"You'll see but will make you laugh."

Later that morning Mike arrived stinking of alcohol. He had brought his wife with him, which wasn't the deal and I explained the next time he would have to come to work alone. He didn't like it, but had no choice. Bryan then approached him and asked if he would like a coffee.

"Yes please, Bryan, thanks," Mike said.

"No problem, bud. Will go and get coffees with Robert now, anyone else want one?" Bryan asked.

A few others indicated that they also wanted one, and Bryan went off with Robert, returning moments later with the orders. Bryan handed the coffee to Mike and then turned to me and said in Dutch, "I need to see you quickly in your office."

We proceeded to my office where Bryan said to Chris and I that he and Robert had dropped crushed laxatives in Mike's coffee. Bryan also said, "Yeah we also jerked off into the coffee so when he drinks that fucker he's gonna be drinking mine and Robert's sperm, bruv," he said, laughing hysterically. I didn't laugh and just thought the place was becoming a joke.

We went back into the office where everyone was, and Mike said, "Coffee tastes a bit sandy and salty, got better coffee in Canada, Bryan."

I must admit that did make me smile and Bryan then said, "Mike we are going to the beach at Zandvoort after work for a drink, wanna come?"

"Yes sure, Bryan, would be great."

The next day, Bryan gave me a very graphic report about how he had bought Mike plenty of drinks and gotten him rather drunk. He went on to talk about how Mike had shit his pants, and had left a trail of brown bloody shit all along the beach. Once again, I was not impressed and thought it was terribly childish.

There were no deals going through at all; no decent leads and the costs were mounting week in week out for the running of the office and the salaries being paid out. Even though the Managing Director, Graham was humble and good-natured, he admitted that he was worried that Bill might pull the plug and close the company.

I turned a blind eye on everything and went back to Bradford to hang out with Roger. Chris went on holiday and things went from bad to worse. I wasn't a director nor did I have the means to produce quality leads; those two tasks were down to Bill and Randy, but they weren't performing, which in turn meant our sales team wasn't performing. It was one broken chord after the other.

When I returned I decided to try again and I called Bill on numerous occasions, but he was as stubborn as a mule and insisted the leads that we were sent were great. It was not true. Those working under me told me the numbers never worked or the name didn't fit the number or they just didn't exist anymore.

People like Sander, Alan and Bryan were using different names because they were worried the leads weren't qualified and didn't want to be cold calling potential clients, but Chris and I procrastinated and did not interject.

It was all getting too much for me, and luckily I had an excuse to go back to Bradford; I was having laser surgery on my eyes in Leeds. While I was recuperating at Roger's apartment, I received a call.

"Hey, Frans, it's Bryan."

"Yeah what's up, B?" I asked.

"Yeah well me and Robert decided to sort out Mike Swift once and for all."

"Bryan what the fuck, you are supposed to be working not doing crazy shit like this," I said.

"Yeah well Robert felt he was disrespecting things, so we tied him up at his apartment and we both beat the shit out of him."

I froze with the receiver to my ear, and my heart in my throat. "Are you crazy, what the fuck are you doing?"

"Calm down, Frans, he's okay. We let him go and just gave him a beating."

"For what Bryan? Are you insane, who the fuck does that Robert think he is?"

"Well he knows his shit, Frans. You know he legally carries a gun, so he's the real deal, Frans. He reckons Mike was stealing from the office. Anyway the cunt deserved it."

"Bryan this is too much. Fuck Robert and his bullshit, I'm coming back soon, he can't do this..."

I hung up and got to my feet and decided there and then to go straight back to Amsterdam. Bryan and Robert were totally out of control.

On top of that I had a huge mortgage to pay off and I had to keep making money to sustain my lifestyle, so I could carry on looking after my family. The stress was getting to me as it dawned on me that because I had been doing nothing, the company was heading down the drain.

I arrived back and by that time Graham told me that Bill would officially be pulling the plug on the whole company. Additionally, Graham had informed me that Bill and Randy were discussing how they could get the signing on bonus back from Chris and me. If I lost my job, I would have to use the signing on bonus to pay the mortgage until I sold the house and also use that to live off.

What was worse was that Robert was asking questions and wanting to know things about the running of the company and who Bill was and what kind of deals were being offered. He claimed he knew nothing about sales, but then wanted to know everything? He was terrorizing people and had even kidnapped Mike and tortured him while I was away. It was a red alert crisis, and Chris and I had to intervene.

"Robert, we need to speak with you now mate," I said to Robert.

"Yes, what's the problem?" asked Robert.

"Firstly Robert, Bryan told us what you and him did."

"Yeah I can explain," Robert said.

"Nothing to explain, that's some sick, fucked up shit, on top of that the company is a complete failure and Bill the boss in Canada has informed Graham that he's closing the company down."

"So what does that mean?"

"Simple mate, you are fired. One because of what you did and secondly because there's no more work."

"That's fucked up, Frans, we should sort out that Graham and Bill," Robert insisted.

"No, Robert, it's over so just leave it."

Nobody was happy about being laid off. After speaking with the entire staff, we all decided to seek legal help regarding our jobs. We were all desperate and worried. Personally I stood to lose everything that I had built up, but looking back I could only share the blame with Chris, Bill, Graham and Randy. We just had no idea how to run a sales company.

We all arrived at the lawyer's office and the lawyer confirmed that Bill wouldn't be able to just fire us, but the biggest problem would be bringing a case against him because he was in Canada and we were in Amsterdam. Until we could figure that out, there wasn't anything we could do.

The company finally closed down, and by doing nothing I was back to square one.

CHAPTER 39
Crashing

The grape had indeed turned sour, such that by October of 2001, I no longer had my job at Bentley. There was no promise of a better tomorrow, as the year 2002 got underway. I had to somehow bring the signing on bonus back into Holland to use for my mortgage and everyday living costs.

I needed a top accountant, to assist and advise me how to retrieve my sizeable treasure abroad. I knew of a firm not too far away from Nadia's home in the South of Amsterdam.

The firm was called Perfect Partners and was run by a gentleman called Charles van Veen. Once all the pleasantries were exchanged, I proceeded to explain my predicament regarding the mortgage and costs of living. I paid a retainer fee of ten thousand Euros so that Charles could handle my taxes and always be on call.

"Frans, the tax has already been paid, I reckon you wouldn't have to pay tax again," Charles said to me, a few days after I'd put down the sum of money. By that time, I was completely paranoid, and rightfully so. I wanted to make one hundred percent sure that I would have no issues with the tax authorities.

I confessed my concern to Charles, who insisted the tax was paid and I would in fact be paying for taxes again, but I was persistent and he therefore suggested I start my own company, pay the signing on bonus, which was sat offshore in Gibraltar, to my Dutch company and then pay income and any other relevant taxes. That way everything would be done correctly.

I would later be advised that I had actually paid tax for nothing, because the money was signed and agreed with tax being paid by Bill. Those grass snake Dutch Authorities had somehow managed to rip me off.

I followed through with Charles' suggestion, and decided to call my company Ramone Marketing and Consultancy BV. It was named after my second son Ryan; whose middle name is Ramone. A huge weight was lifted from my shoulders, as I started to pay myself a consultancy fee to Ramone and from that money, my Dutch taxes were paid.

In the meantime, I was on the lookout for any sales work available. Spantel had closed their office in Amsterdam down, but the weasel Jerome could still be found on my contact list.

I consulted him, and he informed me that his office Goodman Hart and Associates were still doing IPO for Spantel, as they were preparing for the company to go public. He told me that he was also doing the new IPO for Ad-Rent-A-Car, so he was making a lot of money and he made that clear by saying, "You should never have left us, Frans."

The struggle carried me through all the way to the summer, which arrived in heat waves and cloudless, blue skies. There were still clouds a plenty obscuring my path ahead, however. I hadn't told Nadia or anybody else about my situation, so everybody actually thought I was doing great things, and was making a steady climb each passing day.

I had to have at least one confidant to vent to, and release the frustrations upon, and I maintained my strong bond with my Consigliore Chris. We spoke regularly, and had a hearty laugh about how people put huge amounts of money in IPOs. Some would make lots of money, whereas others did not, and I thought to myself, selling shares was like a casino.

As for my other good friend, Bryan, he had finally come back down to Earth and admitted he had lost the plot while at Bentley. He regretted many things, especially then since his girlfriend was pregnant. That would be Bryan's first child, and he was panicking because there were no funds availed to him, and he, too, sought to act fast.

"Frans, I'm so fucked, Michelle is pregnant. She thinks I got money, but I haven't got shit. I blew everything that I made, and now I gotta make money mate. The baby is due in October, I'm so fucked," Bryan said, the fear blaring in his wide eyes.

"Let's see what happens and hopefully something comes up. In the meantime I'm gonna lend you some money, but we'll have to pick it up in cash at the bank in Gibraltar," I offered.

"Yeah whatever, just say when, can you lend me about eight thousand mate, can you do that? Will give it back once I recover it."

I pitied and assured him, "Yeah no problem, need to ask Chris and Sander to come along. A person is only allowed to carry up to ten thousand cash and Sander said he would carry ten for me."

"Okay. Thanks, Frans, I won't forget this," Bryan replied, breathing a long sigh of relief.

I went on to ask Chris, and he agreed, as he too was low on money and needed some cash. Neither of us had handled our finances particularly well. Chris had bought a mansion in Canada, but he, too, couldn't keep up with the mortgages. The lingering burdens piled on the misery, and the stress forged tensions all through my body.

We set off to Gibraltar. All the demises in my life were at the core of my focus, and once again something did not feel right when we arrived to Gibraltar. I ignored the feeling. I did nothing, nothing but pick up my money in cash from the bank.

Once I arrived back in Amsterdam I gave something to Sander for helping me out and lent Bryan his eight thousand Euros. He told me that he had been in touch with Jerome in Spain and was trying to figure out a way to work without going to Spain, because he was insistent upon staying in Amsterdam, what with his baby due and everything.

Unable to maintain my own finances, I had moved back to my apartment and the house was up for sale and with all the renovations I had done I was expecting to sell at a profit.

As I flicked through my thoughts, the phone rang and it was Bryan.

"Frans, listen I need to see you, can I come round?" I agreed and we met at the coffee shop 'Goed Goed' at the corner of my street. "I have spoken to Jerome and he has agreed to let me speak with some existing clients and try and load them. Problem is I've got nowhere to call them from. Michelle won't let me work from her house and I've got no phone line at my house. Would it be okay to call from your place? I mean like this I'll be able to make money and pay you back quicker."

"I don't know, B, what you selling?" I asked.

"I'm selling the Ad-Rent-A-Car IPO to the existing clients who bought Spantel, so they are all existing clients and no cold calling. Will be easy for me plus if I need any help Jerome said to call him, but he will fax all info over. Come on, mate, let me do this, at least I can make some money and get out of the crap," Bryan said.

I said, "Okay, B, if I can help, I will."

Although I did not personally want to work for Jerome, I could help Bryan out every now and again, and maybe get my money back from him. Bryan also explained to me that he would be using a different name as the clients had been speaking to other account openers and loaders and as Jerome put it, "Clients won't know the difference and feel comfortable speaking with people they've spoken with before." Bryan loved the idea as it would mean he could earn money in cash from Jerome and nobody would have to know.

It was the 27th of August, 2002 and Bryan was at my apartment, calling existing clients. He had asked me to help him out with a few clients to which I agreed as these were clients that had already bought Spantel through Jerome's company Goodman Hart & Associates.

I was in the middle of dialling a client's number, when I was interrupted by a loud and sudden bang at the front door. I hardly had time to react, as I was tackled and pinned to the floor. There was screaming, thick Dutch accents and the unmistakable sound of safeties been flicked off on several nine millimetre pistols.

Nothing was said as I was held on the floor of my apartment.

I was cuffed and cast out of my apartment. The whole street beyond had been roped off, and there were blinking lights on copper vans and cars everywhere. They tossed me into the backseat of a car. "What the fuck is going on?" The copper replied in Dutch, and at that moment, I was so angry and confused I could not even understand him. I had reverted to my mother tongue.

"You know boy," the copper said in broken English, after he received no response from me.

"I don't know, what is going on!" I demanded.

"You are fucked…"

We drove through Amsterdam, past the Leidseplein and onto what was known by everyone as the Police Headquarters. I was brought to the back of the station and thrown into a cell. I could still feel the phone in my hand, back in my apartment. I nearly laughed to myself, and I would have laughed out loud had the confusion not kept me pegged to my anxiety.

It was the same old routine, as I was brought yet again to the investigation room. The coppers in there were trying to play the old-fashioned good cop, bad cop routine. "You want a cigarette?" he asked offering me a stick. I shook my head and he put it back into the packet. "What do you have to tell us, Mr. Merkx?"

"Nothing, I want my lawyer," I said.

"Nothing, what about this ripping people off, taking money from them, printing share certificates, that kind of stuff?"

"I haven't done that; I want to see a lawyer I've got nothing to say to you fucking pigs."

"Shut up, you black shit, you rip off people."

"I've got nothing to say," I said.

The copper nodded his head and gave me a twisted smirk. "I see you don't want to talk, maybe your girlfriend will talk to us, yes. She is in the next room."

"What?"

"That's right, we have arrested her also and unless you talk to us, we will charge her too."

"You low life! I've done nothing wrong and neither has she and you know it."

"Now you are shutting up, you piece of shit, this is our place and you do what we say!" he yelled at me in his broken English.

I felt panic surge through my heart. Nadia was in there too.

"You listen, Merkx, she is part of your criminal organization and money laundering. You black shit, we are going to fuck you up for six years, you will get six years, Merkx, you hear? Now, you both going away for a long time, or just talk with us and we can let her go."

"I want to see a lawyer, you can't do this," I said, adamant.

"There is no lawyer on duty so best you talk with us first boy," he said.

I needed to see Nadia. "I will not talk. I want to see her then I will talk to you, I want to see her now."

"No games, Merkx, after you have seen her we talk, okay?"

"Okay, okay," I said.

"Okay." The copper disappeared and reappeared a moment later with a teary Nadia.

I had never before seen her in such a state. Her eyes were puffy, her mascara smudged. Her lips and whole body trembled. She was hysterical, and her eyes were unfocused. "F... Frans..."

I grabbed her up in my arms and held her tight. She cried loudly into my chest, and I stroked her hair and whispered, "Don't worry about it, it's going to be alright. Don't say shit to them, okay? Listen, Nadia, don't say a thing, you're going to be fine."

The copper came forward and escorted her out of the room by the arms. A minute later her crying was extinguished as the door shut behind her.

"Right, Merkx, what have you got to say?" the copper asked again.

"Listen before I speak I want to see Bryan, I am gonna inform him that I will talk."

"No need, Merkx," he said.

"No I insist, otherwise I'm not talking. He needs to know that I will be speaking with you and understand that he too must speak," I said.

The cop or as I always referred to them 'Pig' agreed to my demands. "Okay wait, Merkx, but after this you talk to us."

A few minutes later Bryan walked in. He didn't look the tough guy and it was clear that he had been crying. I grabbed a hold of him and shook him and just said out loud, "Don't tell these bastards anything, B, they will set us up."

"What?" Bryan Said.

"Don't say anything to them, B!" I screamed at him.

"Okay!"

Before I knew it, the pig was dragging Bryan away and was furious with me.

"Think you are clever, Merkx, eh?" he said.

"I've got nothing to say to you asshole," I said.

"Okay so you've got nothing to say, if that's the case we are gonna charge Nadia."

They took me away back to the cell and in the words of the copper "give you time to decide Merkx." I lay there on that cold concrete bench and the only thing on my mind was Nadia and the shame I had brought her.

The cell door opened and there stood two coppers. They grabbed me by the arms and led me back to the interview room. We sat in silence and then the pig said, "The prosecutor is on his way here and will explain to you, Merkx, the shit you are in."

The Deputy Prosecutor walked in. He looked like a person who would commit serious sex acts. He could pass for an SS officer. He looked me up and down and he said, "My name is Mr. Woudman and I am the prosecutor in this case. I will insist we hold you here and I will be looking for a minimum of six years in prison for fraud, theft, serious assault, attempted kidnapping and running a criminal organization." He looked at me again, with great disdain, and then walked out.

I screamed after him, "This is fuckin bullshit, it's lies! You bastards are setting me up!"

"Right then, Merkx, time to talk and sign statements. Better you go to jail than your girlfriend eh?" the pig said, smirking.

"Okay, okay, just show me what I have to sign."

I knew that whatever they wrote in Dutch could not stand up in a court of law. I was still English; I wasn't from there and they couldn't do anything to me. That's all I had in my head.

I was sat there completely horrified and once again tortured by the unknown. I wasn't thinking straight, and flashing images of Nadia and my kids kept crossing my mind. My thoughts were disjointed and nothing made sense.

During the days in the cell, I was blinded to everything, and the mirage of a happy home and family hovered across me, teasing me with shimmers. I wondered if it had anything to do with what happened in Paris, or what Bryan and Robert had done.

I was brought in again and I was asked about something I did know about, but I wasn't a 'grass,' which meant I didn't snitch or tell on anyone, especially a friend.

"Merkx, we know Bryan kidnapped a man and beat him badly, want to tell us more about this?" the copper asked.

"I don't know anything!" I screamed.

"Yeah we'll see," the pig said laughing.

"You know you will go away for a long time, better you talk now," the other pig said.

"I have rights, you cunts, where is my lawyer?" I screamed desperately.

"You have no rights here, Merkx!" the pig screamed back and then threw me back in the cell.

As I wandered outside for what they called the fresh air walk, I trod in circles. I looked around and the people who were there were bank robbers and other such criminals dressed in blue jumpsuits, so they could do DNA tests on them. I was most definitely out of place there.

I hadn't slept for three whole days. I sat upright on the most uncomfortable mattress imaginable. I felt a huge tug in my heart as I thought about Nadia and the kids. It must have been her first time in a police cell like that. I didn't even know if she was still locked up or if they had let her out.

I was sure she would never have dreamt about it, but she had been arrested from her workplace, humiliated in front of her colleagues, and with no idea, no clue as to what she had done.

I would have liked to have consulted with Bryan, but the only thing I could say to him, like I did with Alan in Paris was to keep his mouth shut.

Finally, the investigating judge summoned me. I hoped that I would make a swift exit so I could find a way to restore order to the mayhem. "Mr. Merkx-"

"Yes, your honour," I said to the judge.

She spoke in Dutch and in English, but it fell on deaf ears. The confusion had reached break-point and I was in no frame of mind to speak in a language other than English. There was no need for a translator for what she said next, however, and I was blown away.

"Thirty days."

"For what, why, what the fuck is going on, I am innocent!" I said as they dragged me away...

CHAPTER 40
Thirty Days and More

My head throbbed as I teased my brain for a clue. Thirty days. Had Bryan gotten that too? Had Nadia gotten home alright? Had Rishi been picked up from school? How would I contact my other sons Carlton and Ryan?

It was the middle of summer, the thirty-first of August was the date, and the sweltering heat drained me of all energy. I sat limp, my head hung as sweat streamed down the sides of my face. It was as though I was in a sauna, the roaring fires of an inferno casting searing heat waves all about me. I was soaked from pits to pants. I felt sluggish, my brain functioning twice as slow as my slowest day, and the cluelessness evaded me entirely, forcing me into surrender.

And surrender I did, as the coppers pulled me out and nudged me into a van. I hardly looked out the barred windows as we drove on and on. I just stared down at my dust-specked sneakers, the heat causing a sharp pain to my brain.

For three hours, we drove out to who knew where. It was a long, long way away from home and my loved ones. The other prisoners that sat there with me did not speak, nor flinch. They just stared at the roof of the van.

The van finally slowed down to a stop. We had arrived at a prison. I could not tell whether it was Holland or Germany, or someplace worse. The block resembled an old Victorian dome, only the cupola did not have a fancy lantern, the drum was thick, cracked and a dismal, murky brown, covered in moss, the pendentive was amiss, and the pier just about held everything together.

The place, as one of the other prisoners said, was called the Koepel and was located in Arnhem. He explained that the 'Koepel Prison' or remand centre was one of the least profitable places to be. All I knew was that my clothes stuck to my body, as the heat engulfed me.

I was processed as per the procedure, and then presented to the dome's interior. It would have been an auditorium, with a stage in the centre, had the cell doors been left open and seats added all around. There were three levels, and I was brought to the top floor.

I hadn't any legal aid, nor any information. Nothing. It was my mistake that cost me thirty more days in that dump. I actually and stupidly thought signing those statements, which were in Dutch, wouldn't hold out because I was English.

After a couple of days in the cells, with just an hour to wander freely in a yard, roaming around and staring down to avoid blinking in the hot, bright sun, everything had gone so awry.

I was desperate for any contact with my family; Nadia and the kids, and finally, after two days, I acquired a telephone card. I dialled the familiar digits, and with each dial tone, my heart beat faster and faster, until Nadia appeared on the line. "Hello?"

"Nadia, it's me, you okay? Do you know what's going on?!" I said.

"Frans! I don't know what's going on but things will be okay. Hang in there, okay?" It was Nadia's turn to reassure me. It wasn't working, but I just went with it.

"Listen, Nadia, I can't talk much, but I'm glad you're okay. They've got me here at the Koepel in Arnhem."

"I'll look it up and come to see you as soon as I can, okay?"

"I can't wait." My spirits soared. Nadia was home, and she was all right.

In the days that ensued, the legal aid lawyer called me out of my cell: in other words a lawyer who had no interest, but had to represent me. He was on the phone, and I got on the other end.

"Frans, look I can't deal with your case," the lawyer said.

"What? Why not?"

"It's too complicated and confusing. They're accusing you of all sorts of things. Money laundering, criminal organization, fraud, all kinds of things and that's not my expertise."

"This is all bullshit, where is everybody getting this shit from?"

"I'll send you the file with the details and will contact another lawyer who will represent you and who is better versed in these kind of complicated financial cases, okay?"

"Okay, I'm waiting."

I was about to hang up, when I heard the lawyer's voice speak. "...Viereck?"

"What?"

The lawyer cleared his throat. "How good a friend is Bryan Viereck, Frans?"

"What do you mean?"

"I'd like to know, how good a friend is he to you."

"He's my best mate, why?"

There was a pause on the other end, and then the lawyer spoke. "He's made seven statements against you, Frans, I suggest you and your family stay away from him because the statements are quite damning."

My heart skipped a beat. Surely I had heard wrong. "What?!"

"That's right, Frans. He's made seven statements against you. Please read the file or get someone to read it."

Bryan. My best friend Bryan, ex-kickboxer Bryan. Bryan who had fought with me side by side, whom I would never have thought a grass. That very Bryan, the same Bryan that I had known for years and years. Bryan, who had cried to me so many times about how he was in a state, and called upon me for a quick fix. Bryan, to whom I had lent money so many times without twice thinking, whom I had let into my apartment so he could earn his own. It was with Bryan I used to mock the knobs that grassed on their friends. It was with Bryan that I had pulled so many stunts and pranks. We had been on a journey of a lifetime together, and had established the sort of trust akin to blood brothers. I had always thought of him first, when it came to assembling a team at a sales company.

It made no sense, whatsoever, that this very same Bryan, and this lawyer had enunciated it correctly: Bryan Viereck, had issued any sort of statement against me. I don't think it was possible to be angry. I was crushed, but I refused to believe that my best mate had turned right round and done the dirty on me. I had to hear it from him or at the very least see it in writing; I wanted him to look me in the eye as he told me each of the seven statements that escaped his crooked lips. Had he been that wolf in sheep's clothing? Seeking to supplant me? Or had the ex-kickboxer tough guy in him failed as he crumbled under the stares of the Dutch police?

Whatever it was, I wanted to know just one thing. "Is he free?" I asked in a slight croak, my throat dry as my jaw had dropped and remained hanging.

"He's free. He's on bail, he's a suspect for the police, but you, you are the chief suspect..."

"Chief suspect in what and how the fuck is he on bail and I'm here?"

The lawyer then replied, "Look, Mr. Merkx, as I said this case is too complicated for me. I will get in touch with somebody who can work on it. Don't worry."

"What is this all about?"

"You'll see in the file, I'll have it delivered by tomorrow."

And the file did arrive. It was so thick, it resembled a yellow pages book. It was all in Dutch, and even though I spoke the language, reading it was a whole new thing that I couldn't do. I put it to one side, deciding I'd better return to it when my brain had somewhat recuperated even slightly from the mental fatigue I had drawn.

I turned to some fellow inmates: a few that I had gotten friendly with on my landing, ones that had the gist of the English language so that they could translate for me.

Broken English or not, the messages were clear, each one as absurd as the next. "I was working for Frans, and I used to wash his Porsche so I could earn money... Frans made up all these false things about the shares... I was getting paid a salary by him from his company Ramone... Making up names to call clients was Frans' idea, he printed share certificates... I needed money so I washed his car, and I got paid... Frans is the one that has been speaking with the clients..."

I was numb, my heart thumping loudly in my chest, but I was bemused as well. If I wanted to wash my Porsche, I would take it to an automatic car wash, of which I knew plenty.

I had paid for his car, I had lent him eight thousand, a bit much for washing a car. I wasn't some slave owner from the Deep South. And as for calling clients, I hadn't spoken to anybody. While at Spantel, the clients were a part of the company and not in Holland. They were situated mostly in Asia, and there was an existing base.

As I had other parts of the file translated too, I came to find that several "so-called" clients had testified against me as well. They'd told the police that they had indeed spoken with me over the phone. I mused myself with the ludicrousness of the preposterous information given in that file.

They had tapped my phones, too, and from what I discovered, it had all commenced right after the Paris incident. The masks were soon coming off. One such mask belonged to the good old kidnapping cunt Robert van der Braak. It turned out that he was an undercover copper, keeping his eyes on the prize and preying on me with spite and spies. He had been working for the police all along: it was a setup, and they were also attempting to pin the kidnapping of Mike Swift on me. That would be easy to get out of; they'd just have to contact my eye doctor in Leeds, because during the day of that incident, I was having laser eye surgery done.

Everything was already in motion, and that file could not be unwritten. It stayed in a corner of my cell. I left it there, away from me, and the more I heard from it, the more the poison spread.

Nadia kept her promise and came down to visit me. She brought with her not only some money so that I could have a positive balance on my jail card to purchase food and cigarettes and anything else I needed, but also a smile and the sort of comforting gaze that soldiers would receive before they headed out to war. Even that, however, could not hide my hatred for Bryan, and she knew it.

On another visit she informed me that Lateef and Roger would be coming along soon. And when he came, Lateef said, "Yeah don't worry about shit, it's all gonna be good." In his eyes I saw that he was worried about himself, because with me behind bars who was going to look out for him in the world?

At least he did not have the sense to let that be known, unlike Zak. For he, too, came only once to see me, along with Nadia. He sat opposite me, and I could see a shadow of dubiousness cross his face. At the time, I needed some money to survive, because all my money was frozen.

I thought to myself: a brother in need is a brother indeed, after all Zak would know that best with the new car he was driving. "Zak, I need some money, just a thousand Euros. Sell the car I bought you and get a second hand one just for the time being? I need the money to survive here."

I saw his face contort with rage and fear, and he got all defensive, spitting the most preposterous words at me, "You don't know how bad I got it man, I got it fucked up, you tellin' me to sell my car..."

I lost it. "What the fuck, I'm the one who bought you the damn car! After all these years I have looked out for you, I have given your kids everything, you have a good life because of me, I've looked out for you since you were a kid, pissing your pants and shit, and you can't give me a thousand Euros! You talk about you having it bad, I am in jail you piece of shit!" I yelled at him.

"You don't understand, I-" I sprang up and reached across the table where he sat. Nadia, besides him, was crying and looked shocked. I sat back down and demanded he sort it out. He didn't say another thing. One of the screws walked over and Nadia begged the screw telling him everything was okay, and he backed off.

I sat in my cell, infuriated. I had but one resolve, and that was I would never forgive nor forget what my whole family done.

I struggled to get to the end of the day, and by the twenty first day, I had landed myself a shitty job that got me out of the cell for a couple of hours at least, to refute the boredom I found myself in. And the battle against this boredom was given more firepower when I started to play football for leisure.

I wasn't much good at it, but I sure knew how to vent my frustrations, and I broke an Algerian bloke's ankle during one game. It made me laugh as I thought, I'm a Leeds United fan and we are 'Dirty Leeds.'

My thirty days were finally up, and I had to go up to the courts to try and get released. They drove me once again in the prison van all the way back to Amsterdam, and kept me in the same cell where they had first held me for hours. I had gotten very tired of it all by then.

I was brought into court, the prosecutor saying to the judge, "We think he will try and make an escape to another country if we let him go-"

I stood up, and glared at the pair of them. "What proof you got of anything? And where am I gonna run off too, I'm from England, you've taken my passports! What am I gonna do? And hey, guess what, I've still got my ID, if I wanted to break out, I'd do that. This is all bullshit!"

The judge peered at me. "Thirty days again."

I screamed back, "Fuck you!"

The procedure was concluded and I was taken back to prison.

Prison would not be prison without a break-out, and it so happened that two Moroccans actually made the leap. It happened during our yard-time, and they slipped away so deftly and suddenly, nobody knew what happened. It was funny, because those two crazy clowns actually sent us all postcards from Morocco.

And again, thirty days passed, and again I went through the same procedure; in the prison bus for three hours, back to Amsterdam and then in the cells for an all-day seating. I didn't even bother to listen as I had lost faith and accepted my fate would be an additional thirty days.

I was mildly surprised, however, when the lawyer called to the prison and explained that the prosecutor, who happened to be the creep I saw in the police station, a Mr. Woudman, had insisted that bail would be granted if I could raise fifty thousand Euros.

They had read the situation well, because I had nothing. Everything I owned was blocked. My accounts were frozen, and I didn't have my house anymore.

For the first time in my life, I would need help. I decided to call up Nadia, as I had a plan. "Nadia, I'll need you to call Chris and tell him I'll need fifty thousand for bail."

I had not known Chris for all that long, but while my messed-up family had left me to rot, this lad from Canada somehow got the money together: fifty thousand of his own money, and sent it along.

He really was like the brother that I never had and it was something I would never ever forget and something I would be forever grateful for the rest of my life.

As I sat there, waiting for the funds to be cleared so I could make bail, I got called out by a screw. Nadia was on the line. "Lawyer said the money cleared and you will be coming home."

"Chris paid for it, man he came through for me," I said.

Before they let me out, I was picked up by a guard, an Indian one and a Breed at that, and he told me, "The police want to talk to you downstairs."

I replied, "Fuck those cunts."

"Well, you go tell them that then and we will bring you straight back here."

I obliged, and found them waiting for me downstairs. "Mr. Merkx, we would like to speak with you."

I gladly kept my word to the guards. "Fuck off, I don't want to talk."

They sat there with smirks on their faces, but that soon changed as I used every explicit word in the English dictionary. Then the guards stepped forward and said, "I don't think Mr. Merkx wishes to speak with you guys." They were furious and I laughed at them, even though I knew as cops they had the upper hand in everything.

And a few days later, I exited the pit, and breathed the fresh freedom once again. Oddly enough, it was an uneasy feeling leaving prison. I thought that it might be because they'd only find another way to bring me back again and take everything away from me.

There was nobody waiting to collect me. I had specifically asked Nadia not to come. I did not want her to go there ever again. I left the gates after withdrawing whatever money I had in my prison account, and I decided that I was going home in style and would take a taxi straight to Nadia's house. I got in and asked the driver, "How much to Amsterdam?"

"Two hundred and fifty Euros."

"Okay just get me to Amsterdam as fast as possible." And we drove, all the way out of the Koepel, all the way up to Amsterdam and to Nadia's doorstep.

CHAPTER 41
Year of Struggle

I had won the skirmish, and escaped the trenches, but the war had only just begun. From the free legal aid that I was receiving, I was advised to get a lawyer that they themselves would appoint. It was a free service, so I went ahead and requested it.

They sent along someone called Marcel, and I set up an appointment with him to meet and discuss matters.

"I'll be representing you, Mr. Merkx. We will do what we can, given everything," he said.

"Right, let's get started then," I said.

"Well, Mr. Merkx, I don't know if the office made you aware of my charges."

"No, they didn't tell me anything about charges," I said.

"Look, Mr. Merkx, this is a high-profile case, and you're going to have to pay me on the side to handle it, if you know what I mean."

I didn't really see any other way out. Private lawyers would probably cost ten times more, and so I said, "I'll arrange the payment, just send me an invoice or whatever."

"Gladly. You can give me the money when we next meet, and then we will take on the case. In the meantime, I'll have a closer look at what we are dealing with."

"Right," I said, unsure of what to make of it all.

"Good day, Mr. Merkx." He stood up and left without another word.

I went about getting the money together, departing with some of my most prized possessions, including my set of highly expensive luxury watches.

I knew that my every move was being watched, and that those Keystone cops had spent a lucrative sum of money to tap into my, Nadia's and even my brother Zak's phones. Zak never knew it, but I did, and I also knew that they were wasting their time because I never spoke to my brother.

Once they realised that, they took their frustrations out on me, and turned my life upside down. They really thought they were dealing with some kind of an Al Capone case, but what they didn't know was that I was more Al Pacino than Capone.

As I walked down the street, I called Chris. "Hey, Bub, how ya doing?"

"Yeah all good, Frans, more so how are you doing?" Chris asked.

"Thanks to you, Bub, I'm okay. Thanks for coming through and sorting the bail money for me."

"Anytime, I know you would have done the same for me. What's happening there? Any chance you can get Nadia and yourself out here to Canada?" asked Chris.

"No chance, Bub, these dumb mother fuckers won't let me leave the country. My passport has been confiscated so I'm stuck in this hell hole," I said, seething.

I had spoken out intentionally, and sure enough just as I was explaining the situation, I noticed the car across the street and knew it was undercover police. "Hold on, Bub…" I walked over and banged hard on the car window, "Hey, you dumb fucks, don't you think I know who you are?!" I yelled at the two pigs that sat in their unmarked car like some kind of FBI agents. "You jokers…I informed my brother that cunts like you are trying to frame him like you are doing me…" I laughed at them, and they sat uneasily not knowing where to look.

I heard Chris shouting on the phone, "What's going on, Frans!"

"Nothing, Bub, just have two keystone cops shadowing me here and thinking I didn't see them, but I blew their cover," I said, laughing.

"What is it with these Dutch idiots?" said Chris.

"I dunno, but they've tapped my phone, so you know, and the lawyer said they have issued an international arrest warrant for you, too."

"No way, okay thanks for telling me, Frans, I will inform my lawyer here," said Chris.

Chris explained that he had gotten money from his childhood friend, Frank, on the basis that Frank could live in his house and help pay the mortgage, because like me Chris had no job.

Frank agreed, and then went ahead and ripped Chris off, taking full advantage of him and extracting a sure of a lot more than what my mate was expecting to pay in the first place. He might as well have continued paying off his own mortgage at that rate. Like me he had lost everything.

"Chris, I gotta tell you that Bryan made seven statements against me filled with lies. The fucker really framed us, Bub."

There was a long silence, before Chris said calmly, "I always suspected him to be a piece of shit. If he was standing in front of me right now I'd do him in. Look what he did to you, forget me I wasn't thrown in jail and stripped of my dignity. You were, Frans, and look what you always did for him, you always helped that loser, I hate him!" His voice rose in anger.

"It's alright, Bub, fuck him and the rest of them they are a bunch of losers," I reassured him, but I could tell that Chris was upset for me.

"I messed up with Nadia, Frans. I was so stressed I lost it on the phone," Chris confessed.

"I understand, Bub, and she, like you, is under immense stress because of all this."

"No, Frans, it's not about me or Nadia. It's about you. I don't know how you are holding up, but I respect you so much. I'm with you, maybe not in person, but mentally. I am there, Frans. I miss you, brother," Chris said.

"I miss you too, brother, you really are my brother from another mother. Anyway take care, Bub, and we'll speak soon," I said.

"Alright, bye for now."

I'd hustled some money together and I set up another appointment with my weasel lawyer. "There you go; the amount you'd requested."

Marcel took the cash from my hand, folded it in half and pocketed it. "Right, let's get to it."

I thought that we were finally on to something, until: "Frans, you might as well forget about this case. Don't bother fighting it. It's going to take years, firstly because they're running a general investigation and until that's closed, it won't be submitted to court. I am going to try and get your assets unfrozen but that's going to take time."

I rubbed my eyes with the tips of my fingers, which calmed me down ever so slightly, and addressed him. "Anything else that might be of use here?"

"I'm afraid not, Frans, not for the moment. I'll update you, and in the meantime if there's anything you need, don't hesitate to get in touch. I'm sorry, Frans, this is Dutch law: it's very bureaucratic."

I dismissed his apology with a wave of my hand, and that concluded negotiations.

It was back to the old days, to the hustle, back to having nothing, only this time, I had three kids to take care of, not to mention Nadia and I were a lot older.

It was a major headache, the lot of it. They snatched my Porsche, and even got a hold of Nadia's car. They had charged her with receiving suspected criminal finances, which was just another ingredient to the concoction of bullshit that was being brewed by the system. She had even lost her job, because she was working at the job centre, which was classified as civil service, and once they'd arrested her from there, it was a one way walk of shame to the exit.

I did not have access to my income, or anything that could give me financial leverage in the situation. Had it not been for Chris' contribution for bail I would have still been in jail. I knew Chris's resources were limited, because not only did he lose his own asset, his house in Canada, but his accountant also ran off with the rest of his money and forgot to let Chris know that his taxes weren't sorted out properly.

I had already paid Marcel, and I wanted to make full use of him. I was determined to get my passport back, as part of a major resurgence plan, and so I got a hold of that prick lawyer and told him of my intentions.

"I'll work on getting that back for you first, Frans…"

While he was working on that, I did not take his advice. I did not let the case go, but started building it myself from scratch. I got hold of anything that would assist me in proving my innocence. I tracked down bank statements, proof that the companies they invested in were real and that they had paid the companies and not me and that the companies sent the share certificates.

After a few months, I received my passport, which meant I was free to travel as I pleased. The lawyer had been useful, but it was a flash of brilliance. He told me that he was asking for an application to the court for a refund on the bail money that I'd paid, but that was in the future and so I couldn't think about that at the time.

As for Bryan, my once trusted ally, my former best friend, he had had a nervous breakdown. He was living with the guilt of telling lies so he could get himself out of jail. I was his trump card, the misused alibi, one that fell with no honour.

He had left me with but one thought on my mind, and that was I wanted put a bullet right in his head, and keep it lodged there. I wanted to watch him bleed out on a sidewalk, for what he had done. And I would have done it, with pleasure at that, something I never took pride in, for to that date, I held violence in the greatest contempt, but what he did was unforgivable.

I was advised by my lawyer to stay cool with Bryan, and this time I obliged. It was a simple matter of not wanting to get behind bars again, although that wasn't quite enough motivation, and that's when I thought about my kids, and exercised restraint.

Nonetheless, we encountered one another, months after the incident. He very nearly got down on both knees, and he literally cried as he saw me. "Bruv, I'm sorry, I'm so sorry bruv, please, bruv, I…You know I would never, bruv…it was…they said…it was a case of do I protect you or my daughter, do you know what I mean? And bruv, you can take care of yourself, I know you, you can get out of anything…but my girl, my little girl that's not even been born yet, that's due in October…bruv, they told me…they said that if I didn't testify against you, they'd never let me out, and they'd put my girl behind bars. My pregnant girl, bruv…"

I closed my eyes and took his words with a grain of salt. There was genuine remorse in his voice, which shook horrendously as he stammered, but that did not change the fact that I still wanted to kill him. My own kids came to the fore of my thoughts, and I unclenched my fists, and let him off.

I would of course never trust him again, not after what he had done. It was an easy decision to make, but tough to live by, because I'd trusted him through and through prior to all of this. On the other hand, I took a sick pleasure seeing him suffer.

I had to put Bryan behind me for the time being, and get back to building the case. It was a nuisance and a tease because the lawyers did not do a single thing. The prosecution went through cases from the police and they usually saw what they can make stick, and they stuck to that. In good old Holland, you'd have to do that yourself if you wanted to clear your name, and that was my agenda.

I got back in touch with Bill, who on top of demanding I return my signing on bonus that he'd paid out to me, was reluctant to speak with me altogether. I wanted to somehow get him to say that the money was all from the clients, that there was no evidence whatsoever to show that I had taken any of that money from anybody. It was all just pinned on me, like a big Mafia case, and to make matters worse, they'd won over the public by printing it in the papers.

Slowly, but surely, I could see that progress was being made and that I was compiling my case, record by record. I even got an international tax advisor to confirm that I didn't owe anything in tax, that there was no money laundering on my part. I had all the papers to show that my money would come from work, from my commissions and bonuses and that was that. I even got a hold of the bank in Gibraltar and asked them to release statements from there, which meant I had a third party confirming my accounts and where my money came from.

Every time I called my so-called lawyer for advice, He insisted that I drop the case entirely and not bother pursuing it. All that did was motivate me to keep on going, determined to clear my name, but I was still frustrated with the fact that I had paid Marcel, which might even have been illegal because I was promised free Legal Aid.

It boiled down to a heated argument, which resulted in the termination of our work agreement, and I turned instead to another lawyer. I also reported Marcel to the Dean of Lawyers, and they in turn demanded I get a refund on what I had paid for his services. My guess is that asshole

Marcel would have been disbarred and dismembered from the Dutch Law Association, so he'd rather pay.

I got a hold of a Mr. Vink, and the lawyer came on board. He was an emotional wreck, and never thought things through, such was his level of stupidity. Vink pulled a Marcel during our very first meeting, and demanded I pay him or he would not proceed with the case. I assumed that this was going to be the case with all the Dutch lawyers, and so I got the money back off Marcel, and paid Vink instead.

What Vink suggested was, in hindsight, not only stupid, but outright preposterous. "Okay, Frans, let's go and speak with the police."

"You sure, Mr. Vink?" I asked.

"I've been practicing law for enough years to tell you that I am certain." They always said to leave it to the professionals, and that's what I did.

We went down to the central police station, and the police specifically asked me about my money, and asked if I was supposed to disclose it. Vink said it should be done, and so I did it and that only exacerbated the bullshit, because it enhanced the case and gave them new weapons to keep shooting me in both feet. It seemed then that I had to go solo, because nobody was seriously fighting for me.

Vink turned out to be a real idiot. I would call him once a week to see if there was any change, but what really did it for me was his performance in court. I was summoned for opening arguments and there I was sat, while my clown lawyer was torn apart by the Gestapo looking Mr. Woudman. He was humiliated as he stammered, sweating profusely and looking a complete novice.

My fight was countered effectively by my opposite numbers. They knew my vulnerabilities, and questioned Nadia as well, requesting statements and the like. They asked her about her car, and the fact that she possessed a number of valuable items, and specifically asked whether or not she'd ever questioned me about how I got my money.

She responded saying that I had a fantastic job, and then they asked if I ever talked about tax, to which she inadvertently replied, "Why would he talk about tax, people who talk about tax don't pay it."

They took her words, twisted them around, and made it look like I never paid my taxes, which added tax evasion to the constantly growing case against me.

Absolutely nothing added up whatsoever. I was named chief suspect, Chris was a chief suspect and Bryan, who had been charged with the same allegations as I had been, was merely a suspect, and the outrageous Robert was totally ignored in the investigation.

When I asked why Chris was being charged, the accusation was that Bentley was a boiler room; a twisted, no good, illegitimate operation. I wasn't sure what their definition of legitimacy was, because Bentley had been set up by Bill and Randy and authenticated by Baker and McKenzie and even the Canadian embassy.

There was, of course, no use in trying to explain any of it to the police. I was informed by Chris that undercover police had pulled him over on a street in Canada, but because I had informed Chris he hadn't panicked and was prepared.

There was one thing that the Royal Canadian police had gotten right, however, for they had looked over the charges and the case with raised eyebrows and told him that it was all bullshit, and they could not quite believe how the police and Justice department in Holland could pull such stunts. They even advised him not to go to Holland. I was happy for Chris, but it confirmed the pigs in Holland were out to get me no matter what.

And once more, my life was at a standstill; I was moving neither forwards nor in reverse. I was buried under piles of paperwork as I worked to plead my innocence. 2003 had gone from bad to worse. I was still looking for work, selling off most of the stuff that I had already bought.

My own apartment was a complete shit hole thanks to the coppers. When they had first arrested me they bust down my front door, which I never really fixed because I just didn't have the money to do it. They stepped over my furniture with their dirty boots, threw potted plants across the rooms, broke things left, right and centre, threw my clothes all over the place and stepped all over them as well.

Pathetically, they took my plasma television, my car, cash that I had stored in the house, but at least they spared my Cartier watches, that were worth quite a small fortune themselves.

I actually didn't care a damn that they had raided my apartment, but I reached boiling point when they did the same to Nadia's house. Exactly what they were looking for, I had no idea, but they certainly never found anything of interest, and just left a mess behind. If I had to guess, I would say that they were looking for false share certificates and the like.

After my bust-up with Zak, I had developed an intense animosity with him in particular. I seethed and loathed him, and just like Lateef, whereas all those times I had his back, he left a knife in mine. I had pooled them all into one category: the garbage bin, non-recyclable, and I had lost complete interest in them.

In the midst of furiously compiling evidence for myself, I ended up at the coffee shop called 'Goed Goed' just around the corner from my house. I got on well with the owner Said and the shady boys coming there. They actually looked at me as some kind of gangster because they had all seen how the police had arrested me and the bullshit written in the local rag.

That was my recuperation place, and I'd sit there every morning reading the Sun newspaper while sipping on my coffee, thinking about what else I could do for my case, and I'd often end up chatting with a lad that used to frequent the place called Jamal. He was some sort of drug dealer, but not the typical sorts. He was an easy going fellow, beneath the crazy gangster talk, and he showed me respect and a hint of friendship as well.

"Bro, I want to go to England, man," he once said to me.

"Yeah, bruv, I'm from there, and let me say you can't do your shit there, bruv," I said, laughing, as he joined in.

"Yeah, yeah, I know bro, man if you can link me up with somebody from back home, I want to visit next week and go out there."

"I can ask a mate of mine, Roger, let me call him and see if he's around."

I did end up calling Roger and told him that a good friend would be passing through and whether or not he could take him out. "Yeah, Zid, just give the guy my number and he can call me when he reaches, alright?"

"Okay, will let him know," I said.

I told Jamal all about Roger, and that he should call him once he got to the UK and Roger would take him out. Jamal was thrilled. He bought me a coffee as he asked me a thousand things about England: the usual shit, girls, drink, girls and the night life.

"Thanks, bruv, won't forget this," Jamal said.

That very same night, I was sat in my apartment, my eyes half closed on the back of another tiresome day of case-building, when all of a sudden I heard a popping sound, which I recognized straight away as gun fire. I sprang up to my feet, and peered outside the window with caution.

Down below, I saw the figure of someone with a familiar posture. I could not quite see his face in the dark. He had his hands up and was backing away slowly, when all of a sudden there was the drilling sound of an automatic weapon, and the victim was sprayed head to toe in bullets. He fell to the floor and I saw the shooter running away.

My heart leaped up into my mouth, and I sprinted down the stairs to the street, while at the same time dialling the emergency number, "I need an ambulance now, there's been a shooting in my street!"

I arrived to the scene, and laying in the street with blood everywhere was none other than Jamal. I knelt on the ground beside him, as sirens rang behind me. The street shone with the same red substance, and his body had literally been split in half by the bullets. Unbelievably, he was still alive, his eyes wide open while the same time taking short quick breaths.

I had just been talking to him, not too long ago, when all of a sudden there he lay, the ghost of a smile hovering over his lips, and his frightened eyes almost obscured by the blanket of darkness as he began his pass into shadow of death.

Two coppers were shouting somewhere overhead, "Stay with us, what's his name, do you know him!" they screamed at me.

I steadied my breathing, and kept calm as I replied. "Yeah, his name's Jamal."

"Jamal! Jamal! Stay with us, Jamal!"

Jamal did not look at the police. He was looking straight up at me. His short breaths began to slow down as his life slowly faded away. The look in his eyes would haunt me from that day on, and as his breathing finally ceased, he died right there in front of me. I had just witnessed a guy, somebody that I knew of, being zipped from head to toe with an automatic weapon.

My life was a tumbling, fumbling roller coaster, yes indeed it was, but there and there, somebody had been robbed of his life at a moment's notice. Whatever he did or didn't do, nobody had a right to take another man's life.

I retreated to my side of the street as I sat on the porch steps with my neighbour next to me asking who had been shot and if I had seen anything. I just answered, "Dunno mate and I don't want to know."

Later on, a crowd had found its way around Jamal's body. The police had covered him with a white sheet, which had gone completely red within seconds. The blood, the weapon, none of that frightened me, but what did was a piercing, blood-curling shriek that made the hairs on the back of my neck stand up, as Jamal's mother pushed through and fell to the floor beside her son, screaming and shouting in Arabic.

While I was grateful not to be lying in a gutter, unable to respond to anything ever again, it did not make things easier for me. It did give me clarity, and had shaken me up to persist with the case, and go all in with it.

CHAPTER 42
2004: The Worst Year

While I was building my case, I had received word that my sister, Yasmeen, had had a run-in with her sanity, and was pushing it too far with the bottle. My mother had taken it upon herself not to let my brothers and I know that her husband was beating and abusing her to the point where she had literally become a manic depressive.

The drinking had gotten excessive, and she had even been arrested at Dallas airport for public disturbances. And now she was back in Holland, but had been arrested again and sent to jail for shop lifting. I decided to go visit her in jail. Nadia was with me, which I was so grateful for.

I could see that my sister wasn't well with the gibberish she was speaking. The sister I knew was obsessive about her appearance and always looked fantastic. Now she looked freaked out, crumpled, sporting rags and looking gaunt.

I tried to ask her what had happened, but she jumped from one subject to another at lightning speed. I was left with one thought: How could they put my sister in jail? Here was a woman who had helped and loved old people all her professional life, but now she was the one that needed help and guess what this god-forsaken country did?

The hatred for Holland grew inside of me; they had locked up my abused sister even though it was crystal clear that she was mentally not well.

Her abusive husband, Peter Baas, did not help make matters any better and often drove her up the wall. He had a certain affinity with Asian hookers and was fond of the drink himself. He would strike Yasmeen with everything from bare knuckle to belt buckle. He would constantly bully her and throw her out of her own home, into the streets.

I don't know how long it went on for before their marriage ended, but it must have been difficult for her. She got her part of the money and assets, then she went back to Bradford. I heard she returned to the place where we had lived all those years ago and was freaking out the neighbours there. I could scarcely laugh as I imagined her stalking the streets in the dead of night, wailing like a ghoul, causing hairs to prickle and shivers.

Lateef did not help and in the end, she somehow made it back to Holland. It was then that I received a call that she had been admitted to a mental asylum in Amsterdam.

Of my siblings, she had always somewhat been the closest to me, even though we had drifted apart over the years. I recalled the days she deputised in my mother's stead, and put the clothes on my back and fed me. I took time off my own problems and paid her a visit at the clinic as well.

There I was with Nadia and I did not recognize Yasmeen. The smell from her was like she hadn't washed in a century and she had a tooth missing. I stood there trying not to make a big deal out of it, but inside I was falling apart seeing my beautiful sister turned into something of a zombie.

When I was permitted to enter the room, and she saw me, leaped up off the bed, and charged into my arms, saying, "I knew you would come, Zahid, I knew it, and look I have your photo with me. They are trying to fuck me up in here, Zahid. Why did daddy have to die, why did he leave us. You know I speak with him a lot."

Her unfocused eyes stared at something in the distance that only she could see. The clinic was worse than the borstal, the prison in Arnhem or even the French prison in Le Santé.

The nurses came in to give Yasmeen her medication, and when she did take it, she started to speak more coherently and would tell me about a woman who I had seen walk around with her hands held up showing her wrists.

Yasmeen would say to me, "She scares me, Zahid, she's nuts and they are going to let her out. She's told me if they let her out she will kill everyone." For my sister to say another person scared her meant that person was definitely sick. In the end, all I could do was encourage Yasmeen to stay away from her.

Nadia and I met with the doctors there and they promised she would have the best care.

On another day, I turned up and was informed that Yasmeen had escaped and had come back drunk. I asked what they meant by "escaped," and whether or not this was a prison and why they weren't looked after properly? Like with most things in that city, they did not have a respectable answer to my queries, and I demanded they release her from what I declared "holding cells."

They tried to calm me down and explain the situation to me, but I hushed them up and asked them if I could just go in and see Yasmeen. When I saw her, she looked even worse than she had before. Her eyes were sunken, and emptier than ever before, and her thin, chapped lips mumbled words in a language only she understood. It infuriated me that in spite of all the promises they had made to take care of her, they hadn't done a thing right.

I had another word with the staff, and told them to step things up. Sure enough, the next time Nadia and I visited, I actually thought things were looking up, but then Yasmeen said to me, "Remember the woman I told you about, well they let her out today. They are crazy, Zahid, she is going to do some crazy shit, but I'm glad she left here."

I told Yasmeen to keep on taking her medication and in no time she would be out of there and get her life back together and she could be back with her two sons, Thomas and Oliver. She agreed and said she missed them so much and couldn't understand why they hadn't been to visit her, but I actually was glad they didn't because nobody wants to see their mother like that.

The following day, I was watching the television, when I noticed there was news about a killing in the Bijlmer of Amsterdam. The description of the killer sounded familiar to me. She had stabbed her own sister, and her sister's daughter, to death, before calmly waiting for the police.

I sat there shocked thinking Yasmeen was right. On the news bulletin they had asked for character witnesses. I called the police and explained what my sister had told me and what I had seen. The police asked me to come down to the station, which was ironic. I hated them, but this was something different. Innocent people had been butchered and if I could help in any small way to make sure this person was never released ever again then I would do that.

As I entered the police station I explained to the officer behind the front desk who I was and why I was there. I waited for a few minutes until the detective appeared and we went into the interview room. I told him what my sister had told me. He thanked me and said, "I have photo here. Is this the woman that was at the mental institute with your sister?" I looked at the photo and there stood a lady dressed in a blue jump suit, looking absent-minded.

"Yes that's her," I said.

"Okay, Mr. Merkx, thanks for your time. It helps us paint a picture and shows this lady is a very sick woman."

It did feel strange conspiring with the police to bring somebody else down for a change, but it did little to help my own case.

For a few weeks, I popped into the hospital to check on Yasmeen. She was getting neither better nor worse, then again you just cannot tell what goes on in the mind of another person.

As I sat in Nadia's apartment one evening after having paid Yasmeen a visit, I turned to her and said, "I have a really bad feeling that something bad will happen to Yasmeen."

A few days after that, my phone rang and on the other end was Lateef, sounding exasperated. I did not need to actually hear the words to know what had happened. "Zid, Zid, Yasmeen's dead, she's dead, Zid…"

My entire body was paralyzed and I did not know what to say or do. I put the phone down and for no apparent reason, ran outside towards the coffee shop. The owner Said, who was tending to a customer outside, looked up and saw me. "What's up, Frans?"

"My sister is dead, Said, my sister is dead." I saw him struggle with his words, looking as shocked as I had been and before he could answer, I ran right out of the coffee shop.

There was only one place I knew I could go where somebody would understand. I went straight over to my mother's house, my mind on auto-pilot as I somehow managed to drop onto her doorstep. I saw a couple of police cars and knew that they had just arrived.

They explained that Yasmeen had gone to Zaandam train station and had thrown herself in front of the train. I did not want to think of the aftermath, or that my sister had been mutilated by a speeding train. The police said witnesses, who were school kids, had said she was sat on the platform bench then calmly got up and jumped in front of the intercity train.

As for my mother, for whom I put aside all contempt and pitied, it seemed as though her heart had been wrenched right out her chest and thrown down a drain. The only thing she could say was that a child should not go before the parents.

Later we found out those imbeciles at the mental clinic had not taken care of my sister and had given her the wrong medication, which turned out to be the reason why she freaked out. Holland had robbed me not only of my freedom, but my beautiful sister too.

I would have fallen apart entirely, had it not been for Nadia. She was my rock. She had seen Yasmeen messed up and had supported me by coming with me to see her when nobody else did. Of all the silver linings, she was the best one, and I look back on those times and recognize how fortunate I had been to have somebody beside me during the crises.

As tears shifted to bureaucratic matters, Yasmeen's funeral had to be paid.

Not one of my brothers gave even a pound towards the funeral costs, which summed it all up in the worst-tasting nutshell. In the end, I agreed with my eldest sister Soroya that I would pay for the funeral and she would pay for the up keep of Yasmeen's resting place.

It disgusted me that throughout the negotiations, Lateef and Zaker, both of whom worked, remained silent and non-committal, feigning interest in trivialities such as a branch on the floor, or their shoelaces.

I was there for my mum and, at that moment, I let go of the past. I needed to support her. I wasn't working, which meant I would have to hustle again to get the money. I didn't care; this was my sister and she deserved a decent funeral.

On the day of the funeral, we gathered at my mother's house, which was a true concoction for nuisance and peeves.

Surprisingly, my mother had contacted my father's younger brother whose name was Cara. He claimed that he had taken care of us when we were little, but I didn't know or remember him. I just appreciated the fact that he was there for Yasmeen. When Yasmeen was buried, he said Islamic prayers, which with the Christian prayers from the Catholic priest just about summed up how confusing my life was.

During the funeral, I looked up and was taken aback to see Yasmeen's abusive husband was there, along with their two children. I was about to advance on him, when my mother made me swear that we wouldn't kill him. She explained that she wanted Yasmeen's kids there and that was the only way it would happen.

I glared at that piece of shit standing there in his jeans and t-shirt. He didn't even have the decency to dress in black and the only thing that saved that scumbag was our promise to our mother.

As we left the cemetery I overheard my mother saying something, which would be actually quite accurate. "That's the last time I will see my all my kids together."

She was right.

CHAPTER 43
Circus Clowns and Change of Guard

I woke up one day and unfolded the copy of the morning newspaper. The year showed 2007. I was startled to find how fast three years had gone. Three years of the same shit, just different days.

I had decided that enough was enough, and I contacted my lawyer, Vink. Over the phone, he explained that there was a hearing coming up where he would ask for the case to be dismissed based on the fact that after five years nothing had happened.

There had to be some sort of an explanation about why, for five years, I had heard nothing about my case and none of my stuff had been returned to me, in spite of my numerous pleas.

The creases on my forehead were evidence of the painstaking effort that had gone into the work. I was fighting because I was innocent, and the system knew I was innocent. Fact is if I was guilty, they would have had me in court as fast as possible. There was no justice in Holland for an immigrant like me. I was a guy who had, with no education, become successful, and that didn't go down well in conservative and racist Holland.

I had proof where my money came from, that I had actually paid too much tax, the investments were real, I didn't control anything and like the other people working for these companies, I was just a worker. How could it be that they would go after me when the owners were not charged and nobody else was prosecuted? One thing every single lawyer said to me was that the prosecution service had fucked up big time, spent huge amounts of money on a wild goose chase and someone had to pay and that someone was me.

Vink and I arrived to the court. I inhaled deeply and collected my thoughts. I stood there, in front of the prosecutor, whom I would gladly have throttled with my bare hands for the misery he had caused my family, but I was instructed by Vink to say nothing.

Vink proceeded to ask the prosecutor why after five years nothing had happened and then directed his questions to the judges.

"Your honours wouldn't it be prudent and correct to have the case dismissed? It is a burden on the public purse that after five long years there has been absolutely no movement."

The response from the prosecutor was one that he did not expect. "I sent you an email outlining what we were doing, sir."

Vink grew fidgety, and I felt his body begin to quake as he struggled to make up excuses about not seeing an email from the prosecutor. My hands had curled into balls, and I steadied my breathing so as not to make a scene in the courtroom.

"Well, sir, I am afraid that isn't my problem," insisted the prosecutor with a sick grin on his face, much to the agreement of the juvenile judges. Vink's motion was zapped like bug spray. He just stood there, fiddling with the papers, looking as though he was about to urinate on himself.

I did not know who had the worse end of the bitter stem. It was appalling that in five years, only one email had been sent. One email that may even have found its way in the Junk folder, lost under clutters of promotions and offers from online clothing shops. And in the other corner, was my talented and extremely professional lawyer Vink, who had not bothered with the case at all.

And the circus act did not end there. They made me a number of offers; cooperating with them on other cases in exchange for lesser charges. I consulted with my top-notch lawyer, Vink, who told me not to accept any of their offers. Once again, they called my bluff, and I had dug myself an even deeper hole.

I had to get a new lawyer; the man was the star in the circus. I could not afford any more clowns. I had my accountant, Charles, source a top-of-the-pile lawyer. He returned to me a few weeks later with one: a Mr. Cees Van Bavel.

I took Charles' word and hired him. He was absolutely fantastic. He had worked on cases in the UK and knew how to deal with financial cases. I felt I would have a real chance of winning, but my biggest problem was keeping up the payments. After checking through my accounts, Charles suggested I drop van Bayel, because he would be too expensive for me, and recommended another lawyer in his stead.

I was caught up in a real dilemma, and in the end took up Charles' advice, even though in hindsight, it would be the biggest mistake I could have ever made because Van Bavel was an expert in international finance cases.

After consulting with Charles again, he advised me to approach one: Abraham Moszkowicz. The name was already familiar to me because he was possibly the most famous lawyer in Holland.

He appeared many times on national television with his own show, giving legal advice to viewers. He was Jewish and was also known for representing some of the biggest gangsters and thugs. An example was the far-right politician Geert Wilders; a racist who spread his racist rants and his islamophobia nonsense. He also represented Willem Holleeder, one of the most dangerous and infamous criminals in Holland.

"I would say take Moszkowicz, Frans," Charles said as we sat at a table piled with papers. "He can really get people to notice you, which will be effective in sorting out your case, and he demands a one-off fee."

"How much is that mate?" I asked Charles.

"Seventy thousand euros," Charles said.

"Fuck, okay I will sell whatever I can and raise the cash."

I made myself believe that everything made sense then because my world had turned upside down and I was never thinking straight. Here was a lawyer with a proven track record, and even though I did not want to be affiliated with gangsters, I thought if he could get them out of trouble, he could surely help me in some way. I took Charles and Nadia's advice, and agreed to approach Moszkowicz.

He was a man as dubious and as corrupt as any, and it started with the fees he was asking for. Seventy thousand. Up front. In cash. As I entered his office it was like entering something out of a Sherlock Holmes movie; the place was done out in a classical style with a Chesterfield couch and loads and loads of books to give the impression that he knew Dutch law.

The only things he knew was fucking women, doing coke up his nose, and talking out of his ass, but I was the desperate one wanting to believe him.

I was apprehensive, but naively excited that he may just be able to pull the rabbit out the hat and make the case disappear.

"Come in, Frans, how are you today, want a cig?" he asked with his sickly smile.

"No thanks, Mr. Moszkowicz, I'd like to know how you see this case and what your plans are," I said.

"Well I see it like this, Frans. We play the waiting game because the longer this goes on the bigger the chance we have of the case being dropped. I would say not to worry. Let it run its course and you go back to do what you were doing. You were selling shares, right, so go back and do that, my friend," he said with that stupid car salesman grin.

The meeting where I had paid seventy thousand euros was over and he had told me exactly what Marcel and Vink had told me, only difference was I was sat in a fancy office and I was physically and emotionally drained.

I felt ridiculously stupid, but I had no choice but to stick with him. It was my own fault taking advice from Nadia who had recommended him because she had worked for his wife and Charles because the stupid idiot was star struck.

Every day whether I was with Nadia, with my kids, walking on the street, the damned case consumed me. When I was sat in my apartment I was constantly thinking about it. I listened to the sounds of the cars rolling by outside and thought about Jamal at the coffee shop and how he had died.

Months after I had approached Moszkowicz, I had not heard a single word from him. He did not answer his phone, nor did he return any of my calls. I could not sit about forever, waiting on a lawyer that had placed my case at the bottom of his to-do list, or so it seemed.

I rose early the following morning, and fixed myself a cup of coffee. My brain, which had been dormant for a long time, was finally becoming active again. I got together sheets of paper, and jotted down what I needed to do to keep building my case.

The main thing I had to do, what I was paying these lawyers for, was to gain solid evidence that everything Bryan said against me was a lie. That meant client's statements proving all our dealings were legal and systematic, that everything went through the company and that I had not scammed anybody, or issued them with fake share certificates.

The challenge was approaching the clients in a way that was not hostile or pressing. That's where Chris came in. He actually got on with a few of my former clients, but he, too, had to be subtle, and casual about the business.

Within a few months, he had gathered some astonishing evidence for my case. Confessions by clients that they had been coerced by the police into giving false statements against me, and there were no off-the-record deals made during my time at Spantel, Bentley or anywhere else. I sent everything to Moszkowicz and he brushed it all off and just said he would add it to the file and present it at the correct time.

I was stuck, but I had to do something because nothing was happening.

CHAPTER 44
Drifter on the Move

It was nearly the end of 2007 and there was still no word from Moszkowicz about the case.

While I worked with Chris on building the case, I decided to get my act together. I was a great salesman, and I needed to find a job to gather my capital again. I started looking for work, but I couldn't get a job in Holland because aside from not speaking the language properly, I had not graduated from any school. When it came to the school of the streets I was a professor of the hustle.

I noticed an advertisement in the Daily Mail for a job in Malaysia. It seemed like a great opportunity and if I didn't take it, I'd end up the same way as Yasmeen did. So I answered the ad and spoke with a guy called James. He explained the company was a fully licensed investment company.

I actually chuckled and thought I've heard that before but this time I did my checks. I asked if they could produce the necessary licenses, to which he agreed. He also explained that the company was based offshore due to the tax being a lot lower.

It all looked great to me and I was eager to start and even bought my plane ticket to Kuala Lumpur. Nadia wished me luck in whatever I was doing; I hadn't told her anything just in case the Amsterdam keystone cops would try and screw me and set me up again.

I had informed Chris where I was and what I was doing, and he asked me to keep him up to date on everything. I arrived in Malaysia, hoping for a renewed start and after dropping my things off at my temporary accommodation, I made my way to meet James in person.

The office was not half-bad, but what was truly bad was how the sales people there worked. They were nothing like my old team back in the day at Spantel. My boys were efficient, fast talkers and just great salesmen.

These losers focused on their salaries, not realizing that through commissions they could really earn some money. They were dry and monotonous, reading off their scripts like drones.

I went to James's office. "James, thanks for seeing me. I wanted to explain that we can do a lot more in terms of sales, but the guys would have to use a different approach."

"What do you have in mind, Frans?" James inquired.

I told him about how things were done at Spantel, and that the sales should and would have to be based on a sense of urgency.

"Alright, Frans, we'll give that a try. Glad to have you on board," he said.

Lo and behold, he started to make huge profits and was becoming very wealthy. He and his partner Mr. Taylor had bought huge amounts of the stock we were promoting and like the clients, they cashed out and made big bucks while we the workers made our usual shit salaries and shit commissions. Even the clients that had invested did massively well.

Over time, James got greedy. I asked him for a proper salary reflecting the sales I was doing and a proper commission because he was paying one percent on all the deals which was peanuts and I had requested at least five percent. He refused. That for me was the end of things and it was time for me to give it up and get out of there.

I handed in my notice and as soon as I left, the sales went belly up. James panicked and contacted me, asking what I wanted. I explained my dream was to have Nadia with me and all my kids. Having all my kids with me wasn't possible, but having Nadia with me was.

I explained we should open an office in Jakarta, Indonesia, which would be great for Nadia as she had family there and I knew it would make her happy. I also demanded a proper salary, accommodation and a proper job for Nadia. James agreed to everything.

I asked Nadia's sister to contact a proper law firm who could not only help set up the company in Jakarta, but also arrange all the necessary financial permits. Nadia would be an executive secretary and everything seemed fantastic. I found a flamboyant apartment in the South of Jakarta, near the business district and James accepted an office in the Jakarta stock exchange.

I had even arranged for my sons Carlton and Ryan to come over for holiday and put Rishi in school in Jakarta.

The books weren't adding up and it was clear James's Personal Assistant, a Miss Lai Quen, had been creaming off huge amounts of money from him. Before I could act and let James know she had somehow convinced him to stop with the office, even though he'd spent thousands upon thousands of dollars setting everything up.

I asked what was going on and his weak response was, "The law firm is ripping me off, Frans." I tried my best to explain that his PA was the one, but he wouldn't listen and everything fell apart, meaning Nadia had to go back to Amsterdam before anything had started. It felt like another failure and I shouldered the blame, soaking in the humiliation.

However, my reputation as a salesman had spread not only throughout Europe, but now in Asia. I was in demand and so not all was lost. Some time later, I was contacted by a few shady operations and turned them down. And then one day my cell phone rang, and on the other end was someone called Mr. Swift.

He explained that he had heard about the excellent work I had done for James and wanted to offer me a senior sales position in Kuala Lumpur at his asset management company. He explained he would pay a great salary and good commissions and that I would be expected to put a team together. I called my buddy Chris and asked if he was interested.

"Hey, Bub, got an excellent opportunity to run an asset management firm in Kuala Lumpur, no bullshit and fully licensed, what do you think?" I asked Chris.

"Sounds great and good timing because I am so fuckin broke. What's the deal and do we get salary and commissions?" he said.

"Salary is great and the commissions are good plus accommodation will all be sorted, but for the time being we will live in a five-star hotel," I explained to Chris.

"I'm down for that big time sounds great," Chris said excitedly.

"Okay will sort things out. Will be good seeing you and maybe we can get our shit together and make some real money."

Kuala Lumpur it was.

CHAPTER 45
Back from the Brink

It was nearing the end of 2006 and things had taken a turn for the better. My relationship with Nadia seemed to be heading in the right direction for starters. As I left for Kuala Lumpur, I was a man on a mission.

I met with Mr. Swift and his partner John. They told me what they were expecting and we told them the kind of people they should employ. Chris and I had made it clear that we would not under any circumstances get involved in recruitment or the running of the office in any way. Our job was to speak with the company's existing clients and that is what we would do, nothing more, nothing less.

The first few weeks were great as the office was prepared and I enjoyed going back to work. We broke up for Christmas and I headed back to Amsterdam to be with Nadia for the occasion, and to see the boys.

In came 2007 and I went straight back to Kuala Lumpur to my new job and even though the salary was good and the commissions were decent, I knew I wouldn't get rich. There was cause to be grateful, at least Chris and I had jobs and we were living in the five star Westin Hotel.

I had asked John when we would be going into an apartment as it was mega-expensive at the hotel, but John insisted that I shouldn't worry about it and everything was under control.

We took his word for it, and for a total of seven months, we lived at the hotel. After work, I'd eat and train at the gym there. John told us to put everything on the tab and to be honest their company was earning big bucks so I don't think it put a dent in their wallets.

For a few years, I was having this intense pain in my shoulder, but every time I went to the doctor in Amsterdam the idiot would brush it off and say it was nothing and that I should take a paracetamol. On one particular evening, the pain was excruciating and I was feeling very ill. I called Chris to let him know I wouldn't be coming down to eat, as I sat there watching the television and I suddenly felt like vomiting.

It was extremely violent and my insides felt like they might be coming out through my mouth. I started to scream and writhe. I needed to see a doctor and quick. I got to the phone and managed to dial John's number, whom I knew would be able to recommend a good doctor.

"John, it's Frans. Mate, I'm in terrible pain and I've thrown up quite a few times," I said, panting and sweating.

"Did you eat something bad, mate?" John asked.

"No, mate, I haven't eaten since this morning, hang on, mate, got to throw up again." I dumped the phone and ran to the bathroom. "Mate, I need a doctor can you help?" I was starting to really panic.

"Hang in there, Frans, I will contact our doctor, Mr. Abdul Fahmi and he will call you as soon as he can."

"Okay, mate, hurry." I put the phone down. The pain was getting worse and I called Chris, who said he would come to my room at once.

The phone rang. "Hello this is Dr. Abdul Fahmi, is that Mr. Frans?"

"Yes, it's me," I said.

"Can you tell me what are your symptoms?" he asked.

"I am in a lot of pain, my insides feel like they are being ripped out, I keep vomiting and I have this massive pain in my shoulder," I said.

"Okay, Frans, stay calm I am sending an ambulance from the hospital to pick you up."

"Okay, Doc."

Chris walked in and freaked out. "What the fuck is wrong with you, you look terrible!"

"I dunno, Chris..." my head spun, and I panted to get in as much air as I could. I told Chris that I had spoken to John's doctor and the ambulance was on its way and if he could come with me.

"Yes of course, Frans! I'm here for you, you better call Nadia or I can call her if you like?"

"No, Bub, I don't want her stressed and worrying, things will be okay," I said, but with an unsure voice while in serious pain, clutching my stomach.

The ambulance arrived and if I wasn't in so much pain I could have seen the funny side of things. It was built for the 'Oompa Loompa' race; it was so small that it was a challenge getting in there and as we sped through Kuala Lumpur I was thrown around the ambulance. Chris had somehow squeezed in too and was also thrown around like a rag doll. I came out of that ambulance with more injuries than when I first got in to it.

When we arrived at the hospital, I could not stand the agony. I screamed for painkillers and through my pain I could see that Chris was panicking. I was rushed into the emergency room. I kept yelling at the nurses to get me something for the pain, and the next thing I knew, I was laid on the bed and a drip was in my arm and I remember they were trying to get a tube into my penis.

The rest was a blackout, but from what Chris, the nurses, the doctor and the security guards told me later, I had suddenly freaked out and ripped the drip out of my arm and the tube they had stuck into my penis.

Chris said that there was blood everywhere and when the security tried to stop me it was like I had superhuman strength and picked up the guards like they were teddy bears and threw them around the emergency ward. Then I ran off and locked myself in the toilet. Later it would come to light that I had been given too much of a drug called pethidine, which made me freak out.

When I regained consciousness, I was in the hospital room and the pain picked up where it had left off. I pressed the panic button besides the bed and screamed. The doctor came rushing in with the nurses, and as they held me down the doctor explained he was giving me morphine. The pain subsided and I felt relief. I asked the doctor what the hell was happening to me in a weak, exhausted voice.

"You have had a pancreatic attack, Frans, and for the two and a half weeks you will not be allowed to eat. In the drip you will get all you need, but for now no eating or drinking as your pancreas needs complete rest," the doc explained.

"What happened, Doc, how did I get a pancreatic attack?"

"Usually this comes about from two things: one is that if you are an alcoholic and two if you have had a gall bladder infection and blockage of the bile tubes and the enzymes that your pancreas releases to break down food are not passed through and that means they go back and start destroying your own body."

It was very serious and I guess I was very lucky that Doctor Fahmi was there for me and that I was still alive. I stayed at the hospital for over twenty days. I didn't eat or drink, but what kept me going was the thought of the pain I had had and that there was no way I wanted to feel that again.

Finally, I was released and John invited me to stay at his home with his wife Rhonda and three kids. I wanted to go back to Holland, but I wasn't allowed to fly and was instructed that I would have to wait at least a week before I could do so.

They were wonderful people and like the Blacks from many years ago they were honest and worked hard for a living. I would never ever forget what John did for me; he had saved my life. I thanked Rhonda, John and their kids for making me feel so welcome at their house and headed back to Amsterdam.

I was unrecognizable in the aftermath of the attack; I had lost a huge amount of weight, close to thirty kilos, but I was determined to get back in shape. The doctor had warned me it would take on average eighteen months to return to normal.

It took me six weeks.

CHAPTER 46
Resurrection

It was the beginning of January and as I headed back to Kuala Lumpur, I was as focused as ever. I had survived a life-threatening situation, which gave me greater perspective.

I arrived upon a hostile scene. John and Swift had had a falling out, and it looked as though mine and Chris' jobs were in jeopardy. Sure enough it was announced that those two had decided to close the company down.

I did not hold Swift in contempt, because he had offered me the job and I certainly did not have any hard feelings towards John because he and his family had saved my life and looked after me. What I absolutely loathed was the fact that, once again, I was left in the crap and the only thing that I had left to do was to pack my things and head back to Amsterdam. Chris explained that he would stay on and finish up whatever work he had and see if any other offers would become available for us, but he understood that I wanted to get back to see Nadia and the kids.

I arrived back in Amsterdam and found the task of explaining it to Nadia was getting harder and harder. She was a patient person, but even she was being tested to the limit and she wanted stability. I, too, wanted stability, but that seemed to always evade me. After a few weeks, it seemed as though things were settling down.

As I sat there with Nadia I noticed her looking rather nervous and worried. She stood up suddenly and said, "I'm going to take a test to see if I'm pregnant, I don't think I am but I'm late." She went ahead and bought the kit.

As I sat there watching the television, she called me into the bedroom.

"Frans, I'm pregnant," she said nervously.

"Really?" For some reason I was stunned. Happy, yes, but stunned.

And it fell upon me once again, the mission of getting things sorted. I think Nadia didn't understand my reaction. I was ecstatic: it was what we always wanted, but my brain went into overdrive as I knew I had to make a quick move.

In such a situation, there was only one person on my speed dial. I called Chris knowing I had to make money and I didn't care how.

"Bub, we need to work, you heard of anything?" I asked with urgency.

"Hey, well as a matter of fact I heard there's something going down with Swift in Malaysia. Wouldn't be on the same level but a job is a job."

I gave myself no other choice, but to head back to Malaysia and see if we could work with Swift's new enterprise. Swift explained that he had decided to set up his own asset management company and that it would be a lot more stable and that he could arrange things a lot easier himself instead of always waiting for John.

Swift rented a fairly big office and hired other sales people, but the actual deals were pathetic. I turned to Chris and said, "Chris we won't make shit here, what's the point in doing this? What's the point in me leaving Amsterdam for this crap?"

"Yeah I agree, but what do we do, Frans?" Chris asked.

"We gotta go to the Philippines. There're shit jobs, but they pay good money. I don't want to go down that avenue, but what choice do I have? Nadia is pregnant and I gotta take care of her and the baby and my other three boys."

"I understand Frans. I'm gonna make some calls and see if anyone knows anything," Chris said.

"Okay, Bub."

That weekend we planned our departure and it was right on time because the secretary told us that Swift hadn't paid the office rent, the rents on the apartments and even her salary. Ours was due at the end of the month, but we both knew we weren't getting diddly squat.

As we got to packing, pausing here and there to recuperate our energy, Chris got a call. Two positions had opened up in Manila. He looked at me for approval.

I whispered, "Let's do this, Bub."

Chris confirmed to his contact that we would go first thing in the morning and hung up the phone.

Some very shady and nasty looking chaps met us at the airport in Manila. They held a board up with Chris's name, but strangely not mine. As we sat in the car they explained that we would be brought to our living quarters and later on we would meet the boss who went by the name Sanjay, who had to be Indian with a name like that.

We entered our apartment and it was the giant rats and roaches all over again. It was as though I had gotten used to the heat waves, because I hadn't noticed it until I scratched my armpits and found my shirt was soaked through. Chris was freaking out. "What the fuck this is the worst, Frans!"

"Don't worry, Bub, we make quick money then get out of here," I assured him.

"Okay, Frans," he said, cringing as he accidentally stepped on a roach.

I quickly showered and got myself clean clothes and then met Chris downstairs and waited for our pick up to take us to meet the boss.

As we sat there discussing our predicament, in walked the biggest Filipino I had ever seen. He looked the spitting image of that wrestler, "The Rock."

"Boss is ready to see you guys," he said.

"Okay cool, where are we going mate, anywhere nice?" I said jokingly, but he didn't answer.

We drove for about twenty minutes and pulled into a steak house restaurant. It looked decent and expensive, so at least we would eat well. We were instructed to take a seat and wait.

After about thirty minutes a plump Indian fellow walked in. He greeted Chris, but didn't say anything to me. When I asked him questions, he didn't answer to my face and just spoke with Chris. I did not just feel uneasy, but I also wanted to knock the obnoxious man out. I got up to go to the toilet and our so called new boss insisted that he would order our food. I walked over to the toilets and Chris followed.

"What the fuck is his problem, Chris?" I asked.

"Fuck knows, Frans, but it's clear he doesn't like you."

"I don't give a damn. I am here to make money that's it, looks like he fancies you though," I said laughing

"Shut up, Frans," Chris said, also laughing.

As I walked back to the table I noticed our food had already arrived. The chubby Indian had ordered on our behalves. This time he did look at me with a grin and said, "Dig in, Frans, hope you enjoy it."

"Okay, bruv, thanks."

I ate the steak, which was lashed down with a cold beer, and I thought maybe I had gotten off on the wrong foot with him. All of a sudden Sanjay rose and explained he would be retiring for the night and he would see us in the office the following day and then he left. I was feeling a bit queasy and thought: it must be the heat.

We were driven back to our quarters and by then I was feeling sick. I knew it wasn't the pancreas as that was a different kind of pain. I sat in the apartment and violently started throwing up. I couldn't stop, and clutched the edge of the sink as I struggled to regain myself. I stumbled downstairs and made a dash for the seven eleven to get some water to stop myself from dehydrating.

The whole night I was sick: constantly throwing up until the only thing that came out was air because there was nothing left in my stomach.

In the morning I couldn't go to work and informed Chris. He understood and said he would go once I was better. "We came here together, we go to work together," he said.

One of the lads who had picked us up from the airport came to me and said, "Look, sir, I want to tell you that Sanjay the boss spiked your food and drink yesterday. Sir, he is crazy, he tell us he didn't like you and want you to suffer. Then he want you dead, he want we shoot you, sir. He is crazy because he have money."

My blood boiled, and there was just nothing reasonable about it whatsoever. I had known him for less than a half hour, in which time he had hardly glanced at me, and yet he had the nerve to try and poison me.

When I asked why the fat monster had done that, he just said that Sanjay was a sick man that took pleasure in seeing others suffer and he enjoyed being the big boss.

I remembered my time doing military service, and how I had always taken out the strongest guy at camp. I hadn't killed him, of course, I would never dream of such a thing, but the concept stood. Suddenly, it made all the sense in the world, and I decided I would confront the fat Indian, when what I should have done is gotten the out of there.

By the next day I was feeling better and stronger, and I told Chris what went on. His jaw dropped, and he wouldn't stop asking the same questions. Even though I had figured it out, he did not give me the chance to respond.

Our pick up was a blacked-out van, where we couldn't see outside the windows and had no idea where we would be going. The driver assured us that it was alright, and that they did not have other cars to spare. To be fair to him, a lot of cars were blacked out in Manila, and so we just shrugged it off and got in.

We drove for what seemed like an hour and when the car finally slowed down and stopped, we were in the middle of nowhere. We got out of the van and in front of us was a kind of broken down villa. On the doors were two guys holding machine guns. It could have been the set of that 'Scarface' movie.

We entered the villa and inside there was an admin area with lots of computers and people were making calls in separate rooms. Chris warned me to not confront Sanjay yet and wanted to see what we were going to do. I couldn't care less for the blacked-out van or the machine gun men at the entrance. I was adamant about setting the record straight with that fat lump, and let him know he was not the big boss he thought he was.

Then the fat boy walked in with that twisted smirk on his face. I glared at him and he knew that I knew what he had on his deranged mind. Chris nudged me and nodded towards the machine gun toting nutters standing at the front door, and for all my bluster I was no match for them.

Sanjay sat down and as usual spoke to Chris. He explained his operation was so sophisticated that Asian people would be thinking that when they spoke with his people they were speaking with a real bank. He gave us a stack of leads, but this was something neither I nor Chris wanted to do. These people were playing with fire and didn't give a damn.

When he was done briefing us, I pulled Chris over to the side and told him that wasn't for me. He agreed and said, "How the fuck do we get out of this, Frans?" I was dealing with some Indian wannabe Tony Montana, who clearly wanted me dead.

The situation weighed down on me, but I refused to stand down. "Screw this, Chris, I've had enough of this I'm out of here," I said.

"You're nuts, Frans, they've got guns out there, plus the entrance is guarded!"

"I don't give a damn I want out of here now." I stood up and walked to the front door and there stood "The Rock." I wanted out and would not be held prisoner.

"Sir, you cannot leave," he said as he pointed his gun at me.

"Fuck this if you wanna shoot then shoot, I want out of here now!" I screamed at him with rage.

He recoiled, startled. "But, sir, I can't let you out!"

That was the final straw; I barged past him and through the front door. Chris followed me outside and we demanded to be taken back. I think those guards either admired our courage or just thought that we were crazier than they were.

They brought the van around. Strangely Sanjay was nowhere to be seen, but at that moment I didn't spare a thought for that fat lump. We drove back to the apartments, collected our things and headed for the airport.

We were able to change our tickets and got on the flight to Kuala Lumpur. What a relief it was to get out of there; I hadn't left with a pile of cash like the last time, no this time I had left with something even better.

I had left with my life intact.

CHAPTER 47
Happiness

As I arrived back in Amsterdam, I realized just how lucky I was to be alive.

It didn't turn out all bad, and in the end there was a surprise package waiting for me, as Swift actually sent my due payment along. I had enough to buy the baby things and for Nadia and I to take a holiday in Indonesia.

I went back to Asia, to Indonesia; a great place which I had long cherished in my soul. Friendly faces beamed at me from all corners, and it was refreshing after my run in with that evil-grinned psychopath Sanjay.

As Nadia and I sat around the dinner table, with loved ones close by, I watched her talk and soon got lost in an enchanted trance. Coming face to face with fat "Tony" and his gang of nutters made me realize just how beautiful she looked. It also made me appreciate my kids more, and suddenly the news of having another baby was more than I could have asked for from life.

While in Indonesia, we paid a visit to a specialist to find out the sex of our baby. I had my fingers crossed for a girl, but was just as overjoyed when they announced it was going to be a boy.

Our refreshing trip came to an end, and as we headed back to Amsterdam to prepare for the birth of our son, I felt a rush of excitement run up my spine. I tabled the stress about how I would look after my family and let it all go.

My son was due to be born on the eighth of the eighth, two thousand eight. On the first of August, Nadia decided she needed a foot massage at the Chinese place and after the massage, the contractions started. On the second of August, two thousand eight my beautiful son Jay-Jamal Merkx was born.

I peered into his tiny face, with his eyes closed, and savoured the moment. He was the most precious thing in the world to me at that moment, and I felt so proud to have fathered four boys.

It didn't matter that the Dutch authorities were still stalking me, that I was struggling, and that all my possessions had been taken from me. That I had my liberty taken away from me, that my family had stabbed me in the back so many times, that I was bullied every day of my youth by pea brain Lateef and that my so-called best friend had lied and gotten me locked up. I had contemplated ending it all myself a few times, and had even nearly died from pancreatic disease and to top it all off some mad Indian had tried to kill me.

At that moment, while I doted over my newborn, none of it bothered me whatsoever. Because when I looked into his eyes and saw my other boys, I realized that they were all worth fighting for and for me that was happiness.

CHAPTER 48
Did Nothing!

I had accepted that there was nothing I could do or say and that the case would make and take its own course. The legal battle tagged along as everyone else got on with their lives, but no matter how hard I tried mine stood still.

All I wanted, and the only thing I wanted, was what most of those people had. Freedom. I wanted to break away from the binds that kept me obligated under Dutch law. I wanted to break away from peering over my shoulder at every conceivable minute, thinking somehow, somewhere, a dirty copper was going to pull a fast one on me.

Screwed for tens of thousands, it didn't matter that I was screwed for hundreds of thousands. Moszkowicz was a no-show, time and again, and had done nothing on my case. Money was lost, and the waiting was agonizing. The court gave me ridiculous offers to hand me my freedom, offers I refused outright. The worst of it: time was lost.

When I really thought about it all, how nobody in the family wanted to contribute to paying for my sister's funeral, how Bryan sold me out, I realised the harshest, and most bitter truth: I was alone in it all. Yes, there was Nadia, and there was Chris, and my accountant, but there was only so much those fine folks could do before I came back to the inevitable, inescapable truth.

But I didn't despair. I worked various meaningless jobs, but disaster seemed to rear its ugly head when it came to business.

Of all places I had gotten to know someone from the gym who went by the name Martijn. He was a strange fellow, but likable, and the funny thing was he looked exactly like my old friend Caleb Black, even though he was no Caleb. While sat in the sauna at the gym he explained his company Facet Vision had invented a kind of new television module, that later that would come out to be real time television.

He explained he wanted to sell it in Asia, and was trying to find a way to do it. I told him I had been to Asia quite a few times and that in my opinion Malaysia was a good place to go about doing business. The people spoke English and the infrastructure was supportive and it wasn't expensive. He agreed and then asked if I was interested in working for him. He explained he needed someone for the sales department and, from our conversation I fitted the role perfectly. I would be given a salary and company car, which at that point sounded too good to be true.

I was just glad at the prospect of having a normal job in Holland. Our meeting in the sauna room concluded, and he asked me to drop in to finalise the deal and get working.

I reached out to a few different people who were interested in Facet Vision and I arranged various presentations for Martijn in Kuala Lumpur, where he went with his team to present. When he returned, he was pleased with the way things went, and with my presentation preparation, and then arranged to go all the way to Croatia where we would meet an investor called Ferdinand Perko.

We flew into Zagreb and when we met with Mr. Perko it was clear he didn't have the money to buy a loaf of bread. I had the sense that things were going sour, but neither I nor the Man of Steel could do anything to stop things falling through.

The saving grace was the pending deal with telecommunications companies in Malaysia, but again something went wrong and all that fell through as well.

Facet Vision had four partners, and something had stirred there. What was discovered was that one of them was cooking the books and with that came the inevitable. The company went bankrupt and everyone lost their jobs and the same clown fraud police who had stalked me for close to eight years charged him.

It was back to square one for me, or maybe square two because I was entitled to a kind of benefit because for six months in Holland, the government pays you eighty percent of your original wage, after which it's normal dole.

I took the six months thing, but didn't take the dole, and kept up the routine with more sales jobs here, and more sales jobs there.

One morning, I stared at the reflection in my bathroom mirror. It felt like only the previous day when I saw a rosy-cheeked lad about to go to Caleb's house and play with his action figures and ride his bike. The face that now looked back at me was tired, hardened by twelve years of fighting the system, and soldiering on down the path to freedom.

It was a special morning, too, for at long last, my case had gone right through to the Supreme Court. The final showdown was imminent, and what I hoped would be the end of the longest saga of my life, would finally be concluded. It had been tantalizing, not in the least because I had to balance it out with my family life and my work, but mostly because I had to cover all my bases all on my own, with no help whatsoever from my corrupt, lazy lawyers.

To sum it up, I was now being represented by Moszkowicz's assistant because he was disbarred for taking money illegally. I had neither the resources nor the energy to embark on yet another legal battle. I found it hilarious that this same man wanted to be the next Prime Minister of Holland, but I would not be surprised if he was elected because the country just never failed to amaze me.

I sighed deeply, and closed my eyes. One way or another, I was walking away with an answer. It had taken twelve years, twelve long, stupid years, for the legal system to crack the code, and finally do something about my case.

I could give myself a pat on the back for the way I had handled things. I had been persistent, and tracked down every single bit of evidence that could be applied to my case. I had gone from end to end, called every single person I had been affiliated with during my time at Spantel and after that, when I worked for Bill at Bentley.

I tried to look my best and I put on some formal bits of clothing. Dress for success, they always said and I made my way to the Supreme Court.

The assistant to Moszkowicz insisted I say nothing and do nothing. Do nothing. All the hard work I had put in to build my case and the asshole assistant didn't even bother to present anything.

In the end, the year was 2013, and I ended up winning ninety-five percent of the case. The five percent I lost was down to the technicalities, but the battle, the hard-worn battle, was finally over. I was, to my utter dismay, found guilty of some lesser charge so they wouldn't have to give my assets back, which was devastating because I had the hard evidence to prove my innocence. The system doesn't change; it's all corrupt.

Bryan was unbelievably found not guilty, as I was told by various lawyers. From what I gathered through everything I was told, Bryan was the dumb broke black guy with nothing to get, and I was the dumb ass brown guy, but I had money and assets and that's what they wanted and that's what they got.

I was sentenced and it felt as though I continued to tango with prison. From Armley to the Borstal, and then there was Le Sante and the Koepel in Arnhem.

Sitting there, for the umpteenth time in a lonely cell, I came to my own conclusion that life itself was prison. I did nothing, but everything, good, bad and ugly, happened to me. There was no justice, no winners and no losers, just nothing. Things were taken away from me, and things were given to me. There were betrayals and conspiracies, but there were also magical moments of insanity, where I stood to gain. The only thing that remained a constant in my life, whether it was in a cell or out, were my kids, and that was something I could be eternally grateful for.

In the end, I walked out of prison, a free man. It all seemed a bit of a waste of time to me, and I rued the days I spent buried in evidence. I missed valuable time, and didn't get to see my boys grow into young, strong men, going from strength to strength and getting to do something with their lives. Seeing them again, tall, bold and waiting to hear my story, I saw mirror images of my own childhood.

That is a mistake I was not willing to make again. There was still precious time with my youngest boy: little Jay.

As for me, I wasn't fazed, I felt nothing. Whether it be a different name or a religion, it doesn't matter because it's all the same shit. In life you live the life on that path that you follow and that path can give you riches, despair, pain, sorrow, hate, betrayal and love, but it's a path where you can do nothing, but just walk the walk.

'Do Nothing.'